PRODUCT SPONSORS

Wheel Vintiques

Classic Motorsports Group

RON FRANCIS
WIRING

A GUIDE TO BUILDING A '33-34 FORD

BY RON CERIDONO

Table of CONTENTS

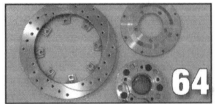

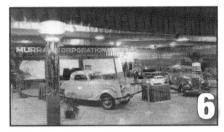

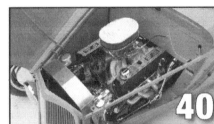

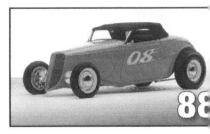

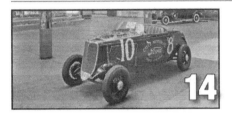

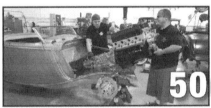

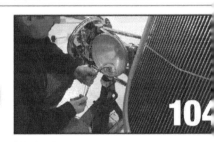

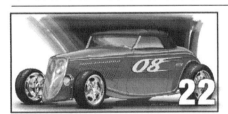

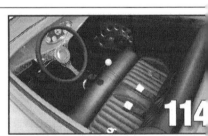

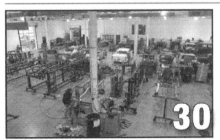

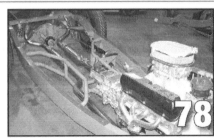

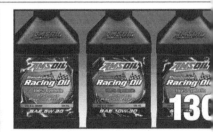

Contributions

Printed in the USA. First printing 2008.

NOTICE: The information in this book is true and complete to the best of our knowledge. All recomendations on parts and procedures are made without any guarantees on the part of the author or the publisher. Tampering with, altering, modifying, or removing any emissions control device is a violation of federal law. Author and publisher disclaim all liability inurred in connection with the use of this information.

ROD & RESTORATION GROUP

SENIOR VP / GROUP PUBLISHER
Doug Evans

PUBLISHER
Tim Foss

EDITORIAL DIRECTOR
Brian Brennan

ASSOCIATE PUBLISHER
John Barkley

WRITTEN BY
Ron Ceridono

PHOTOGRAPHY BY
Brian Brennan
Ryan Manson

ART DIRECTOR
Dan Silverio

GROUP ART DIRECTOR
Aaron Kahan

GROUP MANAGING EDITOR
Noel Wamboldt

COPY EDITOR
Suzanne Baldwin

ROAD TOUR DIRECTOR
Jerry Dixey

GROUP PUBLISHER ASSISTANT
Yasmin Fajatin

Chapter 1
HISTORY OF THE MODEL 40

By Ron Ceridono

Ford relied on several outside vendors to produce the Model 40 bodies. Murray produced the open cars (roadsters, cabriolets, phaetons) as well as the three-wind coupes, Victorias, and four-door sedans.

Henry Ford is credited with saying, "Changing models every year is the curse of the industry," an understandable stance coming from the man who produced the Model T for 19 years and the Model A for four. To the man's credit when he did decide to make changes for '32 they were significant. Ironically, while the Deuce was revolutionary in many ways, at the end of the short model year analysts were saying the Ford Motor Company's glory days were over. It had gone from being one of the largest revenue-producing businesses in the country to one of the biggest losers. Chevrolet was now outselling Ford by a huge margin, Plymouth was closing in, and worst of all, 70-year-old Henry Ford was viewed by many insiders and consumers alike as being out of touch with the car-buying public. But Henry was not the kind of guy to give up, and while his vast personal wealth certainly made it easier for the company to hang on when times were tough, it was his tenacity and mechanical savvy that lead him to make his cars more desirable by improving the V-8 engine. He also realized that to regain his sales lead, a big investment would be required to produce a new, more stylish and comfortable car. Henry was wise enough to assign that responsibility to an extremely talented, and arguably one of the best designers of the era, his son Edsel.

Although its not often pointed out, 1933 was Ford Motors 30th anniversary. It was also a tough time for the United States economy and was considered its worst year. The dollar was removed from the gold standard and unemployment was at 24.9 percent. To put things in perspective, some costs from 1933:

- Hershey's chocolate bar: 5 cents
- Bread: 7 cents a loaf
- Pound of hamburger: 11 cents
- Can of vegetable soup: 10 cents
- Gallon of gas: 10 cents
- First class stamp: 3 cents
- New car: approximately $550
- New house: $5,750
- Average annual income: $1,550

Despite the tough times, once the '3 went into production Henry gave the go-ahead to his in-house designers as we as those from LeBaron, Murphy, Briggs, and Budd to start on another new car. Called the Model 40 (that designation refers to all '33 and '34 Fords), some confusion exists because of the addition nomenclature Ford used to identify the powerplant. Those with four-cylinder

Murray-built phaetons were also available in Standard and Deluxe trim, with a four-cylinder or a V-8. For whatever reason, more Standards had four-cylinders than V-8s (457 to 232 respectively), while the Deluxe versions went the other way (1483 V-8s to 241 fours). Shown here is a Deluxe (note the dual horns and cowl lights) with optional windwings.

With the body by Briggs, more than 45,000 five-window coupes were built. Like most models, they were available in four configurations: the 200.5ci four-cylinder, or 221ci V-8 engines in Standard or Deluxe trim. Deluxe versions had chrome windshield frames, dual horns, cowl lights, and dual taillights. A Standard coupe with a four-cylinder cost $440; a Deluxe V-8 was $540.

Another Murray body was the three-window; this example is a Deluxe version and is equipped with unusual accessory windwings. Almost 16,000 Deluxe versions were sold with the V-8, only 24 had four-cylinders, 6,500 Standards had V-8s, while 189 were equipped with the four-cylinders. Trunks were the norm on Standard and Deluxe models, rumble seats were optional on both.

The Deluxe Fordor carried a hefty price tag, second only to the station wagon in 1933. Although Briggs built the Tudors, Murray built Fordors, probably due to the labor strike at Briggs early in the production run. In this photo, the slope of the '33 grille is obvious. Compare it to photos of '34s.

engines were still referred to as the Model Bs; V-8 equipped cars were called Model 18s.

Essentially another new car from the ground up, the wheelbase was stretched to 112 inches (from 106 inches for the '32) and the frame now had a full X-member. Transverse springs were still used at both ends, but the wheels were 17 inches in diameter. Minor changes were made to the 21-stud V-8, aluminum heads were used, and as a result, compression was increased to 6.3:1 and horsepower rose to 75 at 3,800 rpm. Internally, the pistons were redesigned and the water pumps were now lubricated by engine oil rather than with grease fittings.

Visually the '33 was a huge departure from Fords of the past. The full-width bumpers on both ends dipped in the center, the new grille was at a rakish angle, the headlights were more streamlined as were the fenders, and of course all were equipped with rear-hinged doors that had previously been used only on the '32 three-window coupe.

A strike at the Briggs body plant, along with the problems inherent in designing and producing what were for all practical purposes completely new cars, Model 40s weren't introduced until February 9, 1933. As in the past, Ford referred to Model 40 two-door sedans as Tudors and the four-door sedans as Fordors. Standard and Deluxe versions of most models were available and buyers could choose a 200.5ci four-cylinder engine or the 221ci V-8. A wider variety of paint colors were available and there was a growing list of options including radios, heaters, clocks, dual wipers, and greyhound-adorned radiator caps.

The handsome new body styles were well received, but their late introduction again gave Chevrolet and Plymouth a head start in sales; Ford sold a total of 334,969

Cabriolets were only available in Deluxe trim; however, both the V-8 and four-cylinder engines were offered (only 24 were built with the four-cylinder option; the remainder of the 7,852 sold had the V-8). Equipped with the V-8, a cabriolet cost $585; the four-cylinder version was $535. Here the single hood handle and elongated headlights typical of '33s can be seen.

At $640, the station wagon was Fords most expensive car in '33. Wood for the bodies was milled and cut at Ford's Iron Mountain plant then shipped to Murray for assembly. Note this car has very early fenders without valances. The hubcaps indicate a V-8 engine, while the lack of cowl lights makes this a Standard version (although all wagons had a single, painted horn).

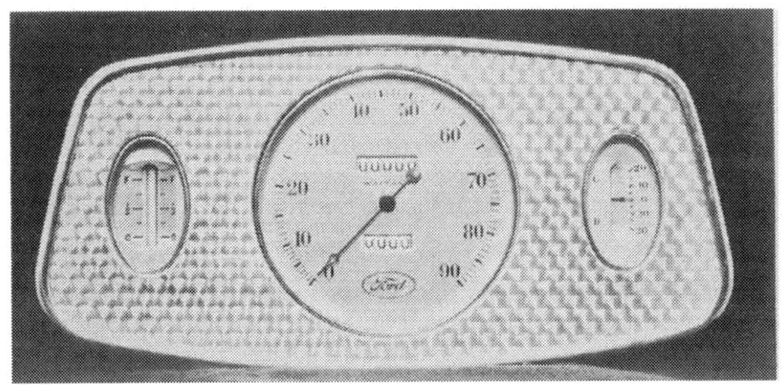

The classic dash of the '33 used an engine-turned insert. Instrumentation consisted of a 90-mph speedometer in the center, a hydrostatic fuel gauge (liquid rose in a glass tube to indicate fuel level) on the left, and an ammeter on the right.

Phaeton bodies were shipped by rail car from the Murray plant; they were painted and the dashboard, instrumentation, and seats were in place. These bodies were unique in that they were the only four-door Fords that had the rear doors hinged in front. Note the front and rear door hinges attach to the B-pillar.

cars for the year. While sales could have been better, the public's confidence in the Flathead V-8 was growing. It's been said that Henry was confident that this was the absolute best car he could build, and that when customers realized this "the market would come to him." But Henry wasn't taking any chances, either, and when 1934 rolled around, Ford was ready to pounce on the competition with an aggressive advertising program.

Beginning in October of 1933, Ford began a promotional campaign touting the virtues of the Model 40, which was beginning its second year of production. The pinnacle of this public relations blitz was the company's display at the 1934 Chicago World's Fair. The Ford Exposition building at the 1934 A Century of Progress occupied 11 acres bordering Lake Michigan with Ford Gardens in the foreground. The huge central rotunda that resembled internally meshed gears stood 10 stories high and three Fords were suspended from a single wire wheel hung from the ceiling. Signs proclaimed this was the same welded-steel wheel construction found on any new Ford car and scientific tests showed that the wheel had strength sufficient to support the weight of fourteen Ford V-8 cars.

For 1934, the V-8 boasted 10 additional horsepower, now up to 85, thanks to the new Stromberg two-barrel carburetor and a dual-plane intake manifold. Inside the cast iron block was a new fully counterbalanced crankshaft that reduced engine vibration considerably. Pistons were also redesigned, as were the thermostats and fuel pump. While the list of mechanical changes wasn't long, there were a considerable number of changes in appearance. Externally all Fords had black fenders. In 1934 they were body color with black as on option, '33s had twin body pinstripes, and '34s had three. The V-8 on the '33 hubcaps was raised and the surrounding areas were painted. In 1934 the V-8 was indented and painted.

One of the more obvious differences for 1934 was the new grille; it wasn't curved like the '33, had a wider surround and

Edsel Ford truly was a genius; he and the legendary E.T. Gregorie designed this roadster built in 1934. Constructed in the Ford Tri-motor aircraft plant, the workmanship was amazing. The front fenders turned with the wheels, while the rears moved with the axle housing. To get the car low, the chassis was underslung, or positioned below the rear axle housing.

In 1932, Ford improved the "banjo" rearend by adding a support bearing to the end of the pinion gear; it stayed essentially the same for the '33s and '34s. This so-called "straddle-mount" design with an enclosed driveline and tapered and keyed axles continued through 1948.

This assembly line shot shows a '34 roadster body being put in place. Note the fender covers on the chassis in the foreground and the grille shell resting on top of the engine. The worker has removed the hubcaps from its wrapper; they were matched to the engine used and had either a V-8 logo or the Ford script for four-cylinders.

In what is surely a testimony to the ruggedness of Ford's four-cylinder engine, a Consolidated Convoy Company '30 Model AA truck hauls a trio of new '33s. Front to back: a Deluxe Fordor, Standard five-window coupe, and a Deluxe Tudor. Evidently the hood sides were removed from the truck to help engine cooling.

fewer, straighter bars. Other changes: '33s had one hood handle, '34s two; '33 hood louvers were curved, '34s were straight; '33 headlights and cowl lights were longer and came to more of a point in the rear; closed car doors were changed in '34 to accommodate windows that moved slightly to the rear for ventilation, as well as rolling down. Inside, the major change was the '33's engine-turned instrument panel insert was replaced with wood grain. Some things that underwent a surprising number of running changes were the door panels/garnish moldings. A ring-style door pull was used during most of 1933, late in that year and into 1934 a horizontal pull strap was installed. 1934 standards had a grip built into the window frame, and eventually door pulls of any kind were eliminated on all '34s.

While Ford fell behind Chevrolet in sales for 1934, there's no denying the Model 40 was a success. For a comparison, here are some examples of automobile sales during that year:

Ford	514,976
Chevrolet	551,191
Plymouth	321,171
Dodge	95,011
Hudson Terraplane	85,835
Oldsmobile	79,814
Pontiac	78,859
Buick	71,009

Certainly one of the best-looking automobile designs of the period, Model 40s speak for themselves. As for performance, the V-8 got an endorsement from an unlikely source. Bank robber Clyde Barrow wrote to Henry saying: "What a fine car you got in the Ford V-8." Evidently he wouldn't steal anything else to outrun the law, and Clyde and Bonnie Parker met their end in a bullet-riddled '34 Ford Fordor. ■

By the time 1934 rolled around, Ford had begun an aggressive ad campaign. The point of many of them was to convey the power and reliability of the V-8. Ford started their publicity blitz more than a month before other manufacturers with a press preview—it was the first Ford-sponsored event where alcohol was served.

As in the previous year, the '34 cabriolet was only available in Deluxe versions with a rumble seat; however, either V-8 or four-cylinder engines were available (only 12 were sold with the four-cylinder, 14,496 with the V-8). Note the straight hood louvers and the grille's more pronounced peak.

While '34 roadsters were only offered in Deluxe trim, there is evidence that Ford built four Standard roadsters. Interestingly, roadster interiors were upholstered in leather, while the rumble seat cushions were covered in "artificial" leather. There were no handles on the rumble seat lid; the release was behind the front seat.

Perhaps the sleekest of the sedan bodies was the Victoria. Built by Murray, the bodies were lengthened slightly for '34; the rear side windows were longer, rear side and the bustle back look of the '33 and earlier Victorias was flattened. Another unique feature of '34 Victorias was the rear luggage compartment. After releasing the inside latch, access was gained by pulling back the spare tire.

By comparison to the other body styles, the Fordor looks a little formal, even slightly stodgy, yet the Briggs-built '34s outsold the '33 Murray sedans almost two to one, 125,451 and 65,906 respectively. This is a Standard (one painted horn, painted windshield frame, and no cowl lights) with a V-8 (according to the hubcaps). Note the "lip" at the back of the front door's window opening. It allowed the glass to move back with the first movement of the window crank making a small opening for ventilation. Continued turning of the crank lowered the glass into the door.

Model 40s had an entirely new chassis. Both ends of the framerails kicked up to lower the car and there was a new X-member to increase torsional rigidity. Transverse springs and Houdaille shocks were still used, as were mechanical brakes.

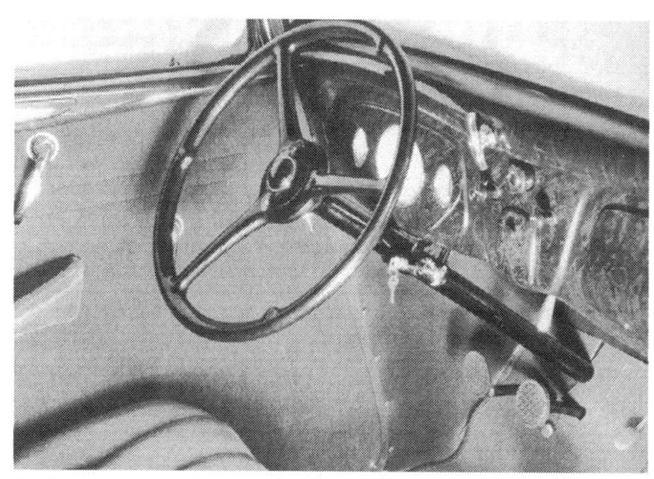

Inside, the most notable change for '34 was the replacement of the engine-turned instrument insert with wood graining that matched the rest of the dashboard. Note the knob in the center to crank out the windshield. In the center of the dash is the cigar lighter, below is the choke and throttle, and at the bottom is the ashtray. The headlight switch and horn button are in the center of the steering wheel and the ignition switch and lock are on the column.

One of the most complicated stampings on the Model 40 was the grille shell; there remains a fair amount of speculation on exactly how it was done. Whatever the process, the results were classic. These are '34s; note the larger surround for the radiator cap, another difference between '33s and '34s

A '34 Deluxe Tudor body is dropped onto the frame. This was Ford's second-best selling model for the year with sales of 121,708 (12 of which had four-cylinder engines, the rest were V-8s). The Standard Tudor was the sales leader with 124,870 V-8s and 185 with four-cylinders. Briggs supplied bodies for both.

Ready to got to a dealership, this Deluxe '34 Tudor would set its owner back $575 with a V-8, while a Standard went for $535. Choosing a four-cylinder engine cut the price of both models by $50. This photo provides a good view of the dip in the Model 40 bumpers.

Who knows how many early cars met their end in screwball comedies of the day. Here Larry Fine, Curly, and Moe Howard, aka the Three Stooges, ham it up with what's left of a Model 40 phaeton.

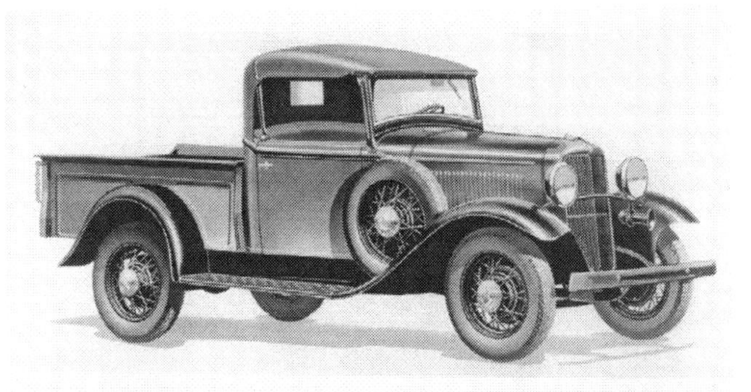

Ford built some pretty good-looking trucks, too. This is a '33 roadster pickup (only 593 were built). Murray and truck-style grille hoods supplied bodies and beds and grille shells were used. Commercial headlights used passenger-car lenses, but the buckets were shallower and painted. In 1934, 347 open-cab pickups sold; it was the last for open cab Ford pickups.

This is a '34 half-ton panel truck (note the V-8 emblem, new for 1934, on the hood side). Just a few over 9,000 panels were built this year (production figures combined four- and eight-cylinder engines). Passenger-car-based sedan deliveries were also offered; LeBaron built those bodies.

Ford offered truck chassis and cab units to companies that built special bodies; roughly 600 were sold in 1933, and about the same in 1934. Production was pretty evenly split each year between four-cylinders and V-8s. The dashboard shown here was typical of all the trucks. The lever under the four-speed transmission's gearshift knob is a reverse lockout.

This is an example of a '34 cab and chassis used for the construction of a fire truck. Although the wheelbase was often much greater than the 112-inch pickups, the Murray manufactured cab and sheetmetal were the same.

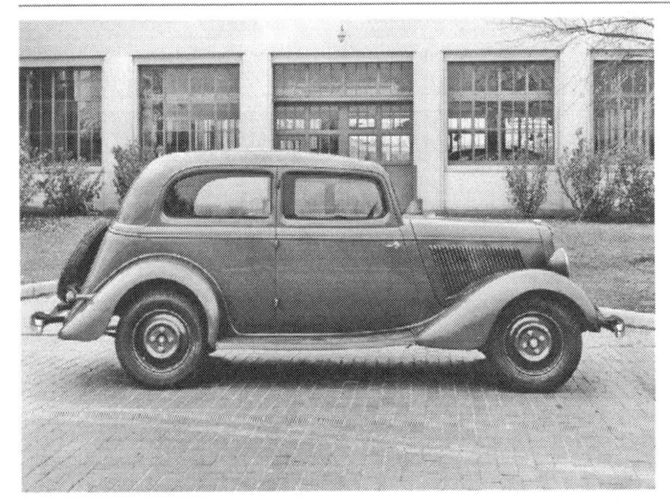

Fords were built in a variety of plants outside the United States. This example has a '34-style body with '35/'36-style fenders. The headlights and grille shell look more like commercial than passenger car pieces. Note the four lug bolts and solid steel wheels.

This '34 Deluxe Fordor has several accessory items installed. The greyhound wasn't particularly unusual, but the spotlight was, an original vacuum wiper on the driver's side uses a rod to operate an added wiper on the right.

ın unusual combination, this '33 carries a spare in the usual rear mount ɔcation along with dual side mounts. Side-mount spares were often found on edan deliveries, wagons, and pickups, but in most cases only one was installed ın the passenger side.

This is a rare glovebox radio with a dial that matched the speedometer. Other radios were offered that fit in the ashtray opening. Note this '34 cabriolet does not have a crank-out windshield.

ilovebox-mounted clocks were also available. Often called eight-day clocks, hat's how often they had to be wound with a stem on the backside of the lid.

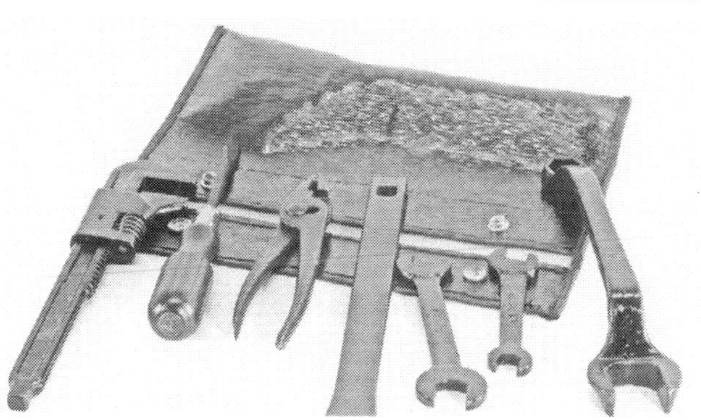

While not intended for major repairs, each car came with a tool kit. On the left is the famous Ford adjustable "monkey wrench." Note the square end designed to fit and add leverage to the tire-changing spoon in the center.

. close-up of the elegant greyhound radiator rnament. They also made a convenient handle for emoving and replacing the radiator cap.

Another example of an accessory clock, this one is mounted in the rearview mirror. This clock also required winding every eight days.

Chapter 2

THE SIGNIFICANCE OF FORD'S MODEL 40 TO HOT RODDING

By LeRoi Tex Smith and Ron Ceridono

Model 40s have been hot rods almost since the day they debuted. The lightweight, stripped-down roadsters were the cars to beat in such races as the Gilmore Gol Cup, which was held on the site of what is now LAX.

From its introduction to the American public in 1933, the Model 40 Ford was far more of a step toward modern automotive styling than the 1932 ever was. The '33-34 Ford styling was a radical departure for Henry Ford; a leap of faith for America's car that transcended whatever else was happening in the automotive world. The Model 40 (as it was known "in-house") was different in dozens of ways from the Model T and Model A—basic transportation devices that Henry had supplied to the world for decades. The 1932 model laid the framework for these changes, especially those of engineering, but the basic styling of the Deuce is not all that removed from the Model A. The '33 is way different, and in some ways, more in step with where American auto styling was going in general. It is elegant; Ford's predecessors were crude boxes.

There are several Ford products that are significant, transitional vehicles for th hot rod fraternity. The Deuce is one, the '34 another, the '40 coupe, and so on. It remains for the '34 to straddle old and new better than any other car Ford has delivered. The difference in appearance a vehicle weight for the "new" '33 was far more profound in hot rodding than mos contemporary street rod enthusiasts seem to realize.

A wonderful contemporary version of vintage styling is this Model 40 roadster with '37 Ford passenger-car vents in the hood side and a '37 truck grille shell.

One of the things about hot rodding is that it's open to interpretation. This channeled '33 five-window has '32 fenders and grille.

Anyone who was on the street rod scene in the 1970s remembers the look of fat tires hanging out of the fenders and a CB antenna for communicating with other rodders on the road.

The 1970s saw an influx of cars built to travel cross-country, so bigger cars like this '34 Fordor became popular. The builder of this one decided to add to the hot rod flavor by taking a little off the top.

When I bought my first '33, a three-window coupe, just after WWII, it was simply a used car. It was tired, the black paint was still shiny, and the stock flatmotor was better suited for mosquito abatement than transportation. At $40, it seemed overpriced. A good A-bone was $10 to $15, and a Deuce wasn't much more. But for me, the '33 represented a step up to the "big car" brigade. Just sand the good paint, apply gray primer, heave the fenders, put in a mildly hopped-up '48 truck Flathead, add some larger diameter Buick (used) rear tires, some (also used) small-diameter Studebaker front tires, and instant hot rod.

All of you taking Hot Rod Philosophy 101 must understand that the automotive era up to the 1930s was broken into three groupings. Early in the 1900s, there were those tiny little cycle car thingies that were popular in England and Europe, but hardly practical for North American motoring. Then came the cars for the unwashed masses, which were a bit upscale, but still rudimentary. At the top were the mega-rides for all the robber barons—big, heavy, somewhat fast for the times, and way expensive. The masses got mass production, and that kept prices down. Lower prices dictated smaller vehicles just as it does today, but such cars responded very well indeed to performance enhancement.

This chopped sedan delivery is a rarity. It rides on '35 wire wheels and has another modification common during the period: sealed beams behind the original headlight lenses.

And then there's really rare—a '34 woody. The resto-rod style was popular, so that meant cars wore vintage accessories such as a grille guard, foglights, and of course, a sweater for the greyhound. Tru-Spoke wire wheels were also the rage.

Speaking of accessories, this '34 cabriolet is equipped with a top over the rumble seat. This car wears Cadillac wire wheels and it too has sealed beams behind stock lenses.

Before drag racing emphasized the importance of big power and small weight, we applied the formula to circle track racing roadsters. The flimsy little Model T roadsters usually put the later-body cars in the pits, so you didn't see many '33-34 Fords on the circle tracks until jalopy circuits evolved. And in the 1930s they were essentially new cars—hardly in the price range for young guys.

You've probably heard how the outlaw element seemed to prefer the '34 Ford. I can verify that my liquor-running uncle found the '34 Tudor to be the best for bringing alcohol across the state line from Missouri into Oklahoma. The car was fast, with a special riser under the rear seat there was room for a bunch of small, flat whisky bottles, and with my tiny mom and aunt in back with me, the border patrol always failed to check our contraband.

There was a smattering of '33-34 Fords in West Coast hot rodding right after WWII. Perhaps the best known was a yellow, fenderless roadster owned by Jack Morgan. This car appeared on the cover of an early *Hot Rod* magazine; I ran across it a few years later when I was running the NHRA National drags in Oklahoma City. It was much the worse for wear, ensconced in an Oklahoma chicken shed and neglected. Perhaps it's still there.

Another well-known yellow '34 Ford roadster belonged to Dean Moon from the Santa Fe Springs area of Southern California. Dean cut away the front fender leading edges, a kind of European styling change that was somewhat popular with '34s. In the very late 1940s, there was a three-window fenderless coupe running around Southern California that got coverage in *Hot Rod* magazine around 1950 or '51. The car was primered, chopped, and had the stock hood louvers chrome-plated. In the *HRM* photo, the owner was standing alongside with his arm resting on the top to emphasize how low the car was. This photo feature got the immediate attention of hot rodders in America's heartland, where far more closed cars remained than roadsters. But perhaps the most famous of all those early rodded '34s is the dry lakes racer built by the Pierson brothers. Also an *HRM* feature car, and still around, it has a dramatic top chop, but in the 1950s it wasn't all that different from the few other '34s running, even down to the racecar nose. Of course the impact of the Model 40 didn't stop there, thanks to a media blitz of sorts. Millions of people saw the *California Kid* '34 slide across their TV screens, and while many didn't know what it was, it was cool and made an impact. The ZZ Top coupe was on album covers, in videos, and audiences followed along as Tim "The Tool Man" Taylor built a '33 roadster in his garage.

In light of history, the Model 40 is a part of hot rodding, but somehow a separate part. For many years, post-WWII hot rodding focused on the dry lakes, where power-to-weight ratios dominated. The dry lakes were short; not at all like the Bonneville Salt Flats. Car body frontal area was important, so the small Ts were good, the '28 and '29 Model A's not bad, and the '30-32 Ford bodies were pushing more air, and they weighed more. On the streets of most hot rod-conscious West Coast towns, the most common of all hot rods would be the A V-8, and the most popular would be the '28-29 versions. There were many Deuces, of course, but the '33 and later Fords were considered "big" cars—more suited to becoming customs than hot street champions. Yes, there were exceptions, but the Model 40s didn't really come into vogue with the emerging street rod hobby until the 1960s.

In a way, the larger Fords started gaining a following as the waistlines of the rodding fraternity began to expand. Still, it could well be argued that the most significant factor driving the growing Model 40 appeal was/is the front-opening doors! While this is a styling cue aimed more at gaining entry foot room (you know, extra room between the front seat and the door opening, and it is significant), it has precedent in European design circles. It is also a design element not at all limited to Ford. Still, the "suicide door" has become synonymous with the '33-34 Ford. Through all the years of Ford production, this style door was used for only two years.

Trucks weren't exempt from the hot rod scene. In fact, it seems like every muffler shop had a hopped-up truck, and many of them served duty at the races as push vehicles. This '33 sports a Buick Nailhead engine backed by a Cad-LaSalle transmission.

There have been a number of cars that have reawakened interest in hot rodding—one was the *American Graffiti* coupe, another was the *California Kid*. Built by Pete Chapouris, not all TV viewers knew what the car was, but lots of them knew they liked it.

Another car that sparked interest in our hobby was the ZZ Top coupe. Lots of red cars with graphics started showing up when this car came on the scene.

A modern-day resto-rod, this '33 roadster proves the point that you don't have to do anything to any Model 40 to make it look great.

Check this '33 out for a comparison. The subtle modifications like removing the horns, louverering the hood, substituting '35 headlights, and a slightly chopped top add to the hot rod look.

This chopped '33 five-window has solid hood-side panels and commercial headlights. The top has also been filled.

While the Model 40 seemed to be a natural to hop up, it took organized street rodding to bring it to the forefront. The smaller, earlier Ford bodies were great for bopping around locally, but the bigger Fords (and other makes) were more suited to long-distance rodding. The Model 40s fit the bill exactly—they weren't as bulbous as the '35 and later Fords, they looked good without fenders, and there seemed to be plenty of coupes and sedans to fill the demand. Roadsters were sparse, however, and into the void came the fiberglass open bodies. In the popularity lineup, '34s run very similar to the other Ford body styles. Number one is the roadster, followed by the convertible, the phaeton, the three- and five-window coupes, the two-door sedan, and finally, the four doors. Mixed in there haphazardly are things like the Vicky, sedan delivery, and various custom one-offs.

There is considerable interchangeability of Ford car parts, body and mechanical, well into the '50s, and it seems that hot rodders always want the latest in styling of any given production. The '34 is better than the '33, the '36 is preferred over the '35, the '40 over the '39, and so on. Given interchangeability, updating a Ford was easy, which is why my '33 became a '34. Off came the '33 grille, and away went the stock hood. On went a '34 hood and grille, with only minor changes necessary. I was styling! The parts came from an abandoned sedan, no cost involved.

In the pages of hot rod magazines during the 1950s, there were '34s shown, but most were full-fendered closed cars—often what we considered at the time to be trophy quality show machines. In the Eastern states, a few heavily channeled '34 roadsters appeared, often with rear fenders relocated higher on the quarters and often molded to the body. Since Ford vehicles have been available around the world, it's not surprising that the '34 is popular in hot rodding across the globe; nowhere more so than in New Zealand and Australia. In New Zealand, Fords were imported through Canada, thus they are essentially the American versions. However, in Australia the Ford assembly plant used a combination of Aussie-made components and imported pieces—as well as a pile of leftover factory parts, which is why the '34 is perhaps more popular in Oz rodding than the '32. While the Aussie roadsters and phaetons look U.S., they differ in many small ways. The Australian '34 sedans use the leftover Aussie '32 sedan body (with front-opening doors).

Interestingly, much of the current popularity of the '34 stems from the availability of custom chassis, fiberglass and metal bodies, and great reproduction grilles. At the same time, there was a very determined swing from the more pointed '34 grille to the swoopy '33. As more and more layback grilles began to appear, they also seemed to move forward. For all of the reasons that the '33-34 Ford has become second only to the '32 as a hot rodding icon, the fact remains that this is one powerfully bitchin' hot rod foundation. It is strong, can be fast, can be comfortable, and it's good looking. What more is there? ■

The builder of this '33 three-window chopped and filled the top, but chose to retain the stock headlights and cowl lamps. Wide whites and '35 Ford wire wheels give it a vintage look.

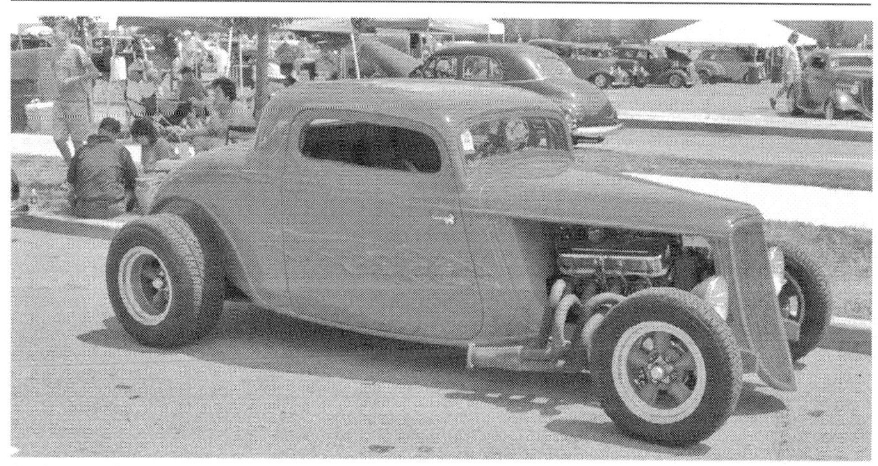

On the opposite end of the continuum from resto-rods, we have a chopped and channeled highboy running a big-block Chevy sans hood sides with American five-spokes at all corners. If you want to go unnoticed, this is not the way to do it.

Clean and simple, this '33 has a custom grille with the radiator cap surround removed and a three-piece hood with a solid top. Note the simple nerf bars and commercial headlights.

This '34 lost the front bumper and gained a set of '36 Ford headlights. Fenders below the grille on a low Model 40 are vulnerable to driveway and other types of damage. Being low and cool can extract a price.

If you want to haul the family to a rod run in an open car, there's no better way to do it than in a '34 phaeton. Note the grille bars have been painted.

Other than the wire wheels, this Deluxe '34 phaeton remained stone stock on the outside. Many rodders in the resto-rod period felt it was a way to protect the value of their cars, while some felt no changes were necessary.

Speaking of family cruisers, this '34 Fordor fits that bill perfectly. The wide whites chrome wheels and '50 Merc hubcaps have a clean simple look that complements the car.

Here's a car that stops rodders in their tracks—a Model 40 roadster with a beautifully executed track nose and a DuVall windshield.

This '34 Tudor combines elements of stock car and street rod for a unique look. Note the nerf bar/chin protector.

Model 40s are hot for rodding down under, too. This '34 Vicky has been built as a highboy, but has cycle fenders to comply with Australian regulations.

An interesting mixture we ran across in Australia, a '34 truck with passenger-car fenders, grille, and a hood that's half of each.

The Australian Ute is half car/half pickup. Sort of an early Ranchero, this is a '34 five-window closed cab version. They were also offered as roadsters.

Every once in a while, you stumble across a diamond in the rough; this '34 cabriolet was at the L.A. Roadsters Father's Day Swap Meet. In very nice condition, it has sealed-beam conversions in the headlights, '35 wire wheels, and an accessory grille guard.

Another swap meet find, this '34 standard Fordor was at the NSRA Street Rod Nationals swap meet. Both this and the cabriolet had unusually good original grilles; that's not often the case.

Chapter 3
AMERICAN SPEED COMPANY'S SPEED33

By Ron Ceridono

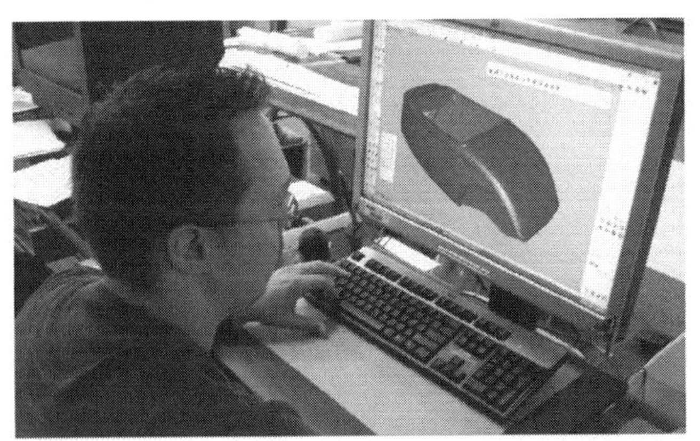

The Speed33 began as a scan of a perfect original '33 that resulted in a 3-D computer image with all the necessary dimensions to duplicate the body.

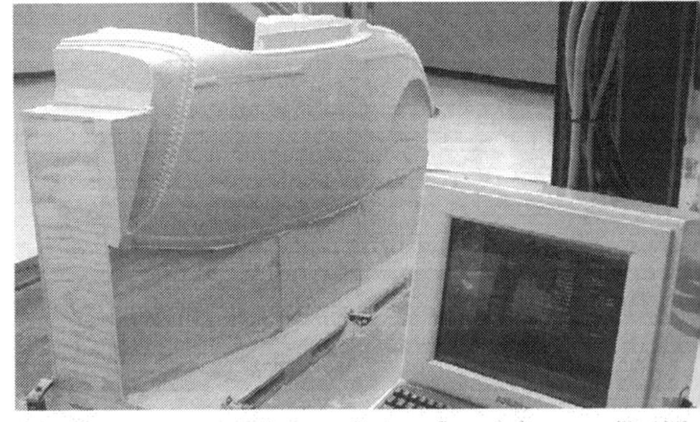

Using the computer established coordinates, a five-axis free-arm mill whittle this half body from a block of urethane foam. The design team studied its sh then made adjustments as necessary.

For many street rodders, nothing beats racking up the miles in a roadster with the sun on your face and the wind in your hair. It's the stuff songs and hot rod legends are made of. Of course, just as legendary are the tales told of sunburns, windburns, near drowning, and if there hasn't been a country western song about a divorce caused by a roadster road trip gone wrong, there should be.

While roadsters are indeed wonderful, there's much to be said for a car with a top; even more to be said for roll-up windows, heat, and air conditioning.

When discussing open cars, they can basically be broken down into two categories: roadsters and convertibles. The main difference is a convertible has roll-up windows and a roadster doesn't (removable side curtains were generally used to keep out the majority of the weather).

While Speed33 body panels won't interchange with originals, the new wheelwells will accept stock fenders. The dies for each panel are carefully inspected before each use.

Speaking of dies, it takes quite a few of them to turn out a Speed33. Body panels are stamped from 18-gauge steel; the inner structure is made of 11-gauge with 1/8-inch wall steel tubing used for reinforcement. The floor is stout and is made from 1/8-inch steel.

Some panels require multiple strikes to achieve their final form, and in most cases there is excess material that has to be trimmed away. The stampings for the Speed33 bodies are manufactured to standards that were impossible to achieve in the 1930s.

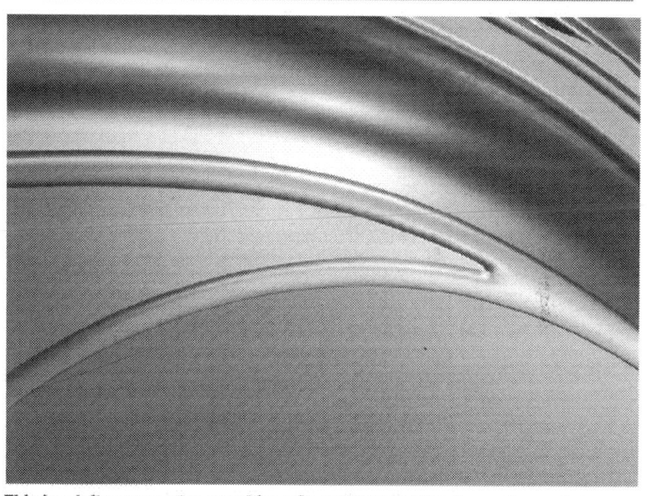

This is a left rear quarter-panel for a Speed33 body. Note how crisp and clean the edges of the character lines are. Although they're not exact duplicates of the original, all that are found on this body match.

Model 40 convertibles, called cabriolets as many others of this body style were referred to in the day, had other differences that set them apart from roadsters. The cabriolet's windshield framework was part of the body, unlike the bolt-on posts found on the roadster. The cabriolet's windshield didn't pivot to open on the posts as the roadster's did; it rolled out like those of the closed cars. Both the cabriolet and roadster tops had zippered rear-window panels that could be opened for ventilation. Although roadsters have always been the most popular body style with hot rodders, back in 1933 there were almost twice as many cabriolets sold. By the end of the 1934 model, cabriolets were outselling roadsters three to one.

When street rodding came on the scene and began to grow, the demand for Model 40 roadsters, cabriolets, and coupes was such that reproduction bodies came on the market. At the outset of the new body boom, fiberglass was the material of choice because it was the cheapest and easiest way to copy an original. But thanks to new technology and a few entrepreneurs willing to make a substantial initial investment, reproduction steel bodies became a reality.

Of course, if you're designing dies to build a new body, there is the opportunity to tweak the basic shape of whatever it is you're going to build, but when it comes to the Model 40, there isn't much you can do to improve upon Edsel's design. It can be a little like putting the Mona Lisa in a tank top. Go overboard with modifications to an original artwork and you end up with less than you had. It takes a good eye and deft hand when making changes in classic automotive

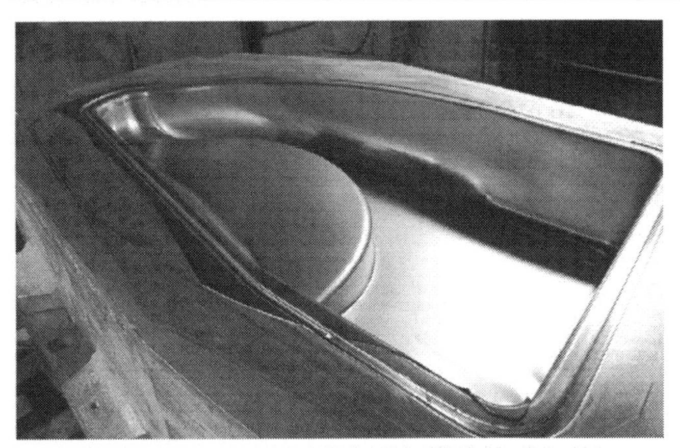

The inside of the same quarter-panel. While original Ford stampings were known to have dimensional variations side-for-side, thanks to modern manufacturing techniques, the Speed33 has the same close tolerances found on new cars.

Kevin McLoughlin and Rodger Hermann inspect an attachment point on a Speed33 trunk lid.

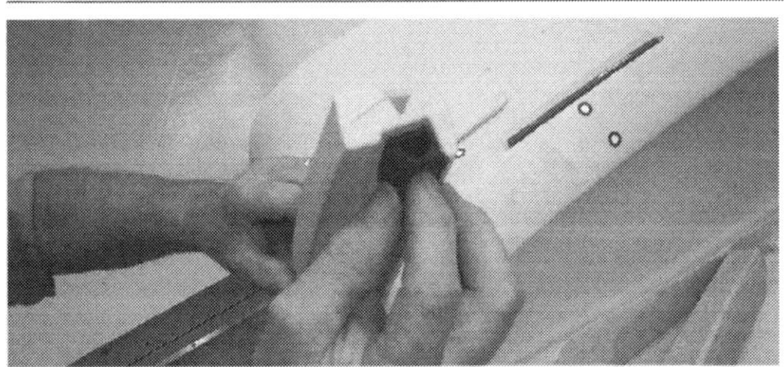

One of the biggest challenges was redesigning the windshield posts to include a window seal, while maintaining a slim, stylish appearance. Production posts are investment-cast stainless steel.

This is a digitizer—it picks up datum points on prototype parts to prove dimensional accuracy of computer-modeled components. The necessary adjustments can easily be made before production begins.

architecture, and one group that has perfected the procedure is American Speed Company, creators of the Speed33, which is the basis of the '08 PPG/Street Rodder Road Tour car. Having designed the Dearborn Deuce, and with 30-plus years of experience with Detroit's OEMs, the company not only knows what to do, but how to do it.

To build its bodies, American Speed Company started with surface scan data from a pristine original '33 roadster. Unlike the old days when a clay model was made and traced to make blueprints, the new procedure is somewhat the reverse. Once the original body was scanned and the necessary dimensional data acquired, a computer controlled mill carved a likeness of the body out of foam. That allowed the design team to see what they had, then they incorporated a variety of refinements using the latest CAD software and hardware just as the major manufacturers do it. Among the numerous subtle changes, the firewall has been modified to accept contemporary engines, the cowl has been reworked to mount a uniquely curved windshield, and access to the roomy passenger compartment (4-inches wider and 5-inches longer than a '32) is through doors that are stretched. But what makes the Speed33 so unique is the fully integrated convertible top and roll-up windows. So cleverly done, these additions take nothing away from the classic roadster styling with the top up or down, yet it offers best of the open- and closed-car worlds.

By combining the latest automotive technology with the vision of an experienced street rodder like Mark Trostle, American Speed Company has done a remarkable job of updating a classic design, while keeping its character intact. It truly is the best of both worlds and we're sure even Henry and Edsel would approve.

hink of this as a certificate of authenticity. Each ody comes with a serial number; they're in stock nd ready for delivery. To ensure these bodies will e around a long, long time, the latest in corrosion rotection, E-coat (electrocoating cathodic epoxy) ipping is available.

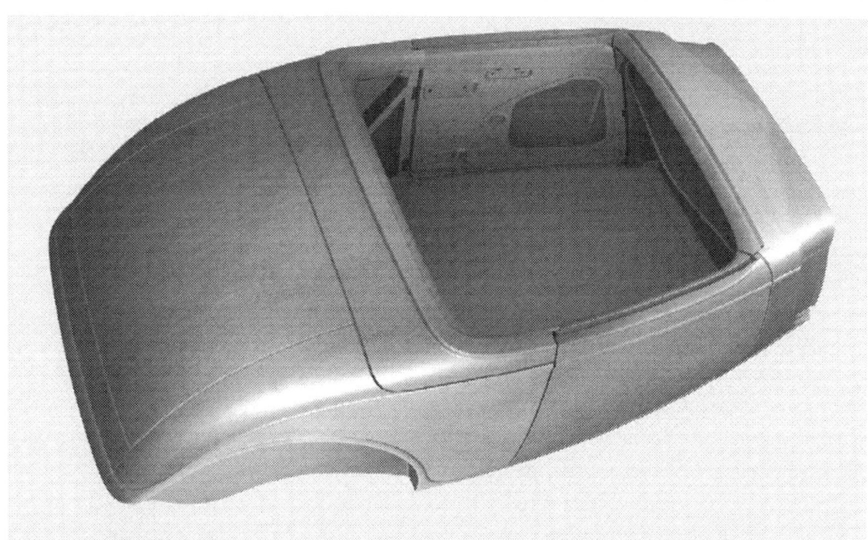

For those building highboys, a no-cost factory option is a repositioned floor that allows the body to be channeled 1 3/4 inches over the frame. This eliminates the gap between the cowl and framerails with stock bodies.

o ensure the panel alignment and body gaps meet urrent OEM standards, assembly takes place on a gid surface plate. A stiff internal structure keeps that way.

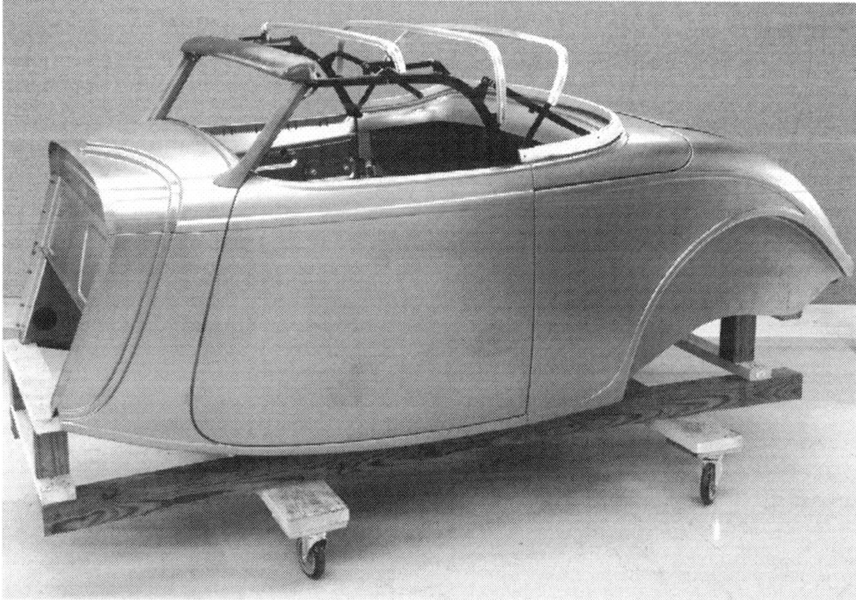

A considerable amount of engineering went into the folding top. Not only does it fold into a compact package when down, it provides plenty of headroom when it's up.

'HE MAN AND MISSION BEHIND THE SPEED33

y Chris Shelton

Mark Trostle, the man behind the peed33, told us: "Somebody could say 's like the Dearborn Deuce, well, that's ecause our group designed that for Hot ods & Horsepower." You see, Mark was ormerly the head of American Specialty Cars when it created the Dearborn Deuce (as well as the Buick GNX and Chevrolet SSR). Mark created American Speed Company specifically as a means to move on in more ways than one.

Both the Speed33 and the Dearborn Deuce are similar because the philosophy behind them is the same. "I love the looks of those cars, but I always wanted to change 'em," Mark began. "Your memory gets a little fuzzy when it comes to this stuff. You look back and you think they were just wonderful, but the reality was there were some shortcomings to them," he pondered. "As we get older—speaking for myself here—some of us like to be comfortable." And, as he muses, the Speed33 is that place where old-car aesthetics and new-car performance meet.

To give the body its old-car aesthetic,

Speed33 tops are covered in Haartz cloth. Black, beige, and navy are standard with custom colors available as an option.

Hidden hinges are standard, but unlike many, these allow the doors to open wide for easy entry.

The changes made to the Speed33 have been so well integrated that none of the charm of the original design is lost, as this full-fendered version proves.

Built as a highboy, there's no mistaking this is a hot rod. Note how the bottom of the cowl fits the chassis. This example will have the fuel tank in the trunk and a rolled rear pan will be added.

Mark and his crew scanned a cherry '33 roadster. But as you'd likely assume, they didn't copy the body gaps, bumps, and all. Second to the top mechanism, the 4 1/2-inch-longer doors are the most obvious clues to a little design slap and tickle. Study the body even closer, and you'll see tight and consistent fit and finish that Henry's body never bragged of. "Because we're based out of Detroit," Mark pointed out, "it was completely engineered in CAD by OE engineering and designers that work in the industry on a daily basis."

As part of that design process, "We actually milled a full-sized foam model that we reviewed, making sure all the character lines and the surfacing was the way we wanted it to be," he noted. The decklid, for example, "...was flat in the middle and wasn't what it should be aesthetically," Mark revealed. So his crew tuned it up before tooling up. For that reason, no Speed33 body panels will fit a true Ford. "But the rear wheel opening," Mark explained, "we wanted that to be an exact duplicate so you could bolt on a stock fender." And that's something unique about the car: While it's tuned to modern standards, the body accepts a stock hood, tank cover, fenders, running boards, and so on. In fact, "This was designed with all the body mounts common with the standard chassis," he said. "Take a stock '33/'34 car, and you can bolt this body right on it with the fenders. In fact, we're in the process of putting one of those cars together."

"One thing that sets us apart is a no-cost option," he continued. "If you tell me that you're going to build a contemporary looking car with no fenders, we offer it channeled 1 3/4 inches," Mark pointed out. "If you just pull the fenders off an original car, the cowl is actually above the framerails. Well, with this (option), the body drops over the chassis."

What makes this car modern is more than just aesthetics and a few cable releases and gas struts. While the body is 19-gauge steel, the floor is roughly 0.100-inch thickness. A network of 1x3 steel tubing reinforces the lower part of the body, and a structure within the cowl supports the steering column and instrument panel, "so you don't get what we call in the industry as cowl shake," Mark noted.

Furthermore, the Speed33 arrives as a complete assembly. "You get all the glass in it; it's already mounted with the power lift system. It comes with cat whiskers at the beltline for the glass. It comes with a safety laminate windshield with a sweep to it—it's not a flat windshield. All that is designed and custom tooled by us. The windshield posts, for example, are investment-cast stainless. It's a lost-wax casting method."

"The other thing we can provide (as a cost option) that no one at this point offers as far as I know, is you can buy this body already E-coated," Mark says. In other words, the body's rust-protected. "It's dipped in a tank, just as all the new cars are today. There's a minimal amount of surfacing on the outside of the body and you don't have to worry about anything on the inside because it's already protected."

As Mark put it: "We've maintained the original look of a roadster, but it gives you all the amenities of a contemporary car, meaning that you've got power windows, and it has a convertible top that's very similar to a Corvette in operation (one of Mark's prior projects at American Specialty Cars)." Speaking of tops, this one's structure is entirely extruded aluminum, making it both light and strong.

While the design and tooling phase consumed more than a year, American Speed Company has produced 18 bodies from September to December 2007—that's six cars a month. "We were getting two bodies a day out at one point," Mark proclaimed. "We don't want to work that way on a regular basis, but I will tell you that our projection is in the 15-bodies-a-month range."

As faithful as its appearances may suggest, Mark said he knows the Speed33 isn't the answer to the purist's prayers. "It's not meant to go to somebody who wants to build an exact reproduction," he cautions. "We didn't want to lose the essence of what the original car was; we just did all the things that we thought somebody would like to see in a hot rod." ■

How about full fenders, a stock grille shell, and a full race Flathead. The body lends itself to a variety of build styles.

The same car from the rear with stock fenders and a custom gas tank cover with an inset for the license plate.

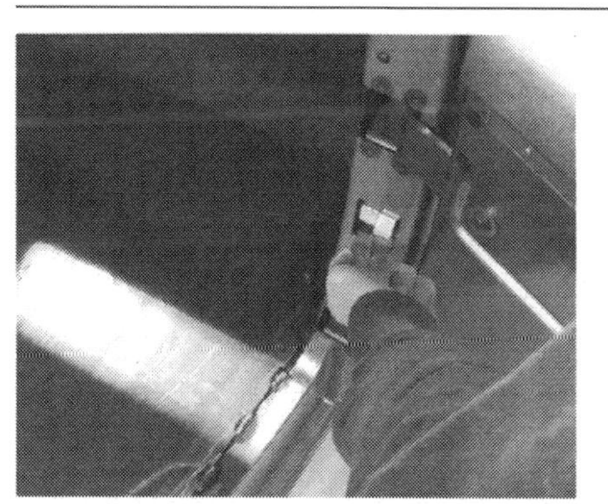

Release levers for the trunk and top lids are recessed in the driver-side hinge post.

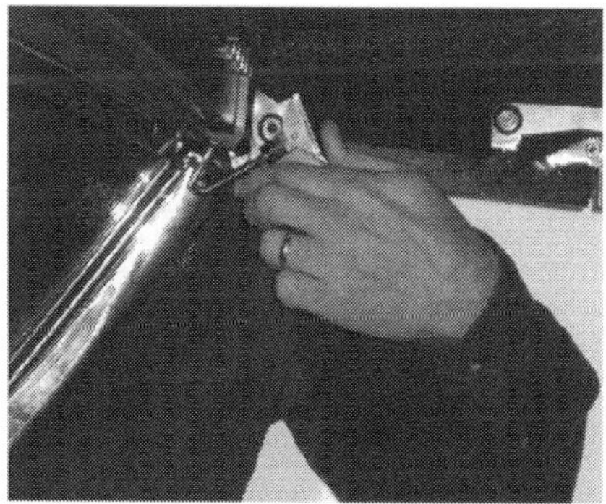

To drop the top, the windshield header latches are released.

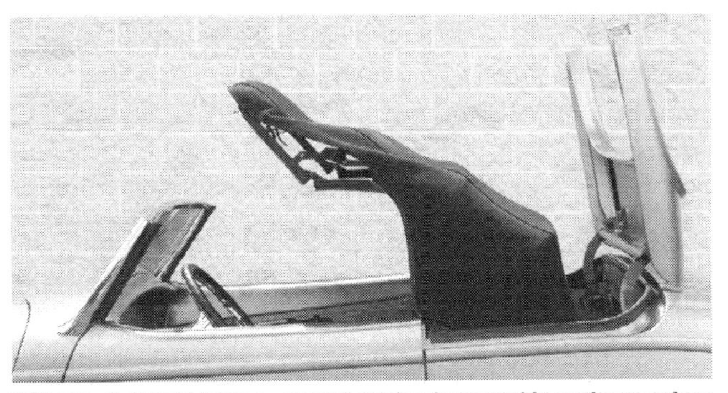

With the windshield latches released, the header assembly can be moved up and back.

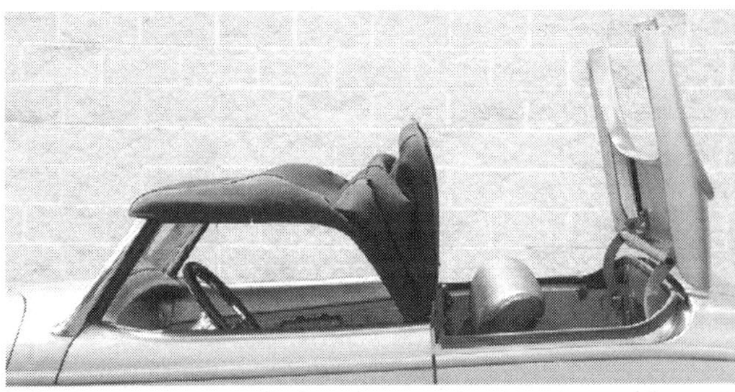

...then it moves to the rear, the front disengages from its guides, and the panel opens fully.

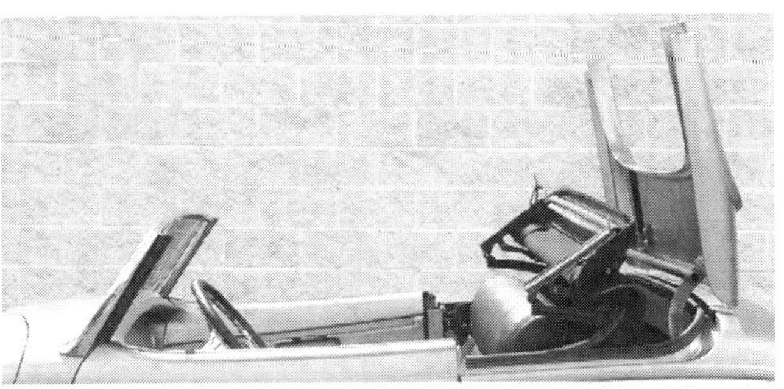

The top assembly folds easily and is completely hidden in a well behind the seats.

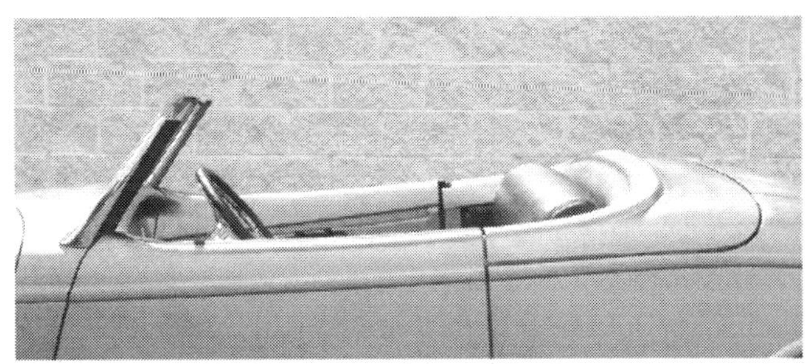

With the top stowed, the tonneau cover/tulip panel is closed and latched, and you're ready to cruise in the sun.

Clever design work allows the leading edge of the tonneau cover/tulip panel to move back as it opens so it and the trunk lid can open simultaneously.

This is the right side catch that secures the front of the tonneau cover when it's in the closed position. Note the slanted slot on the bracket that serves to pull the cover down as it moves forward.

As demonstrated, the tonneau cover goes through a variety of moves when opening. This is the hinge assembly at the back of the panel that makes it all happen.

Compared to the trunk hinges used on a stock Model 40, these are an engineering masterpiece. They operate smoothly thanks to modern bushings, pivots, and a small set of gas rams.

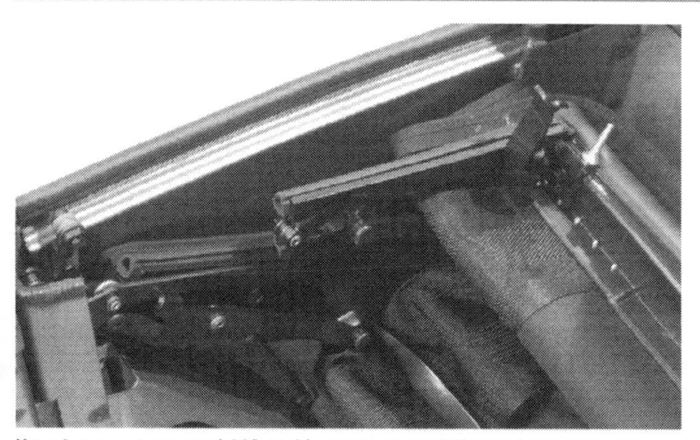
How do you get a top to fold into this compact area? Years of experience building unique drop-top vehicles evidently helped.

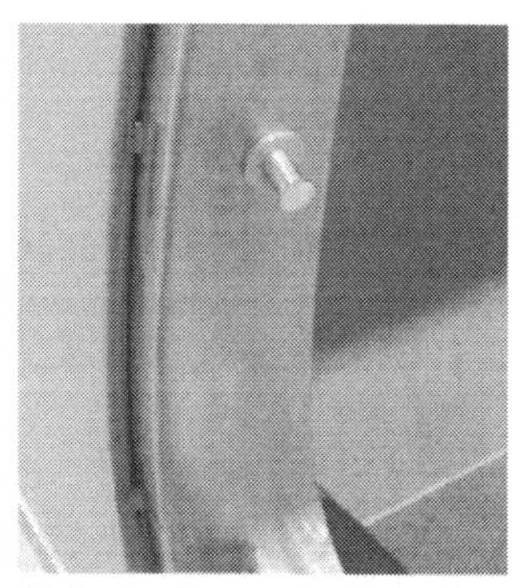
Modern hardware such as bear-claw door latches are used throughout. This is the latch pin at the front of the door opening.

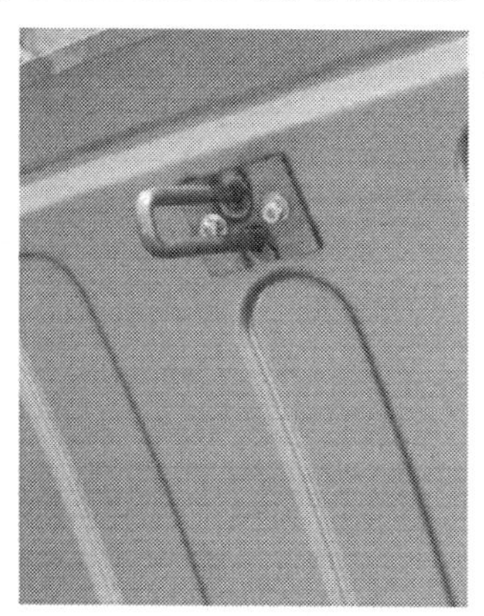
The trunk lid uses a modern style latch with a cable release.

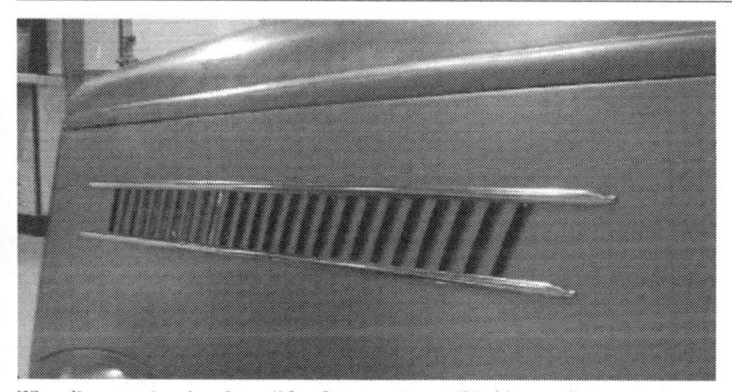
When it comes to a hood, anything from custom solid side panels to a stock original can be used, the reversed louvers and chrome trim are classy and unique.

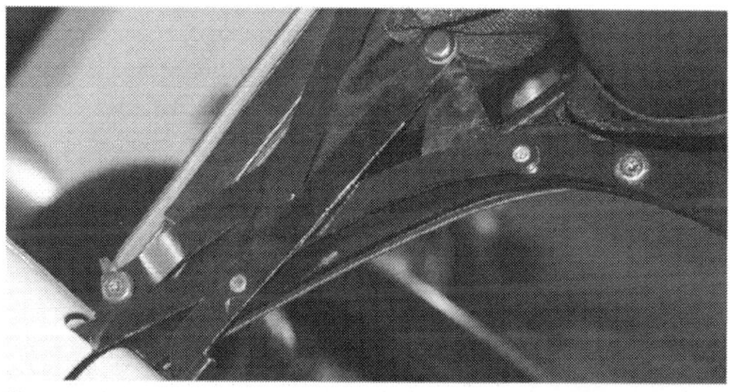
The same fasteners, bushings, and pivots found on contemporary convertibles are used on the Speed33. As a result, raising and lowering the top is effortless.

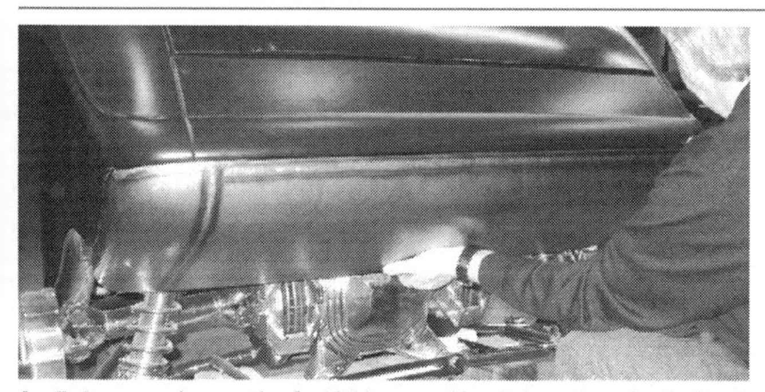
A rolled rear pan is an option for highboys, and is what we chose for the Road Tour car.

Using the rolled rear pan requires the gas tank to be moved into the trunk. It fits below and behind the well that the top drops into.

The Speed33 combines the classic looks of the Model 40, the attitude of a traditional hot rod, and the comfort and convenience of a modern convertible. What else can you ask for?

Chapter 4
BUILDING THE CHASSIS

By Ron Ceridono

It's been said a building is only as strong as its foundation; the same thing can be said for an automobile and its frame. Automotive frames have to be strong enough to handle the various forces applied to them to maintain body panel alignment, to allow the suspension to function as it should, and to keep passengers safe. One of those necessary strengths is referred to as beaming stiffness. Simply put, it means the frame must be able to support the load it carries between the axles without sagging. In most cases, the more section width—or the deeper the framerails are (top to bottom)—the more weight the frame will carry without deflecting. Think of the floor joists in a house: they are installed on edge so the load is applied to the larger dimension. The same thing holds true with an automotive frame.

Another force applied to an automotive frame is twisting. If you've ever driven a street rod through a driveway at an angle and felt the body twist, heard creaking or groaning, or seen the door gaps change, it was due to the frame's lack of torsional rigidity. During the era of the Model T Ford, frames were simple and had little torsional rigidity, but they were curiously effective for the time. Ofte referred to as a ladder design because tha what they looked like (the two side 'rails with crossmembers tying them together made the bare frame look like a ladder), t frames under Model Ts were notoriously flexible, but that worked to the flivver's advantage. Model Ts had a reputation fo handling the poor roads of the era and not getting stuck easily because the frame flexed enough to allow both rear wheels t stay in contact with the road, no matter how rough it was. If the body twisted an the hood and radiator danced about whil

The purpose of redesigning the Speed33 framerails was to enhance the smooth, raked lines of the body. Note how the framerails follow the shape of the body and there isn't a gap between the cowl and the top of the 'rails.

When the body is channeled, the framerails disappear, then reappear and get thin and wide all along the way. The Roadster Shop has changed the kick-up in the front of the framerail to a more gradual curve that follows the shape of the cowl. Compare this profile to the preceding photo.

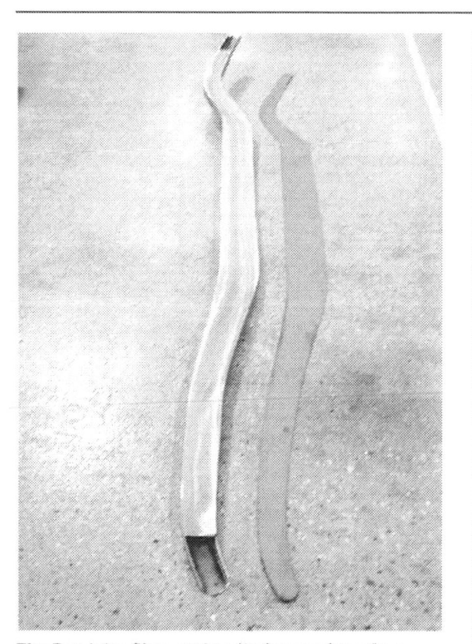

The Roadster Shop makes its frames from four pieces of 10-gauge steel. By using specific patterns for the top, bottom, inside, and outside, any shape 'rails can be created. This is a comparison of the pattern for a Speed33 'rail side (left) and a standard '33 Ford 'rail (right).

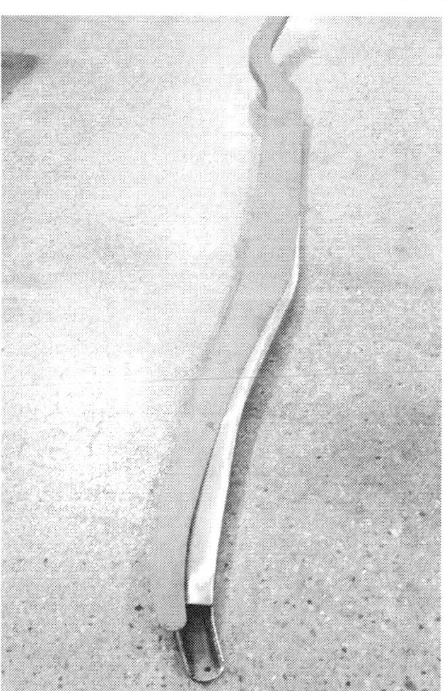

By stacking the two patterns, the differences between a stock frame profile and the Speed33 can be seen (the original is on top, Speed33 is on the bottom).

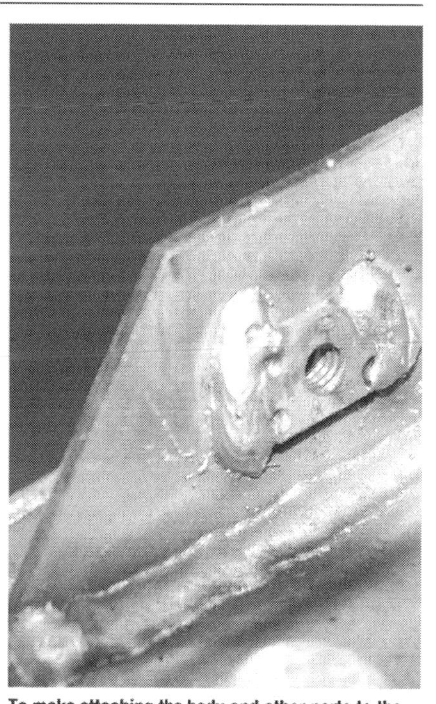

To make attaching the body and other parts to the boxed 'rails easy, threaded plates are welded in place as the frame is put together.

negotiating rough terrain, it was better than getting stuck.

With the introduction of the Model A, the framerails were deeper, which increased the load-carrying capacity, and a center crossmember was added, but there was still a considerable amount of movement that could take place. But thanks to Ford's transverse springs, the chassis worked reasonably well. With the front and rear springs anchored to the centerline of the frame, the suspension was free to travel through its normal range of motion without twisting the frame excessively. Most other cars had the suspension attached at the four corners of the frame and as a result, they had to be stiffer and heavier than Ford's lightweight frame.

Beginning in 1932, Ford framerails were even deeper and a new K-member was added to stiffen the frame, but the most noticeable improvement in torsional rigidity came with the X-member introduced with the Model 40. It worked so well that the same basic frame design continued through 1948.

While Ford frames were vastly improved for '33/'34, the same suspension used on earlier cars was still employed, which meant the springs were still anchored down the centerline of the chassis. But when the type of suspension is changed, as it often is when these cars are transformed into a street rod, the location where the suspension attaches to the frame may also be changed. And as those attachment points move away from the

For increased strength, the Roadster Shop 'rails are completely boxed. The boxing plates are positioned in such a manner that the welds make a rounded edge and little material is lost to grinding.

With the 'rails secured in a fixture, the boxing plates are clamped in place, then tack welded from one end to the other.

Once the 'rails are completely welded, the edges are ground smooth.

Since the Speed33 chassis is unique, special jigs and fixtures are required for assembly.

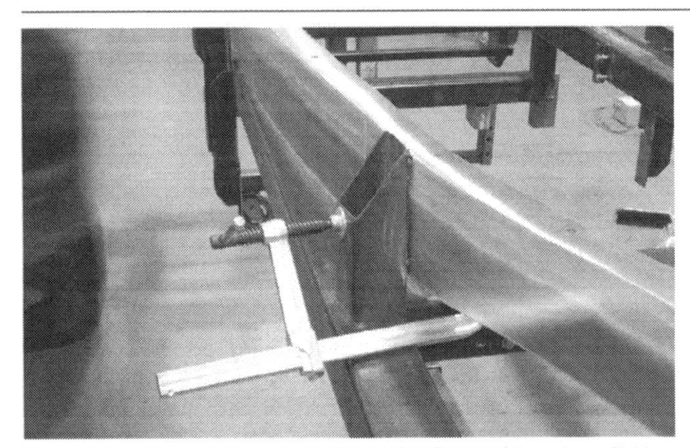
After grinding, the 'rails are securely clamped in a jig, and the crossmembers and X-member are then installed.

Many frames are said to be jig-built, but a frame is only as accurate as the jig it's built in. The Roadster Shop's jigs and fixtures are solid and all frames are checked for accuracy during assembly.

centerline of the frame, more twisting forces are applied to the 'rails. Boxing, or enclosing the open side of the framerails, is one method of strengthening these frames; heavier front and rear crossmembers and a more substantial X-member are also employed when suspension modifications are made.

When it comes to choosing a front suspension for a street rod, the debate on which is right—a solid axle or independent suspension—will likely rage on forever. However, as far as we're concerned, the major consideration when deciding between them is looks versus performance. For a vintage, old school, traditional, or whatever handle you want to use to describe the look, nothing beats a solid axle. They're clean, simple, they're what old hot rods had, and that's pretty much the end of that debate. On the other hand, in terms performance (read ride and handling), a properly designed and installed independent suspension will outperform a solid axle every time. That is not to say a solid axle can't work well—again, properly designed and installed, they will. But the fact is solid axles have limitations due to their basic design—unsprung weight

With the X-member in place, more clamps and fixtures are used to maintain dimensional accuracy during welding.

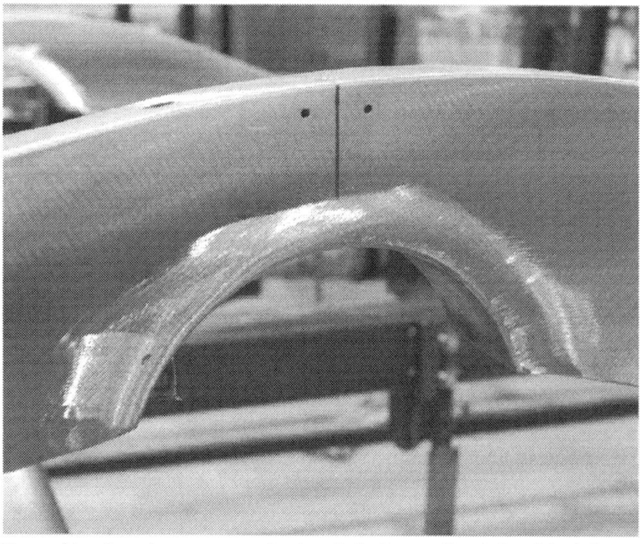

To provide adequate rear suspension travel, the framerails are C-notched above the axle housing.

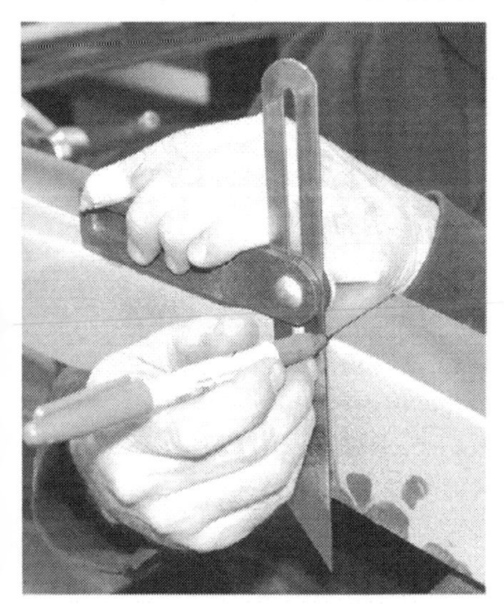

The wheelbase of the Speed33 chassis has been extended 3 inches. This puts the wheels forward in the center of the grille shell for a more aggressive look. Here the centerline for the front crossmember is established.

Part of the Heidt's IFS system is an extremely strong front crossmember. As the forces from the suspension have been moved away from the chassis centerline, this piece must be strong to resist flexing.

is generally higher; when one wheel hits a bump, the other one is affected, meaning both tires' contact with the road is disrupted. On the other hand, with an independent suspension each wheel reacts to irregularities in the road separately; one wheel hitting a bump doesn't affect the other. Coupled with the lighter components for less unsprung weight, it means that an IFS maintains better tire contact with the road for improved handling; the ride will be better, too. And when it comes to aesthetics, the look is just fine with a contemporary-styled ride. So, if you're building a street rod with steel wheels and caps, '39 taillights, and all the pieces that are considered "traditional," a solid axle probably follows the theme better than an independent. If you opt for a more modern approach with wheels, tires, and the rest, an IFS will certainly be keeping with the build style. That being said, keep in mind there are no hard and fast rules for street rods other than those you establish; your car should be built the way you want it, consequently there is no right and wrong.

Although the Speed33 body will fit a stock Model 40 frame, the crew at the Roadster Shop thought something special was in order. As Phil Gerber explains it: "The purpose of redesigning the framerail specific to the Speed33 body was to further enhance its smooth, raked lines. Being that the body is channeled in the front, it has a

The front frame horns have been shortened and reshaped for a better highboy look. The framerails are pinched to end inside the crossmember and there are no frame horns.

Another fixture positions the rear crossmember. Here, the ends of the crossmember are marked for trimming.

By raising the rear crossmember it's possible to obtain the desired ride height while using long coilovers for plenty of suspension travel. Note the C-notches in the 'rail to allow for movement of the rear axle housing.

With all the components positioned and thoroughly tacked, the finish welding is done on a rotating fixture.

natural slope down toward the front. The '33/'34 Ford chassis that Henry built has a slope that goes up in the same location where the Speed33 body slopes down. This area is in the cowl and the engine compartment. We saw two directly intersecting lines and wanted to improve on the design. Another issue that we saw was the fact that when the body was channeled over the frame, the framerail would disappear, then reappear and get thin and wide all along the way." In addition to altering the profile of the frame, the wheelbase has been extended 3 inches up front (however, the stock hood still fits), which results in the front wheels being moved forward. Phil points out that, in normal driving situations, that means the tires will hit any bumps rather than the bottom of the grille shell. To provide the utmost flexibility for those building a Speed33, the Roadster Shop is offering chassis in a variety of configurations—solid axles or independent suspension on one or both ends, fendered or highboy style.

For the '08 Road Tour car, we chose a Heidt's Open Wheel IFS. Designed for fenderless cars with pinched 'rails, the front tubes of swept-back-style control arms are inline with the axle centerline and are longer to accommodate the narrower framerails, and also provide a tread width of 56 inches. Steering is by way of a rear-mounted manual rack from Flaming River. Polished stainless control arms, spindles, ball joint caps, and tie rod ends along with polished aluminum rotor covers are all part of the package we used.

As we've said, one of the traits of a good frame is torsional rigidity; to that end, the Roadster Shop uses a dual-level center crossmember made from 1 1/2 inch 0.120-inch wall tubing. A space frame design, the X-member is stiff while allowing the exhaust pipes, and fuel and brake lines to run between the upper and lower elements. Also part of the X-member is an adjustable transmission mount that allows the fitment of a variety of automatic and manual transmissions and the appropriate combination of floor-mounted pedals. The front crossmember is part of the Heidt's suspension system and is designed to accept the loads from the suspension system that have moved outboard from the centerline of the chassis without flexing.

Just as it is up front, there is a variety of

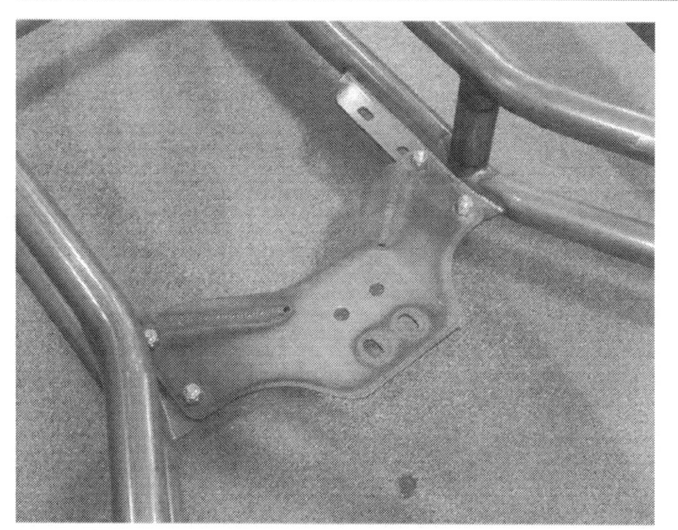

A unique feature of the Roadster Shop frame is the adjustable transmission mount. It allows for the use of just about any automatic or manual gearbox.

Here, it's easy to see how much the rear crossmember has been raised. Also note the C-notch is not done to the extreme that is often seen to maintain structural integrity.

Here, the Heidt's front crossmember has been installed as well as the rear mounts for the upper A-arms.

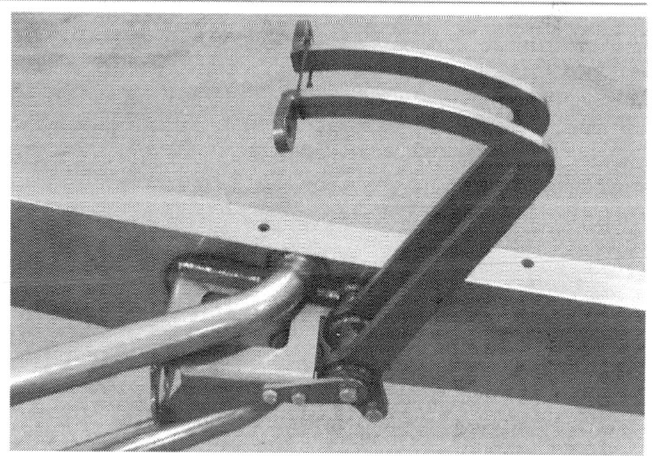

For those who opt to shift for themselves, the Roadster Shop offers brake and clutch pedal combos.

suspension configurations used under the rear of street rods. An original Ford transverse spring, 1/4 elliptic, parallel semi-elliptic, coils, air bags, and coilover shocks will all be found. Of course, the trick with any suspension system is to balance the spring rate with the damping control provided by the shock absorbers, and one of simplest methods to "tune" both is through the use of coilover shocks. We used Strange aluminum coilover shocks on both ends of the Road Tour car for precisely that reason. Strange Engineering developed their line of coilover shocks with the help of chassis builders, racers, and street rod enthusiasts. A wide range of spring rates are available and damping is adjustable. Shock extension is easily adjusted by turning

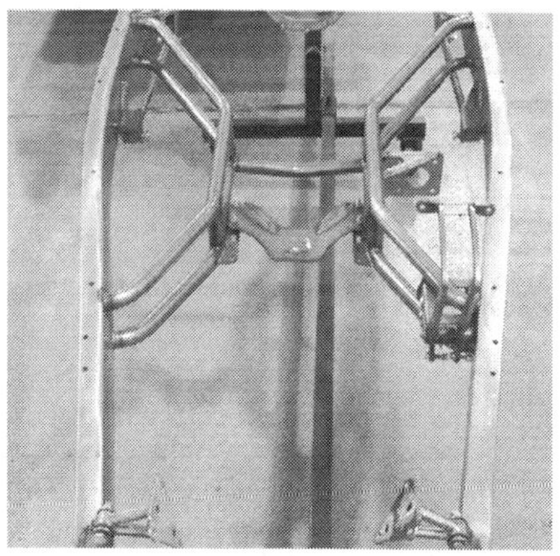

The stout X-member is made from 1 1/2-inch, 0.120 wall tubing and provides ample clearance for up to 3 1/2-inch exhaust pipes. Here the engine mounts have been installed and the body attachment holes are visible.

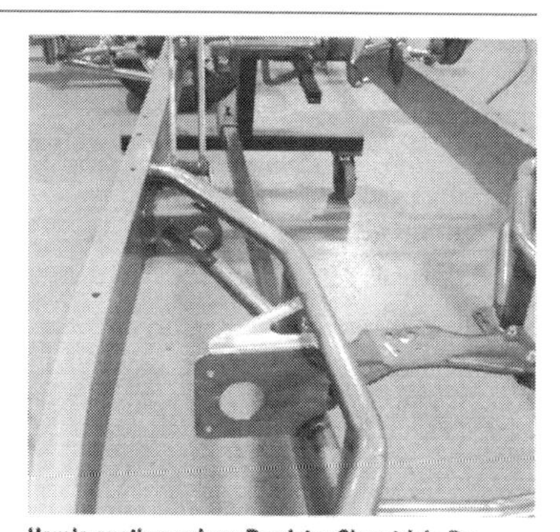

Here's another unique Roadster Shop trick: By moving the chromed power booster and the Wilwood 1-inch-bore master cylinder toward the rear of the X-member, more room is available for the exhaust. A threaded rod is made to extend the throw of the pedal back to the booster

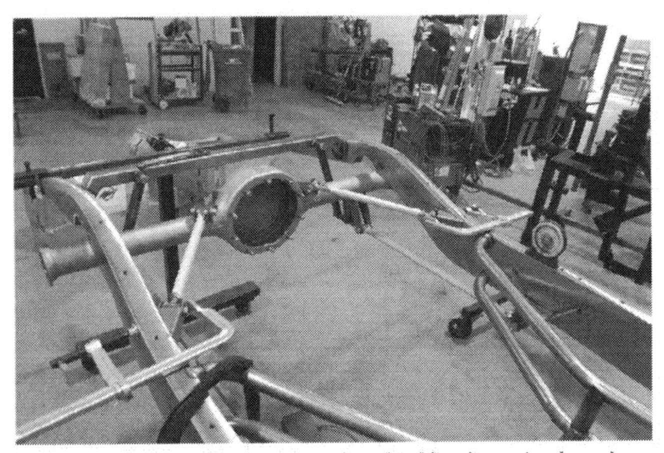
In the rear, a Heidt's polished stainless triangulated four-bar system is used. The angled upper bars eliminate the need for a Panhard bar.

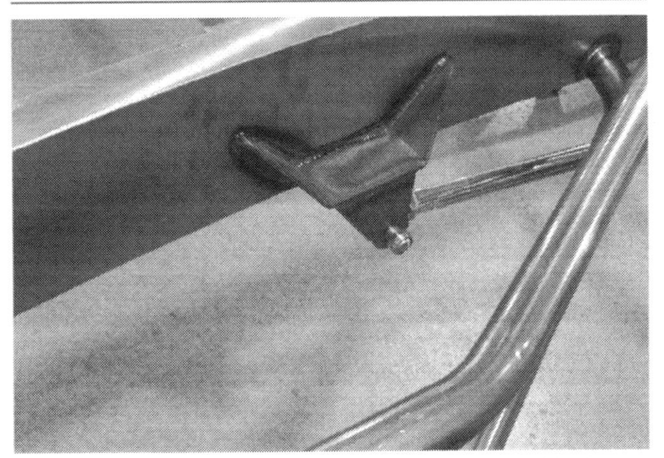
This is the frame mount for the lower bar. All the welding on the chassis is beautifully executed TIG.

a conveniently located external knob that offers 10 precise rebound settings.

Along with the springs and shocks that support the rear of the car, some method of locating the rear axle front to back and side to side is required when anything other than parallel semi-elliptic are used. Ladder bars or four bars are often used for the fore and aft function along with a Panhard bar for side-to-side stability. Another popular option, and the one we chose for the Road Tour car, is Heidt's triangulated four-link. Similar in design to what was used by General Motors, the bottom bars are parallel with the framerails, while the upper bars are at an angle. The angled upper bars not only prevent the axle housing from rolling on acceleration/deceleration, but they also locate it side to side, eliminating the need for a Panhard bar.

While it seems simple, locating the pedals in a street rod can be a packaging problem. Most builders like to keep the firewall clean, but the area under the floor gets pretty crowded. The Roadster Shop offers pedal assemblies for automatic as well as manual transmission applications, and by moving the booster and master cylinder back on the X-member, more space for the exhaust system is available. ■

STAYING STRAIGHT

ALIGNMENT TERMS YOU SHOULD KNOW

As we all know, it takes time, effort, and money to build a street rod, but the reward of jumping in your personal creation and driving it down the road makes it all worthwhile. Of course that's assuming your street rod goes down the road as it should. Nothing is more miserable than a car that you have to fight with to stay on the road.

One of the keys to making a street rod drive as it should is proper frontend alignment. And while that seems simple enough, street rods have one particular issue in that area that is often overlooked: the classic nose-down stance. Adjusting the frontend with the chassis sitting level in a jig won't accomplish anything. The trick is to make sure that the final alignment is done with the same diameter tires front and rear that will be used, and that the car is sitting at the desired rake and ride height.

While aligning frontends is a job normally left to a professional, it will help if you understand the adjustments that can be made.

CAMBER: Camber is the tilting of the wheels from vertical. Positive camber is when the top of the wheel leans out, and negative camber is when the top of the wheel leans in—the amount of camber is usually measured in degrees off of vertical.

Modern tires generate the most cornering force with a trace of negative camber, around 2 degrees, and most contemporary independent suspension systems are designed to gain camber as the car leans in a corner. Excessive camber, either positive or negative, will usually make itself known by wearing one edge of the tire tread or the other.

STEERING AXIS INCLINATION: The amount the kingpins in a solid axle suspension, or the ball joints in an independent suspension, are tilted in at the top is described as steering axis inclination. The tilting of the kingpins, or ball joints, affects handling in a number of ways; it helps keep the wheels pointed straight ahead, and also aids in recovery from a turn. As a result of kingpin inclination, when the front wheels are turned from straight ahead, the front of the car raises slightly. The weight of the car helps the front wheels return to straight ahead when the turn is completed. Steering-axis inclination is part of the suspension design and is not adjustable.

SCRUB RADIUS: If a line were drawn through the kingpin, or the centerline of the ball joints and extended to the ground, then the center point of the tire marked on the ground, the distance between the two would be the scrub radius. Most early cars had zero scrub radius, the angle of the kingpin met the centerline of the tire at the pavement. Lack of scrub made these cars easy to steer without power assist, as the tire pivoted easily without dragging across the ground.

Unfortunately, many modifications commonly done to street rod suspension systems alter the scrub radius. As scrub is increased, by positive-offset wheels as an example, steering becomes more difficult, and bumps in the road can adversely affect vehicle control. On a lightweight car, increased scrub doesn't create a significant problem, but excess should be considered, and the heavier the car, the more of a factor it becomes.

CASTER: In addition to being tilted toward the center of the car, the steering axis also leans toward the front or rear of the car. Forward tilt is negative caster, rearward is positive.

Most cars use positive caster, as it prevents road wander and helps keep the wheels pointed straight ahead. Drag race and Bonneville cars often use extreme caster for high-speed stability.

TOE: The distance between tires, measured at the front and rear, is called toe. Most cars use a small amount of toe-in, that is the front of the tires are closer together than the rear.

Toe-in is generally used to compensate for the tolerances in the steering system. If the wheels were set parallel, as the car moved forward any slack in the steering would let the front of the tires spread apart, resulting in toe-out. Toe-out will cause most cars to wander when going down the road, and contributes to oversteer when first entering a corner.

By setting the front wheels with a small amount of toe-in, generally around 1/32-1/8 inch, the small amount of play in the steering linkage that would produce toe-out in the earlier example is counteracted and the wheels run parallel. Excessive toe, either in or out, will contribute to a peculiar tire-wear pattern called feather edging, the tread looks as though it's been dragged sideways on the pavement, which in effect it has.

For the front suspension we chose the Total Cost Involved custom IFS. This is a worm's-eye view of the crossmember.

TURNING RADIUS: Turning radius, also called toe-out on turns or Ackermann, is the difference in angles of the front wheels when turning. When negotiating a corner, the inside wheel travels in a smaller arc than that of the one on the outside, consequently it must turn tighter.

Toe-out on turns results from the position of the tie-rod ends in the steering arms relative to the kingpins or ball joints. If a line is drawn from the kingpins (or ball joints) to the center of the rear end, it should pass through the tie-rod holes in the steering arms. As a result of the arc that the steering arms travel through when the wheels turn, the inside wheel will turn sharper than the outside wheel. At full steering lock the difference is usually around 3 degrees.

BUMPSTEER: As the name implies, bumpsteer means the car steers itself when it hits a bump. A very disconcerting condition for the driver, bumpsteer is generally caused by alterations to the suspension to lower the car on solid-axle vehicles, and poor engineering for those with independents. Bumpsteer results when the travel of the steering linkage travels through a different arc than the steering arm on the spindle(s).

Solid-axle and independent suspensions usually have bumpsteer for different reasons. Dropped axles are often the culprits that causes bumpsteer in a solid-axle car. The angle of the drag link changes when a dropped axle is installed and passes through a different arc than the one originally designed. As the axle moves up and down, the drag link actually pushes or pulls on the steering arm, causing the car to wander, a classic case of bumpsteer.

Although there are other possible reasons, independent front suspensions usually exhibit bumpsteer when toe changes as the suspension travels up and down. The problem can just about always be traced to an improperly positioned rack-and-pinion steering gear, or tie rod angles that move the steering arms horizontally as the spindles move vertically.

ANTIDIVE: This term is often seen in ads for street rod independent suspension systems. Antidive simply keeps the nose of the car from dropping under braking. The upper A-frame pivot is set at an angle to prevent the brakes from applying compression force to the suspension.

For added strength, the upper four-bar brackets tie into the framerails and the X-member.

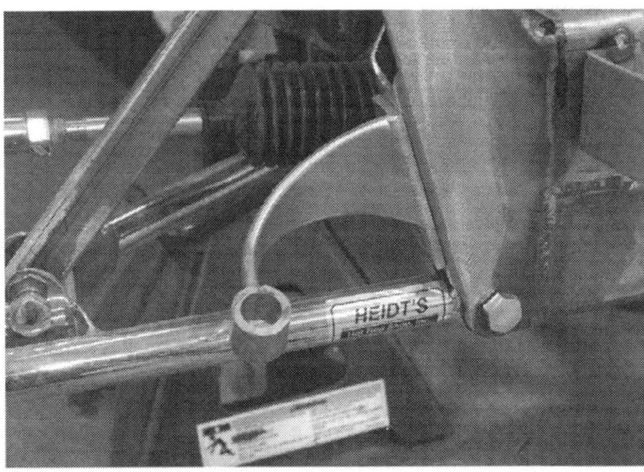

Here's a tasty little Roadster Shop touch: clean and simple headlight brackets integrated with the front crossmember.

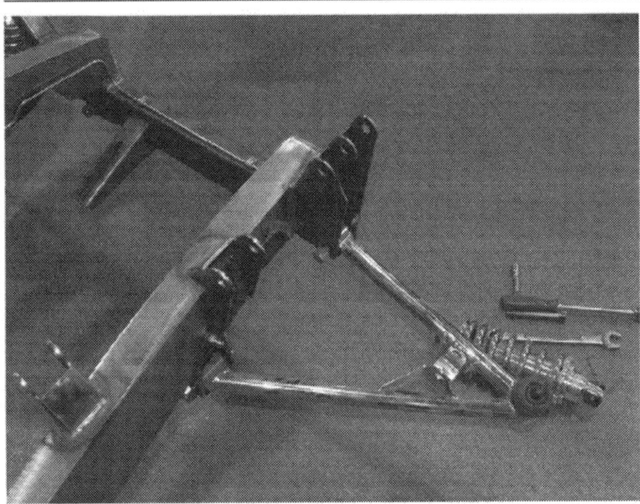

The first step to installing the front suspension is the attachment of the lower A-arms. Note the front leg of the A-frame has a slight sweep to the rear.

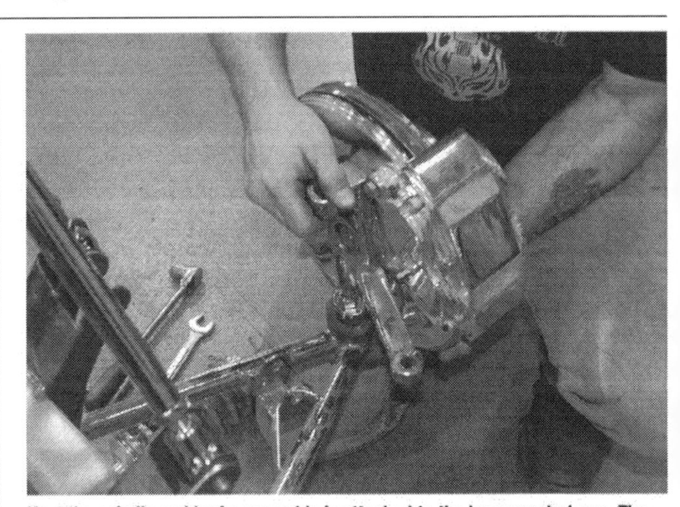

Next the spindle and brake assembly is attached to the lower control arm. The polished stainless spindles have the proper amount of kingpin inclination and the integral steering arms account for Ackermann.

The upper A-frame is next. Note the adjustable ends on the inner attachment points, they allow for caster and camber adjustments.

With the suspension at ride height, the lower A-frame should be level, while the shorter upper A-frame will run slightly uphill for the frame to the spindle.

Without a load, the Strange aluminum coilovers are easily put in place. Strange offers a wide range of spring rates to make suspension tuning easy, plus spring preload is adjustable as is damping.

The front upper A-frame mounts double as an attachment point for the top of the coilover. Heidt's frontends are known for a cushy ride, great handling, and outstanding strength.

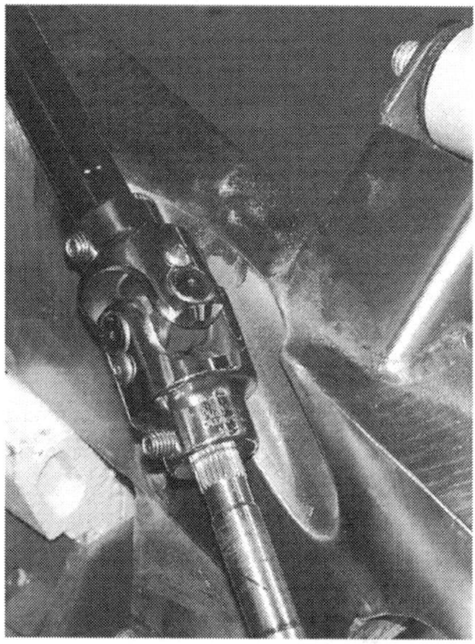
With the pinched 'rails, a cove in the lefthand framerail is necessary to provide clearance for the lower Flaming River U-joint on the steering shaft.

The Road Tour Speed33 is up on its wheels. The combination of the Heidt's suspension, Strange coilovers, and Flaming River rack-and-pinion will make for a smooth-riding and excellent-handling cross-country traveler.

Chapter 5

A FORD FOR A FORD

By Ron Ceridono

What's more at home than a Ford in a Ford? Absolutely nothing. That's why we chose one of the new Boss crate motors to power the '08 Road Tour Speed33.

Although the Flathead was revolutionary in its day, most builders opt for something a little more modern under the hood of their Model 40. Clearly, the small-block Chevy is one of the most popular powerplants to slip into an early Ford, and there are a variety of good reasons for doing so. They're light, compact, affordable, and fit an early Ford like they were made for it. On the other hand, it gets a little boring to see a Bow Tie engine in a Blue Oval car. It's refreshing to see a Ford in a Ford, and the trend is growing by leaps and bounds.

One of the complications when selecting a Ford engine for a street rod is knowing which one to choose. The variety of engines that have been produced since Ford stopped manufacturing the Flathead is truly mind-boggling; there have been approximately 60 different engine combinations offered since 1953.

One of the things that complicates the issue is that Ford built three different engines with 351 cubic inches. There have also been engines with displacements of 427 and 428 in the same FE engine family (the 427 had a bore and stroke of 4.23x3.78 inches, while the 428 was 4.13x3.78 inches), and there was a 429 in another engine family. Ford also built two distinctly different small-block engines: The 221, 255 (an under-bored 302 used in the early 1980s), 260, 289, and 302 referred to as the Fairlane series, and the 351W, 351C

Our engine is equipped with production aluminum valve covers that leave no doubt as to what it is.

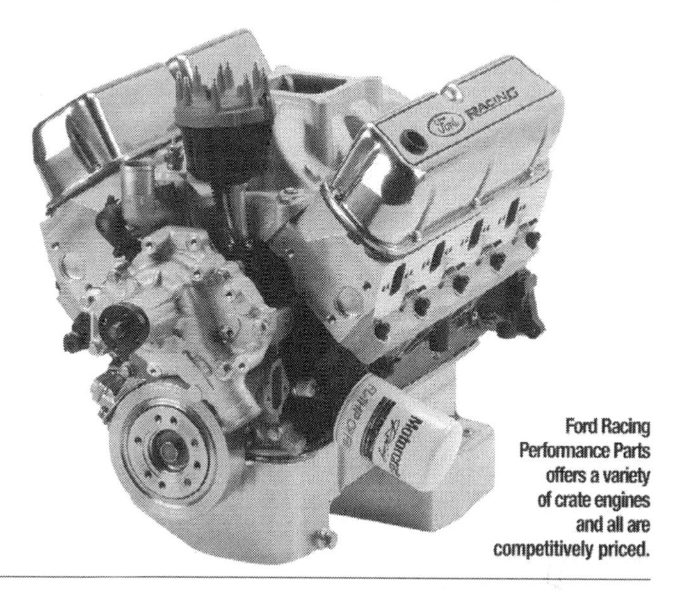
Ford Racing Performance Parts offers a variety of crate engines and all are competitively priced.

The new Boss blocks are made from better material than the originals, have improved oiling, and note the screw-in freeze plugs.

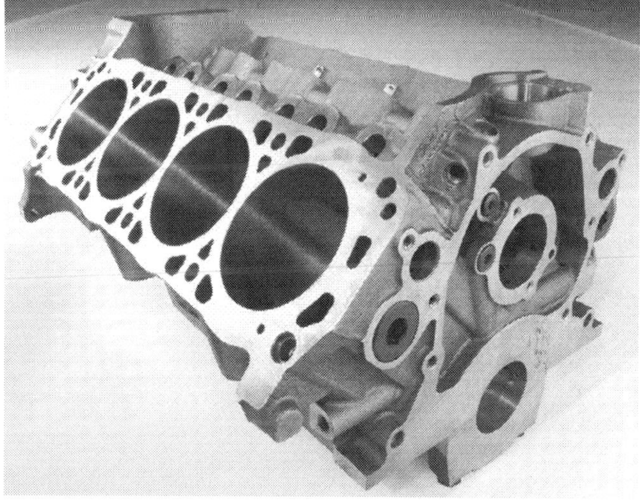
These new blocks feature Siamese bores. That means there are no water jackets between the cylinders at their closest points.

and 351/400M called the 335 series. To further complicate things when mixing and matching Ford parts, within each series there are significant differences. As an example, 221, 260, and early 289 engines had a five-bolt bellhousing pattern. From mid-1965 on, all 289s as well as the 302 and 351 engines that would follow, had a six-bolt pattern.

Something else that confuses the issue is the alphabet soup Ford used as designations and the fact that three different engines had the same displacement: 351W (Windsor, which looks like a Fairlane series, but uses an entirely different block), 351C (Cleveland), and the 351/400M (Modified). All these engines are considered small-blocks (even though the C and M looked much larger due to their canted-valve heads) because the bore spacing and head bolt patterns are the same as the Fairlane series. Toss in the new modular single and dual overhead cam engines (which are a subject unto themselves) and there are plenty of Ford engines to choose from.

Of all the engines Ford has produced, the most popular and frequently modified are the 302 or the 5.0-liter small-blocks. As you might suspect, just to keep things interesting, there's more than one version of the 5.0, the earlier flat-tappet style, and the '85 and later hydraulic roller tappet design. The difference are the roller block has taller lifter bosses and the cam bearing bores are bigger to accommodate the shafts' larger diameter bearing journals and base circle.

Another variation on the small-block Ford was the original Boss 302. Based on Fairlane-style blocks, the heads were the Cleveland style with canted valves. While it appears to simply be a matter of swapping heads (particularly since the bolt patterns are the same), there were a number of other significant differences in the Boss, like a forged crank and four-bolt mains. The other differences that complicate the swap have to do with the cooling system variations. The

Another improvement from yesteryear is the splayed four-bolt main caps along with machined nodular iron caps. Note the Boss 302 logo low on the passenger side of the block.

You can't get the dual-four setup from FRPP, but that shouldn't stop you from trying out this combo on the street. Let's see a pair of 350-cfm four-barrels, some progressive linkage, and *voila*, you have driveability, performance, and that oh-so-important hot rod appearance.

The Boss in any of its configurations comes with a V-belt setup, but by shuffling a few parts you can have a serpentine belt system. We opted for a Vintage Air Front Runner.

This is a preproduction photo, Boss 302s will feature black valve covers with polished fins.

289, 302, and 351W engines use a front timing chain cover and water exits the intake manifold face of the cylinder heads passing through the intake manifold on the way to the radiator. On the 351C, 351M, and 400 engines, the water exits through holes in the combustion chamber face of the heads, then out through an integral extension at the front of the block that houses the thermostat. While the heads and block can be modified for commingling, and the necessary special pushrods can be made, a bigger problem crops up when it's time to bolt on the intake manifold—nothing but a Boss manifold fits. Finding an original could be tough, and while conversion manifolds were once available, we could no longer verify a source for them.

In theory, putting a Ford in a Ford seems like a great idea, but from a practical standpoint, there have always been a couple of hang-ups. One was the overall length of the engine from bellhousing to the tip of the water pump. There were several designs of front covers, water pumps, and vibration dampers used that changed the overall length of the engine. The other complication was the seemingly endless combination of brackets and pulleys Ford used. Getting the correct relationships between the alternator, A/C compressor, and power steering pump, then getting any of them to line up with the crankshaft and water pump pulleys was often the hardest and most frustrating part of the installation. But now there's a simple option, the

SPECS BOSS IS BACK CLOSE

The all-new Ford Racing Boss 302 is the classic reborn in the USA. Known as the greatest production 302 engine ever, the 1969 and 1970 Boss 302 block has grown throughout history as a foundation block for any 302 engine.

Like the original, the new Boss 302 is born of trickle-down race engineering and the best technology in engine block development and production. True to its heritage, the all-new Boss 302 engine block from Ford Racing is redefining 302 performance and setting the standard against which all others will be measured.

Like the original, Ford Racing's BOSS 302 is cast and machined in a Ford production facility and shares many of the same features with the original, including screw-in freeze plugs and 4-bolt mains. With input from Ford's NASCAR engineers and lessons learned from Ford's success in the ASA racing series, the Ford Racing BOSS 302 also features the latest in race block technology.

The next generation of 302 performance is here with the BOSS 302! Good...Better...BOSS!

	THE ORIGINAL 1969-70 Boss 302	GOOD Sportsman 302	BETTER R302 Race Block	THE BOSS Ford Racing BOSS 302
Part Number	N/A	M-6010-B50	M-6010-R302	M-6010-BOSS302
Main Caps	4-bolt cast iron (2, 3, 4)	2-bolt cast iron	4-bolt nodular iron machined splayed (2, 3, 4)	4-bolt nodular iron machined splayed (2, 3, 4)
Siamese bore	No	No	Yes without cross drilling for cooling	Yes with engineered cross drilling
Freeze plugs	Screw-in tapered pipe thread	Press in	Press in	Screw-in O-ring sealed straight thread
Material	Cast iron	Cast iron	Cast iron	Diesel grade heat treated cast iron (41,000psi tensile strength)
Head bolts	7/16"	7/16"	1/2"	1/2"
Recommended Max. Bore	4.030"	4.030"	4.125"	4.125"
Front oil crossover for lifter galley	No	No	No	Yes
Main bolts	7/16" inner (1-5), 3/8" outer (2, 3, 4)	7/16"	1/2" inner (1-5), 3/8" outer (2, 3, 4)	1/2" inner (1-5), 3/8" outer (2, 3, 4)
Oil galley plugs	Pipe thread	Pipe thread and press in	Pipe thread	Screw-in O-ring sealed straight thread
Hydraulic roller compatible	No	Yes	Yes	Yes
Clutch cross shaft pivot hole	Yes	No	Yes	Yes
Rear main seal	2 piece	1 piece	1 piece	1 piece
CID capacity	347	347	363	363
Weight	143 lbs	133 lbs	181 lbs	165 lbs
MSRP	N/A	$1,050	$1,999	$1,759

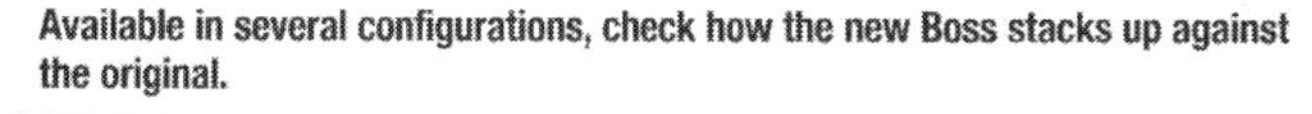

Available in several configurations, check how the new Boss stacks up against the original.

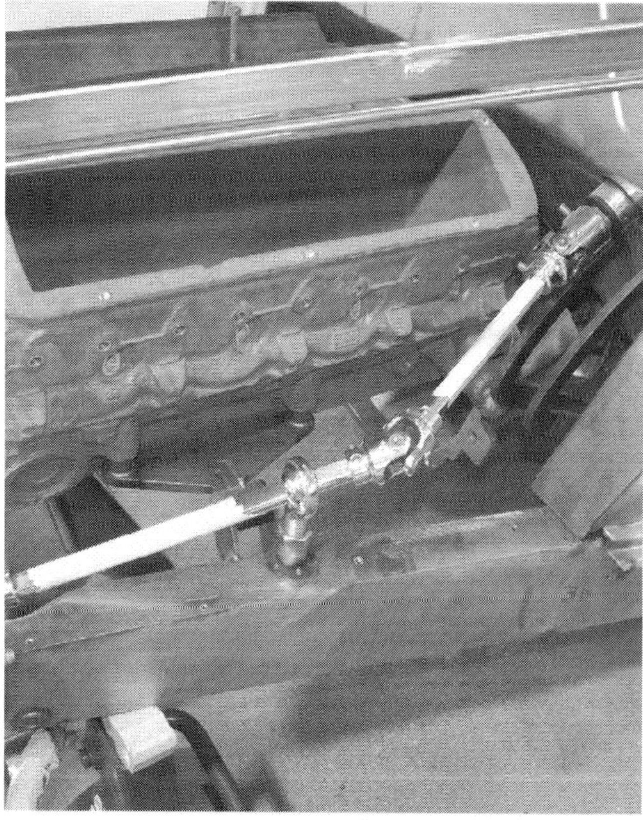

To establish the location of the mounts and route the steering shaft, the crew at the Roadster Shop did a mock-up with a lightweight plastic engine.

Vintage Air Front Runner drive system. It mounts all engine accessories from a unique one-piece forged and machined aluminum timing cover. Nothing else is required.

Included in the Front Runner kit is a high-performance Stewart water pump, 140-amp alternator, serpentine drivebelt, OEM-type belt tensioner, passenger-side refrigerant connections, and all the pulleys featuring optimal accessory drive ratios. Front Runners are available with and without a power steering pump.

THE BOSS IS BACK

One of Ford's most revered V-8s is back and it is better than before.

By Brian Brennan

There can be only one original. The Boss 302 was a two-year (1969-70) production pushrod motor that thrilled Ford fans everywhere and often bested the competition. The Boss was a truly formidable powerplant, but that was 35-plus years ago. What about today? In the age of modular motors there is no denying their performance, but there are still plenty of hot rodders who would like to enjoy the power that can come from a truly potent small-block V-8. When Ford Racing Performance Parts announced that it would bring back the Boss 302, Ford aficionados everywhere were (are) thrilled.

Let us start with a horsepower primer on the original Boss 302 versus the new Boss. The original Boss 302 came out of Detroit with 290 hp at 5,800 rpm, but could be enhanced with Ford factory hi-po parts. Add a low-restriction air cleaner (C5ZZ-9600-W), a larger four-barrel (C8AZ-9510-AD), and a high-rise aluminum intake (C9OZ-9424-D) and an additional 31 hp showed up. An enhanced hydraulic camshaft (C9OZ-6250-C) added an additional 40 ponies. A dual-point distributor (C5OZ-12127-E), and cylinder heads (C9OZ-6049-F) equipped with larger exhaust valves (C9OZ-6505-A) and intake valves (C9OZ-

Although the new engine came with a water pump, it will be replaced with the Stewart pump that's part of the Vintage Air Front Runner kit.

6507) provided another 32 hp. Pop-up pistons took advantage of the improved heads by using part numbers C9OZ-6109-B (left) and C9OZ-6108-AA (right) added to a set of enhanced connecting rods (C6AZ-6200-C). There was a mechanical

There are a variety of front covers used on small-block Fords. Some have provisions for a mechanical fuel pump, some don't. Also, the distance from the front of the block to the water pump mounting surface varies, which alters the location of the water pump and pulleys.

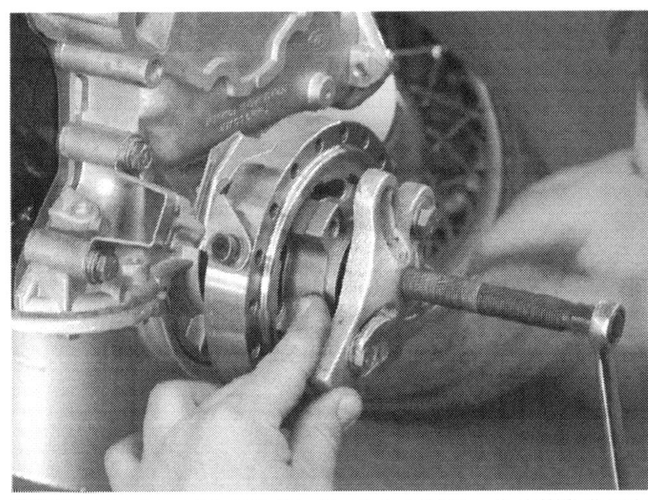

With the pump removed, the vibration damper is next to be removed. The proper puller must be used to prevent damage.

With the front cover removed, the timing chain and sprockets are exposed. Note the fuel pump eccentric on the cam sprocket and that the front cover seals to the pan.

The original pan gasket is one piece. Before installing the new front cover, the old gasket must be trimmed flush with the front of the block.

cam (C7FE-6250-A) for the truly serious performance enthusiast, adding another 59 hp at 6,000 rpm.

Enough of the old, what about the new? Let's start with the new Boss 302 block and see what enhancements have been made by Ford to improve upon a proven package. For the record, the part number on the new Boss block is M-6010-BOSS302. The 165-pound block (old Boss 143 pounds) is made from diesel-grade, heat-treated cast iron (one piece main seal) as compared to the original (two-piece main seal) and cast iron. (Approximate weights for a modern Boss 302 are 543 pounds, while a long-block is 425 pounds.) Both blocks come with four-bolt mains (cylinders 2, 3, 4; and two-bolt on first and fifth main caps), while the new Boss caps are made from nodular iron, and machined and splayed, while the new block features engineered cross-drilling Siamese bores. The new block utilizes O-ring-sealed and straight-thread freeze plugs and oil galley plugs, while the old bock utilized screw-in tapered pipe thread on the freeze plugs and straight pipe thread on the oil galley plugs. The head bolts on the old Boss are 7/16 inch, while the new are 1/2-inch. Coupled to this are the main bolts at 7/16-inch on inner (1-5), and 3/8-inch on outer (2, 3, 4) for the old Boss, while the new Boss employs 1/2-inch inner (1-5), and 3/8-inch outer (2, 3, 4). For those who wish to squeeze out additional cubes, the old block had a recommended maximum bore size of 4.030 inches for a total of 347 cubes. The new Boss has a recommended max bore size of 4.125 inches and max stroke is 3.400 inches for 363 cubes. In its 302-inch configuration, the stroke is based on a 3-inch cast crank, while the 347 version comes with a 3.40-inch forged crank.

The modern Boss 302 can be ordered in one of two cubic-inch configurations: 302 or 347 inches. The Boss 302 can be ordered in one of the following horsepower configurations: 340, 345, 360, or 390. If you opt for the larger displacement 347, then you can have 450 hp. The 340 and 345 versions are ideal street rod motors, offering the greatest driveability. Once you get into the 360, 390, and most definitely, the 450 pony versions, you are in the rarified air of very high-performance motors, and certain sacrifices will be made for everyday street driveability. Now, should you find yourself at the local grudge night or a weekend warrior, then the higher-output versions might satisfy your need for speed.

Obviously, the big-inch Boss is intended to be a competitive motor. The way you order your Boss should be "driven" by the way you want to drive your car. If you like the thrill of power and are willing to sacrifice some driveability, then the 347-inch, 450 hp with 400 lb-ft of torque may be your V-8. You will need to supply the Holley 650-cfm four-barrel for this hi-po motor, while Ford supplies the single-plane Victor Jr. intake, MSD billet distributor, Ford Racing aluminum "Z" cylinder heads (M-6049-Z304A; 2.02-inch intake and 1.60-inch exhaust valves) at 9.7:1 compression ratio and hi-po hydraulic roller camshaft with roller rockers. (Lift is .563 on intake and .584 on exhaust; duration at .050 inch is 232 degrees on intake and 240 degrees on exhaust.) Other FRPP appointments include a Canton 7-quart oil pan, heavy-duty oil and water pumps, and a hi-performance harmonic damper. It is set up for a V-belt accessory drive, but you can change out the front cover and water pump to accommodate the serpentine front drive system.

If you opt for the old fav Boss 302, then you can select from one of four configurations starting at 340 hp and climbing to 390 hp. For instance, there is a 360 hp version (M-6007-Z5OE with camshaft M-6250-E303) or 390hp version (M-6007-Z5OZ with camshaft M-6250-Z303). The 360 hp comes in at 5,000 rpm and has 330 lb-ft of torque at 4,800 rpm and 9.0:1 compression ratio, while the 390 hp comes in at 6,200 rpm with 360 lb-ft of torque at 5,000 rpm and 10.0:1 compression. Both engines are shipped without an intake. Intake M-9424-E302 was used on the 360 hp version, and an intake with Weber carburetors for 390 hp.

Before the new front cover is installed, an abbreviated pan gasket and a new seal are put in place. A small bead of silicone will prevent leaks at the joint.

A clean and simple way to shorten the front of a Ford engine and mount all the accessories is with the Vintage Air Front Runner kit.

TIPS ON INSTALLATION

There are some points of emphasis that we should pay attention to no matter what engine we install, but here are some items to pay attention to when installing your new crate motor.

OILING SYSTEM

Priming the oiling system before starting a new engine is critical. If you change from the recommended factory pan, make sure the new one has adequate capacity, which is generally 7 quarts minimum, coupled with proper baffling. Properly fabricated baffles keep the oil over the pickup screen at all times.

The pickup screen must be the proper distance from the bottom of the oil pan. If too close, cavitation can occur; too far, and the pump will draw air. The pickup screen should be located .250-.375 inch from the bottom of the pan. Make sure to use proper sized lines, while eliminating as many bends or turns as you can. Also make sure to connect your engine's remote oil filter or oil cooler lines correctly to allow oil to flow in the proper direction.

IGNITION SYSTEM

This part of your engine lives or dies with too much or too little. Avoid hooking up the vacuum advance to intake manifold vacuum instead of ported vacuum. Also avoid improper plug wire routing, which means separate plug wires on cylinders that fire in sequence.

According to Ford Racing Performance Parts, the total mechanical advance timing at 4,000 rpm for its crate engines are as follows: 5.0L: 36-38 degrees, 347/351: 34-36 degrees, 392/460/514: 30-32 degrees.

FUEL DELIVERY

According to FRPP, be careful when using oxygenated fuels as it can dramatically affect your jetting requirements. Again according to Ford, it has found in the dyno testing of its crate engines that one point richer on air/fuel ratio equals only a few percent less power. Running an engine as lean as possible produces the best power, but also increases combustion temperatures and the chances of engine damage.

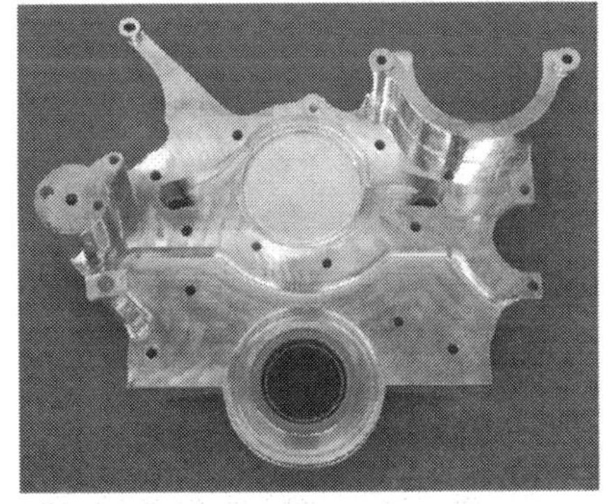

At the heart of the Front Runner is an all-new timing cover that incorporates the necessary mounts for the alternator, A/C compressor, and power steering pump.

Included in the Vintage Air kit are pulleys for a serpentine belt.

An off-the-shelf belt tensioner is used is used for simple, trouble-free operation.

Although the A/C compressor mounts on the left side of the engine, formed tubing make the hose connections on the right side to make routing hoses easier.

Included in the Front Runner kit is a high-output alternator. As the belt is tightened by a spring-loaded tensioner, the alternator and other accessories are mounted solidly.

The Front Runner is good looking and compact; with thousands in use they have proven to be bulletproof. This example uses a power steering pump. The '08 Road Tour is equipped with manual steering so there isn't a pump.

Topping off the Boss is a 650-CFM Holley double-pumper manual-secondary carburetor. Equipped with four-corner idle circuits, this is a performance piece; those living in cool climates may want to opt for a mixer with a choke.

To supply the necessary spark, we chose a complete MSD ignition system. This distributor uses a separate control box mounted behind the dashboard. MSD also has self-contained, ready-to-run distributors available.

COOLING SYSTEM

Rule of thumb: higher horsepower requires more cooling capacity. Something street rodders have to be careful about is the selection of proper pulleys. Improper pulley size makes the fan and water pump turn too slow or too fast. Production water pumps are normally run at 20 percent over engine speed and do not perform well over 5,000 engine rpm. Underdrive pulleys generally reduce water pump speed below engine speed (as much as 15 percent) and may not provide enough water flow to cool the engine.

We have written plenty on the pages of *Street Rodder* about having a proper radiator with enough area to dissipate the engine heat. However, something we see all too frequently are improper sized fans and the lack (or improper use) of fan shrouds.

FLYWHEEL, CONVERTER, AND TRANSMISSION

Installing the wrong flywheel will cause vibration and eventually damage the engine. The wrong length input shaft or "stack-up height" can force the crank forward, damaging the engine thrust bearing. Improperly installing the torque converter can force the crank forward, damaging the engine thrust bearing. This is most commonly caused by improperly locating the torque converter drain plug in the flexplate.

MISCELLANEOUS WOES

Over-torquing of the intake manifold bolts to the cylinder head on 302 and 351W engines can cause head gasket sealing problems.

Installing distributor gears at the incorrect height and/or gears made of the wrong material will cause premature engine failure. Use cast-iron gears for cast-iron flat-tappet cams, and steel gears for steel hydraulic roller cams.

CONCLUSION

The Boss is back and street rodders everywhere, especially those who wish to keep a Ford powerplant in their Ford engine compartment, have lots to cheer about. ■

Our engine came complete with a spin-on oil filter, unfortunately it interfered with the steering shaft.

Gaining more room for the steering shaft was easily accomplished by swapping the spin-on canister for an AMSOIL remote filter adapter.

Between the flywheel and the block is a very important piece called the starter plate. It serves two functions: It's a spacer between the block and bellhousing, and it locates the starter correctly.

The Vintage Air Front Runner makes the front of the engine compact and tidy. Note the lines on the oil filter adapter leading to the remote mount filter.

To make sure that coolant isn't lost even on the hottest days, an overflow tank from Yogi's was installed.

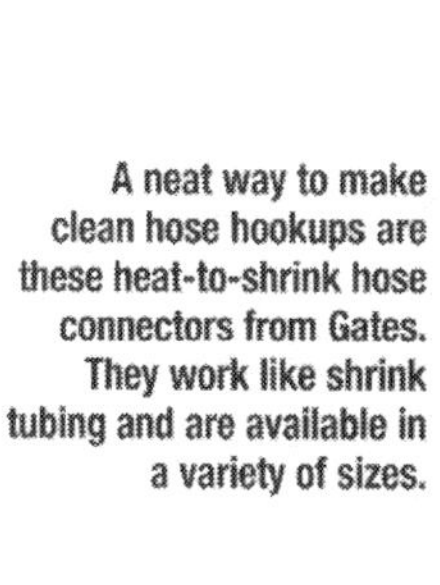

A neat way to make clean hose hookups are these heat-to-shrink hose connectors from Gates. They work like shrink tubing and are available in a variety of sizes.

Chapter 6

SELECTING DRIVELINE COMPONENTS

By Ron Ceridono

Ready for a test fit, the Boss 302 and Classic Motorsports five-speed are heading for their new home in the Roadster Shop chassis.

hen Model 40s were rolling down the assembly lines the driveline components were similar to those introduced by Ford in 1932 and the same basic layout was retained through 1948. Backing up the Flathead V-8 in passenger cars (as well as the all the four- and six-cylinders that were introduced in 1941) was a three-speed transmission; '32-39 used a top shifter, '40-48 had the shifter on the column. While all these transmissions looked similar, gear ratios varied and a common swap was to substitute the gears from a Lincoln Zephyr for a higher Second gear that would allow a hopped-up Flattie to accelerate longer before it was necessary to shift into high.

Examples of early Ford transmission gear ratios:

Lincoln 25-tooth main gear-low 2.12:1; Second 1.44:1, Third 1.00:1

Lincoln 26-tooth main gear-low 2.33:1; Second 1.58:1, Third 1.00:1

Ford 28-tooth main gear-low 2.82:1; Second 1.60:1, Third 1.00:1

Ford 29-tooth main gear-low 3.11:1; Second 1.77:1, Third 1.00:1

Like many cars of the era, Model 40 Ford rearends used an enclosed driveshaft. With this design the rear axle housing couldn't twist under acceleration or braking because the torque tube housing the driveshaft was attached to the back of the transmission with a ball and socket (which also contained the single universal joint). With this system the car was literally pulled around by the engine mounts so longitudinal rods that ran from the block to the chassis were used. Ford stuck with this basic design for passenger cars from the Model T through 1948.

While Ford's three-speed transmission, enclosed driveline, and rearend with its tapered and keyed axle shafts were adequate for the 100 or so horsepower they had to cope with, for the '08 Road Tour car we needed something a little stouter. In addition we wanted a transmission with a wider gear selection. And while there are a variety of automatic transmissions that fit that bill, there's nothing like driving a street rod with three pedals and a gearshift lever that doesn't have a park position. We wanted to shift for ourselves.

Depending on the gear ratios selected the TKO's torque capacity is either 500 or 600 lb-ft of torque. Three available overdrive ratios are available.

When the decision is made to use a manual transmission there are some other components that have to be decided upon as well. First is the flywheel and the choice to be made is between aluminum and steel construction. Aluminum flywheels

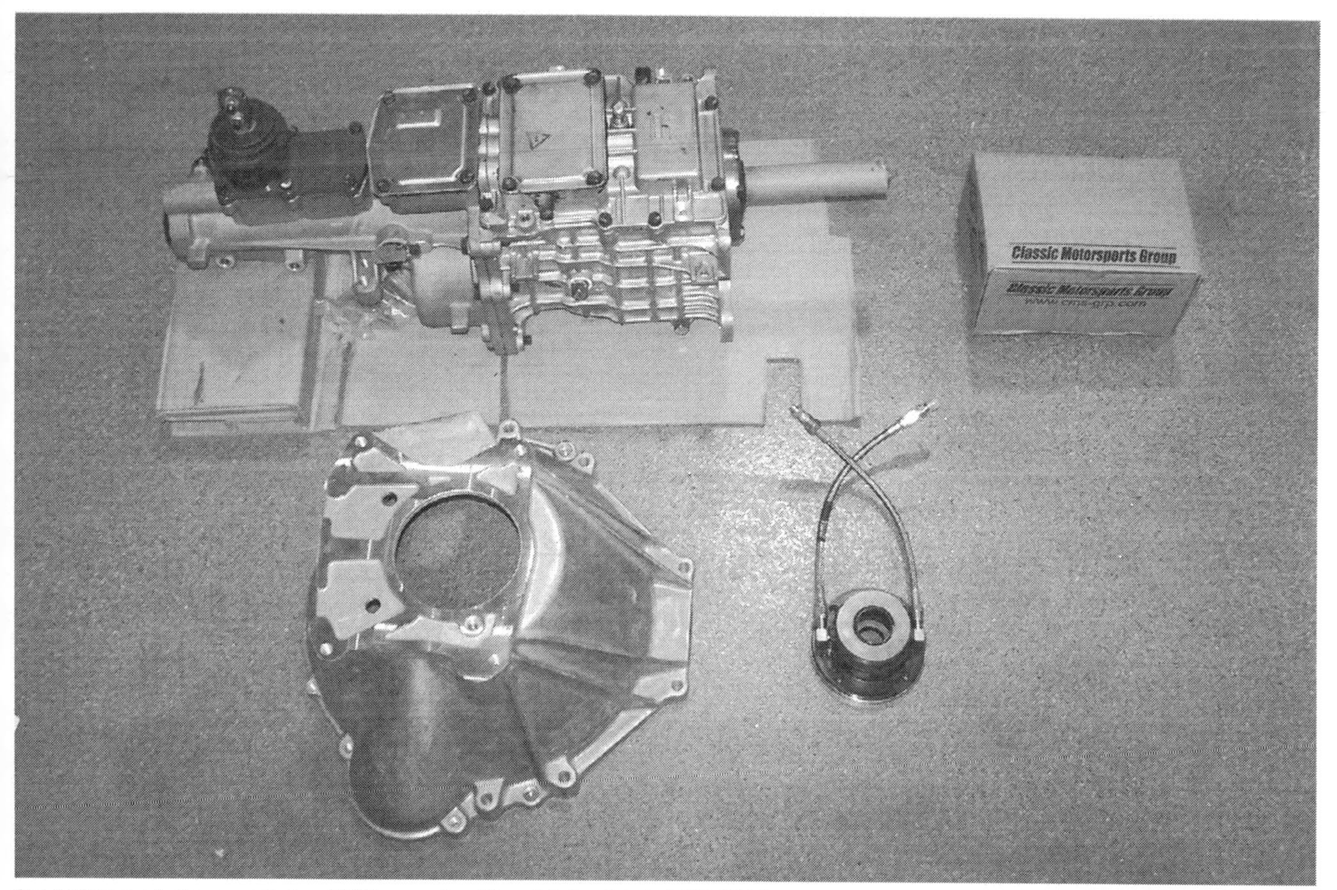

Classic Motorsports Group supplied our TKO five-speed and the related parts to install it. CMG is your one-stop headquarters for a Tremec to fit any application.

Although aluminum flywheels have a reputation for allowing an engine to rev more freely, the additional inertia provided by a steel flywheel works best on the street. Note the spacer/starter plate is in place.

For the best compromise between clamping force and pedal pressure we chose a Diaphragm spring pressure plate. Only the proper shouldered bolts should be used to attach any pressure plate to the flywheel.

When installing a clutch assembly, use an alignment tool that simulates the transmission's input shaft to ensure the disc is properly centered. If the transmission doesn't slide in place against the bellhousing, remove it and double-check the alignment; never force them together by tightening the bolts.

are lighter weight and are typically used in oval track and road race applications, and are also popular in high-horsepower, lightweight drag cars. These vehicles rely on engine horsepower to drive the wheels. On the other hand, steel flywheels are best when engine torque is relied upon for performance. The inertia of a heavier flywheel can help acceleration from a standing start and help acceleration through the gears, in other words the conditions found driving on the street; that's why we elected to use a steel flywheel.

Another consideration is the type of clutch to use. Basically, there are three styles of pressure plates: Long, Borg & Beck, and Diaphragm. The Long-style

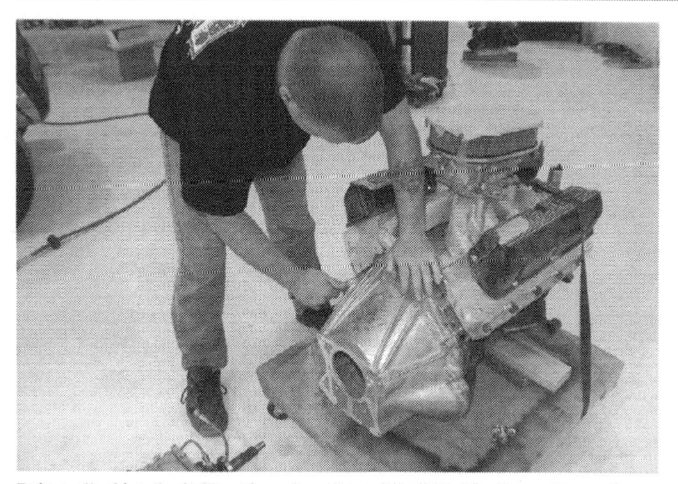

Before attaching the bellhousing, clean the paint off the block's mating surface. Both mating surfaces must be clean and flat to prevent misalignment of the transmission's mainshaft, which can cause vibration and even bearing damage.

If a hydraulic throwout bearing is used, it will be necessary to establish the precise distance from the transmission mounting flange to the release fingers on the clutch.

The TKO comes with a front bearing retainer that also has a snout for a conventional throwout bearing.

Removing the retainer is the first step to convert to a bolt-on hydraulic throwout bearing (slide-on styles are also available).

pressure plate was used by Ford and has three release fingers and coil springs. A favorite of racers, Long-style pressure plates are light and release quickly for speed shifting. Borg & Beck pressure plates also use coil springs and have three release fingers, although they're wider than the Long-style. Some Borg & Beck pressure plates are original equipment on GM and Chrysler cars. They also have three release fingers (although they are wider than the Long-style fingers), use coil springs, and some have centrifugal rollers that add holding power in high-horsepower applications. Last, but certainly not least, is the Diaphragm-style. Easily recognizable by the large number of release fingers, this style of pressure plate offers the best compromise between clamping load and pedal pressure. We chose a Diaphragm pressure plate for the Speeed33.

At one time, opting for a manual transmission meant using an antiquated Ford three-speed, or for four-speed fans, the popular choices were the Borg-Warner T-10, Muncie, or Saginaw. If an overdrive was what you were after, there were a few three-speeds so equipped, but they certainly weren't considered performance gearboxes. But today there are better manual transmission options than ever, specifically five-speed boxes with low First gears, overdrive top cogs and evenly split ratios in between, many of which come from a company called Transmission Technologies Corporation. TTC manufactures a full line of rear-wheel-drive manual transmissions and components for vehicles ranging from high-performance passenger cars and light-duty trucks to 18-speed transmissions for Class 8 commercial vehicles. Part of the DESC group, one of Mexico's largest automotive component suppliers, TTC is a joint venture between DESC's automotive operation and Dana Corporation. With the acquisition of Tremec in 1994, the acquisition of Borg-Warner's manual transmission operation in 1997, and the relocation of Dana's medium- and heavy-duty transmission operation

The new assembly slides in place and bolts to the transmission.

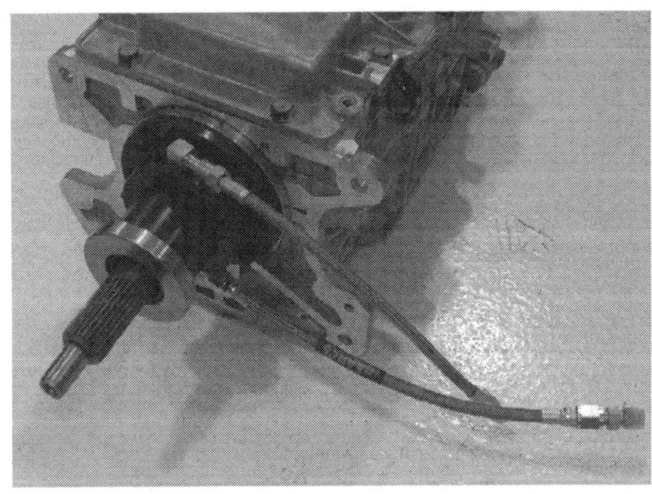

There are two lines: the supply is at the bottom, and the bleeder must be on top.

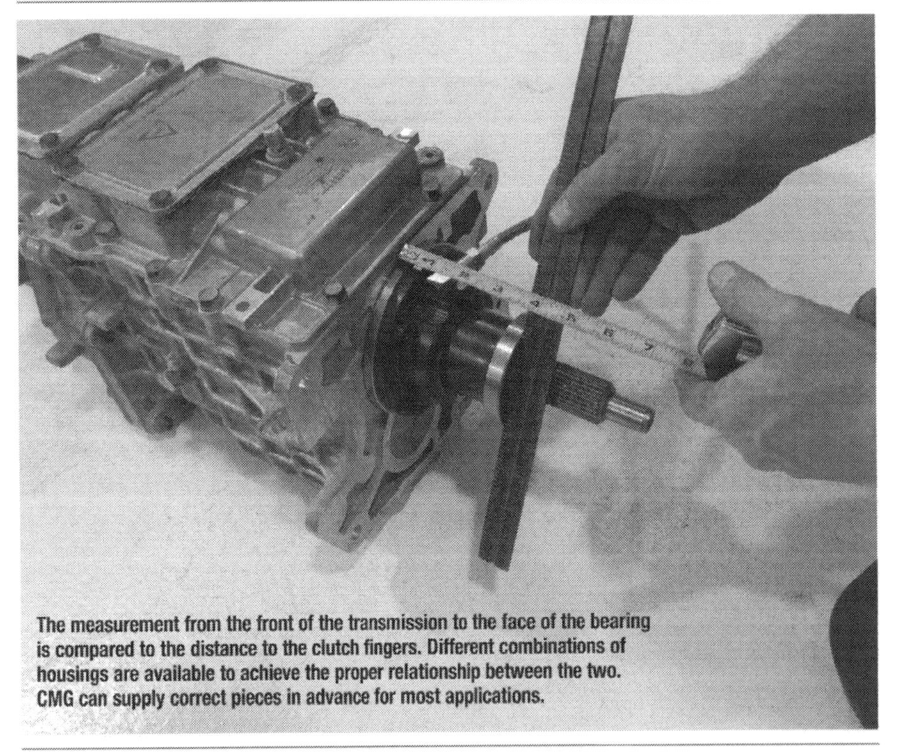

The measurement from the front of the transmission to the face of the bearing is compared to the distance to the clutch fingers. Different combinations of housings are available to achieve the proper relationship between the two. CMG can supply correct pieces in advance for most applications.

in 1998, the company became a full-service, Tier 1 transmission manufacturer with manufacturing facilities located in Queretaro, Mexico and Knoxville, Tennessee.

A variety of transmissions will be found under the Tremec brand name; the following are a few of the most common five-speeds used in street rods. Note that when the specifications of five-speed transmissions are listed in reference to what's called "center distance" may be found. This is the spacing between the shafts in the transmission and in simple terms it means the greater the distance between the two, the larger the gears can be and the more torque capacity the transmission will have.

T5

These are light-duty, five-speed transmissions found in passenger cars and SUVs. Available in a variety of gear ratios, the relatively close shaft spacing limits torque capacity. Although they are commonly used in street rods, they are not suited to high-horsepower applications.

T45

The TREMEC T45 was used on the '96-99 Ford Mustang Cobra and is currently available for aftermarket applications. Its greater 81.5mm center-to-center distance allows for larger gears and therefore increased torque capacity. Found under several part numbers, the torque capacity and gear ratios are the same for all.

TKO

An upgraded version of the TR-3550, the TKO series are high-performance, five-speed overdrive transmissions have extremely high torque capacities thanks to their 83mm shaft spacing. That means they have the capacity to handle a high-torque engine like our Boss, along with better gas mileage and lower cruising rpm due to Fifth-gear overdrive.

Along with their torque capacity, TKOs have a variety of features that make them great options for street rods:

Eight shifter locations available (ranging from 14-27 inches from face of the bell housing).

Three unique crossmember-mounting configurations.

Three different input shafts available.
Three available overdrive ratios.
Aluminum, short-throw shifter.
Speedometer pickups for either mechanical or electric speedometers.
180-day warranty from Tremec.

Over the years we've found that getting related components from one source eliminates problems with parts that aren't compatible. For that reason we obtained the clutch assembly, throwout bearing, and transmission from Classic Motorsports Group. They specialize in five-speed conversions for GM and Mopar cars and are an Elite dealer for Tremec transmissions.

Regardless of the type of manual transmission or pressure plate that is being used, some sort of clutch linkage is required and they fall into two categories: manual and hydraulic. Manual linkage, although common, can be difficult to fabricate for a street rod. There are two types of hydraulic systems; one uses a slave cylinder to operate the release arm and uses a conventional throwout bearing like a manual system. Another option, and the one we chose, is a hydraulic throwout bearing. In either case the source of hydraulic pressure is from a master cylinder operated by the clutch pedal.

SELECTING A REAR END

Without a doubt, Ford's 8- and 9-inch rear ends are the most popular axle assemblies for street rods. In fact, they've become so popular that now they're hard to find. But digging through a junkyard isn't necessary if you're looking for a 9-inch because everything you need is available new thanks to Strange Engineering and U.S. Gear.

Bob Stange began building components for his own racecar and soon others were asking him to build parts for them as well. For reasons that are unknown, as Stange gained recognition for his wares, his name was more often than not misspelled as Strange. When he decided to incorporate his blossoming business, he gave up trying to correct

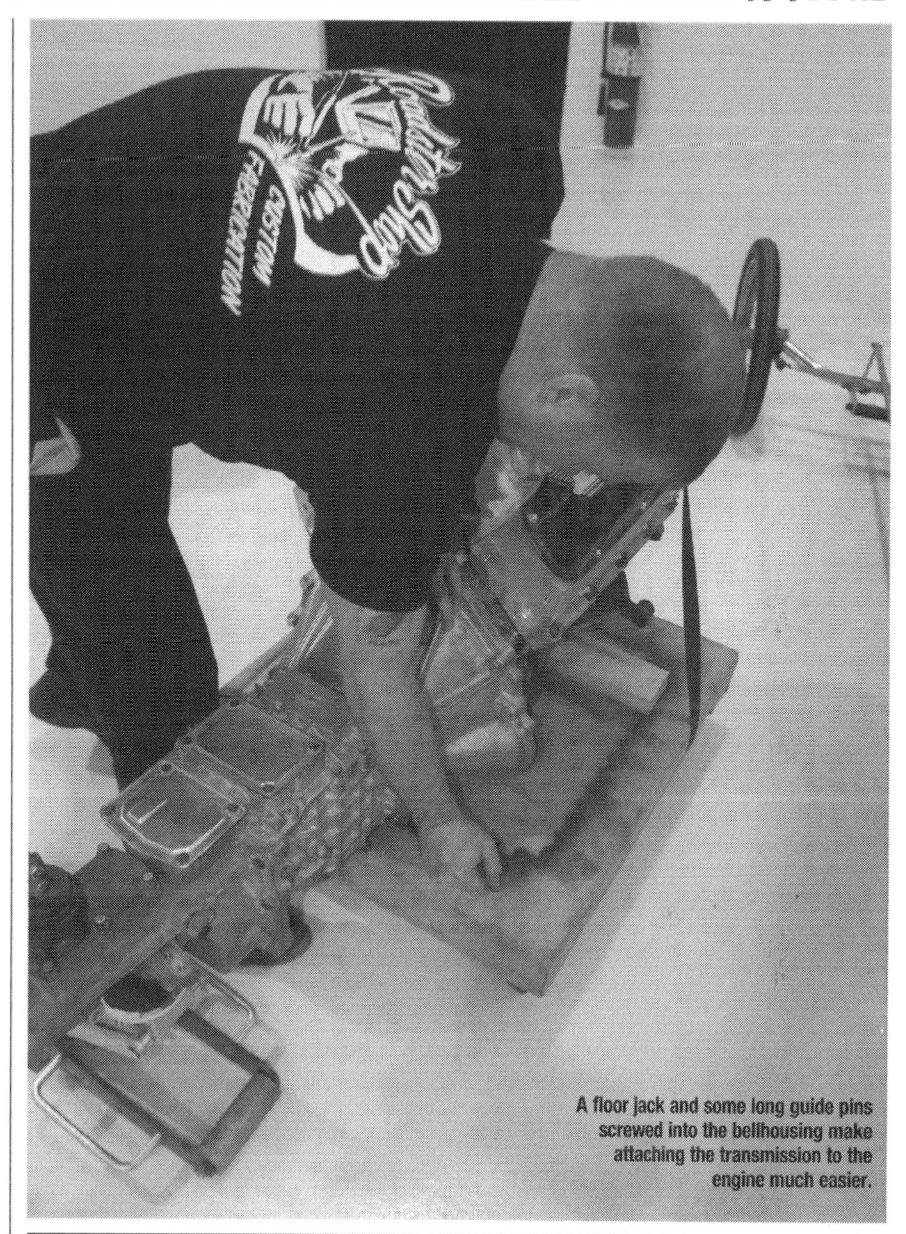

A floor jack and some long guide pins screwed into the bellhousing make attaching the transmission to the engine much easier.

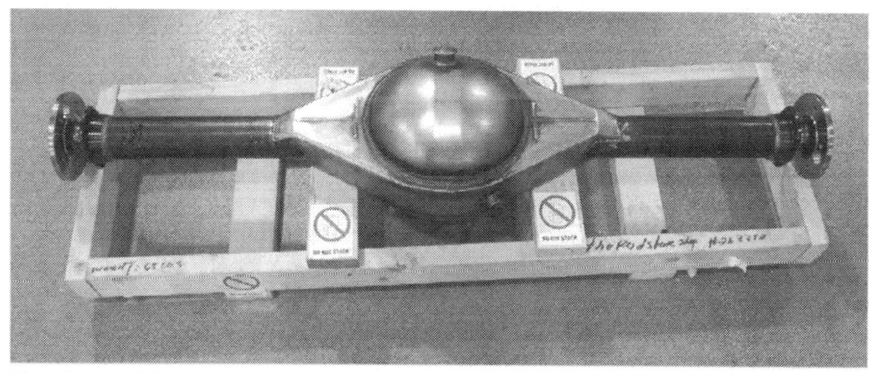
Under the rear of the '08 Road Tour Speed '33 is a new Strange 9-inch rear axle housing filled with all new Strange components and a ring-and-pinion set from U.S. Gear.

Model	Part Number	1st	2nd	3rd	4th	5th	Torque Rating
TKO-500	5201	3.27	1.98	1.34	1.00	.68	500 lb-ft
TKO-600	5008	2.87	1.89	1.28	1.00	.64	600 lb-ft
TKO-600 (RR)	4617	2.87	1.89	1.28	1.00	.82	600 lb-ft

everyone and Strange Engineering was born. Today Bob is semi-retired and his son, Jeff, runs the company.

Although Strange Engineering is known for drag racing components, like the 12-inch top loader rear axle that can be found under most Top Fuel and Funny Cars, they can also supply every component necessary for the rearend of a street rod. All the required individual parts from housings, carriers, axles, studs, bearings, brake kits, and everything up to and including the fasteners that hold one together.

Of course, Strange Engineering also offers a multitude of complete 9-inch rear end assemblies and can custom tailor a rear end to meet your specifications. Strange Engineering offers "packages" of components and will install the parts you choose, so all you have to do is bolt it in. Strange will completely crate your rearend assembly for an uneventful delivery at no additional cost (freight is not included). Here are a few of the steps in a custom rearend package:

First, determine the dimensions necessary.

Housings—Strange recommends 3.250-inch tubing for its increased (23 percent) strength in comparison to 3-inch tubing; however, certain ladder bar and four-link configurations may require the smaller tubes. Please consult with the company that is providing the brackets. Strange will slip (not weld) your mounts onto the tubes before welding the housing ends or, at an additional cost, weld the customer's mounts to the tubes. They require that a weld (location) sheet be completed before this is done. Strange will assist with selecting the proper housing end based on the brakes being used.

Axle Package—S/S Series (31-spline) axles are recommended for street applications and S/T Series (35-spline) axles are recommended for street and street/track applications. Strange Pro Race axles are for drag race applications only! Nine-inch posi units will only fit 31-spline axles and lockers will fit either 31- or 35-spline axles. New assemblies with a 31- or 35-spline locker are the same price, so Strange recommends 35-spline S/T axles when selecting a locker.

Center Section-Center—The S-Series center section is ideal for street or street/track applications. The Pro Iron center section can be used for street/track or drag race applications. Lightweight aluminum center sections are ideal for drag race and select street applications (call to discuss this).

Differentials—The posi unit's smooth and quiet transfer of power is desirable for most street applications. Lockers are stronger than posi units, but are noisier and the transfer of power is more abrupt. Spools should always and only be used for drag race applications. A spool does not permit the outside wheel to rotate at a higher speed than the inside wheel during turning, creating a dangerous street vehicle.

Along with the housings, Strange produces new axle ends. Two Ford styles are available: the big Ford, and the late big Ford. The difference is in the backing plate pattern, which must be matched to the brakes being used.

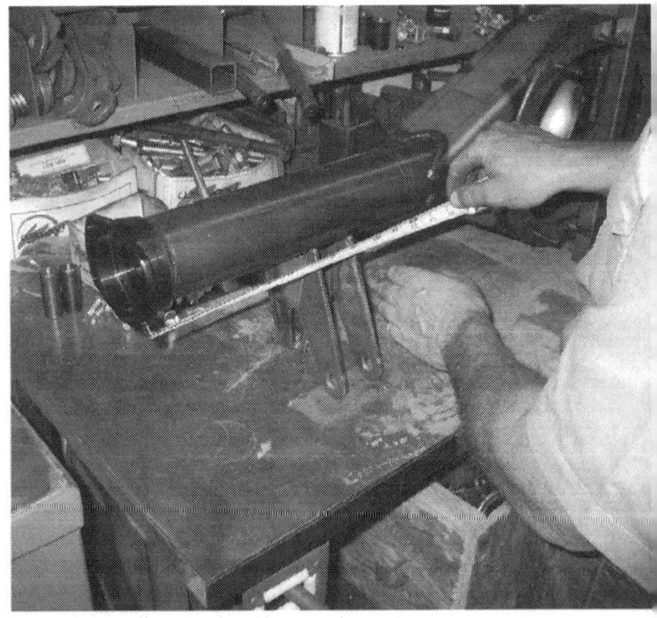

At the Roadster Shop, the housing was clamped in a fixture and the axle brackets were positioned.

Strange Axle Order Information

Strange axles are manufactured to meet each customer's needs. In order for us to produce an optimal axle fit, we have provided the following text and illustrations to assist you with supplying the necessary axle information. Please do not hesitate to call us if you have any questions or need a more in depth explanation of the information that we have requested.

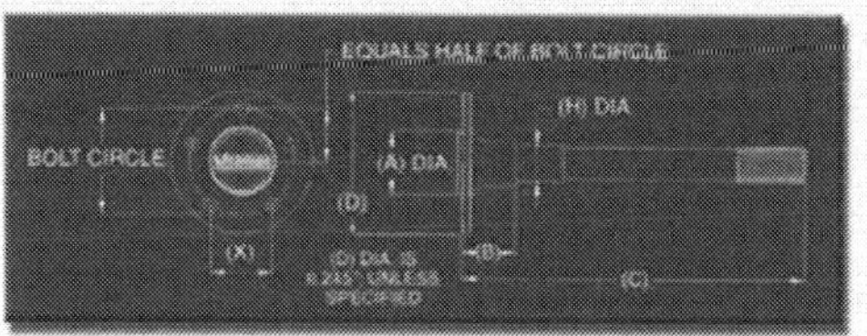

Complete the information for **Rear End/Housing** if you cannot obtain dimension "C". The "C" dimension of an existing axle may be affected by other dimensional changes to rear end (carrier, brakes...)- please let us know of any changes. Provide all the necessary information for existing axles. ***The facing page has a housing end identification chart as well as common OEM and aftermarket dimensions*** .

"X"	*Bolt Circle*
2.645"	4.50"
2.792"	4.75"
2.939"	5.00"
3.233"	5.50"

(1) Application (Drag, Street...). (2) Carrier (Posi, Spool...) and brand of carrier- please let us know if you have given a "C" dimension with an existing carrier and intend to change the carrier. The change may alter the "C" dimension. (3) Number of axle splines. (4) Bolt Circle (above). (5) Tapped for screw in studs (1/2-20 or 5/8-18). S-Series axles may be drilled to accept knurled studs. The knurl size of the stud must be specified. Pro Race axles will not work with knurled studs. (6) Housing end type (note: housing end shape may vary- please verify dimensions). (7) Type of brakes (drum, factory disc or aftermarket) and manufacturer. All aftermarket brake companies should supply you with the brake gap ("F" dimension). (8) Strange axle flange OD (**"D"**) is 6.245" unless specified.

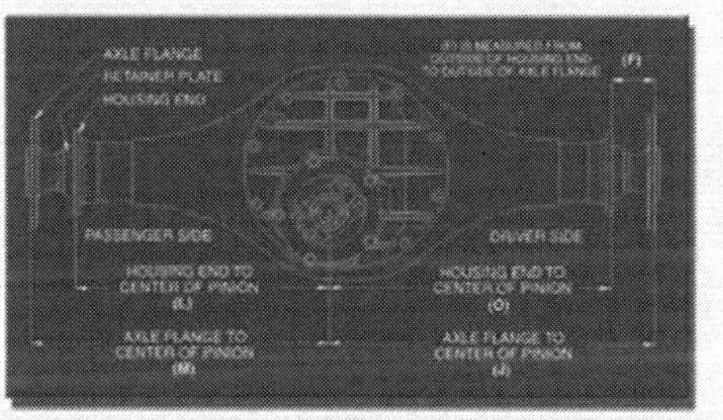

(9) Driver side **and** passenger side **"C"** dimension. (above- axle diagram)
(10) **"A"** dimension (above- axle diagram)
(11) **"B"** dimension (above- axle diagram)
(12) **"H"** dimension (above- axle diagram)
(13) **"F"** dimension (left- housing diagram)
Note: "B" and "F" are not the same dimension. The "B" dimension is from the outside face of axle flange to the bearing shoulder machined onto the axle. The "F" dimension is measured from outside face of axle flange (bare) to the outside face of the housing end. On Chrysler/Dana/Mopar type housing ends, "F" is obtained with the backing plate and gasket installed or combined thickness accounted for. The Mopar type end does not have a step to stop the axle bearing.

Rear End/Housing Information

(14) Passenger side housing end to center of pinion (C.P.)- Dimension **"L"**
(15) Driver side housing end to center of pinion (C.P.)- Dimension **"O"**
(16) Housing end to housing end- Dimensions **"L" + "O"**
(17) Passenger side axle flange to center of pinion (C.P.)- Dimension **"M"**
(18) Driver side axle flange to center of pinion (C.P.)- Dimension **"J"**
(19) Axle flange to axle flange (note: Do NOT add thickness of brake hat or drum)- Dimensions **"M" + "J"**

Notes: (A) *Axle Flange to Axle Flange is measured from the OUTSIDE (Wheel Side) of the axle flange to OUTSIDE (Wheel Side) of the opposite axle flange.* (B) *If you have listed only housing end to housing end or axle flange to axle flange- you must specify pinion offset.*

Strange Engineering • 8300 North Austin Ave. • Morton Grove IL. 60053 •
Phone # 847.663.1701 • Fax # 847.663.1702 • Web www.strangeengineering.net •

Brake Kits—The brake kit is optional; however, the step to select a brake kit is not. Whether you decide to use a Strange brake kit, or another aftermarket brake kit, it is essential they know the specifics. The brake kit affects housing width and several other axle dimensions.

Ring and Pinion—Gearsets from 2.91:1 to 6.50:1 are available. Some Strange gearsets are manufactured in association with U.S. Gear, who supplied ours. Their TORQ-LINE ring-and-pinion gearsets are forged and machined in the U.S.A. Because installation is so critical with this product, each and every set comes with its own set of instructions and pinions marked for checking distance to make setup as accurate as possible.

The United States Gear Corporation is a family-owned and managed gear and power transmission component manufacturer in Chicago with an interesting background. The founder of the company, the late Joseph M. Garfien, immigrated to the U.S. in 1928. Joe arrived in America on a Friday and its been reported he said, "I needed to go to work on Monday." Joe landed a job with Perfection Gear, where he discovered an innate ability to understand the geometry involved in manufacturing gears. In the 1930s, Joe was involved in perfecting the hypoid ring-and-pinion design and during WWII worked with the military and Rockwell Industries to resolve gear problems with "deuce and a half" and five-ton trucks.

Joe left Perfection to start U.S. Gear, which has grown to 200,000 square feet of facilities with more than 250 employees since 1963. U.S. Gear's current products include differential and transmission components for everything from hot rods to heavy-duty trucks. U.S. Gear products can be found in some of the world's fastest race car suppliers' customers including Meritor (Rockwell), Dana, General Motors, Chrysler, and Ford. U.S Gear holds Ford Q-1 quality status and is an ISO9001: 2000 registered company.

U.S. GEAR
U.S. GEAR 9-INCH FORD RING-AND-PINION SETS

PART #	TEETH	Ratio
C0AZ4209A	39-13	3.00
B8AZ4209C	39-12	3.25
C90Z4209A	35-10	3.50
B7AZ4209E	35-09	3.89
B7AZ4209K	37-09	4.11
F9/457	32-07	4.57
F9/486	34-07	4.86

BUILDING A DRIVESHAFT

A driveshaft is a simple but critical part of any street rod. It has to be strong enough to handle the torque applied to it, be true and balanced to prevent vibrations, and finally it has to be the correct length to function properly—that is to not bottom out on, or pull off the transmission splines as the suspension moves up and down.

MECHANICAL AND HYDRAULIC CLUTCH SETUP TIPS FROM CLASSIC MOTORSPORTS.

Setting the Stage

Before getting to the actual clutch linkage system itself, it is assumed that you are using all of the correct clutch components that are known to be compatible with each other such as the flywheel, pilot bearing, clutch disc, pressure plate, bellhousing, clutch fork, clutch fork ball stud, and throw out bearing. It is advisable to purchase all of these components from the same source and that the clutch and pressure plate are a matched set (same brand). Further it is assumed, that all of these parts are either new or in good working order and that they have been installed correctly. Here is a brief checklist of items that must be properly installed for your clutch entire system to operate properly:

- pilot bearing properly installed without damaging it
- flywheel re-surfaced within spec or new flywheel
- bellhousing properly aligned with crank (very important!!)
- pressure plate bolts properly torqued
- clutch disc installed using clutch alignment tool

Make sure to carefully follow the instructions provided with your Classic Motorsports Group kit to properly install these components. For additional, in-depth information on each of the components in the clutch system as well as how to properly install and inspect all components before installation, here is an excellent article: http://www.novak-adapt.com/knowledge/clutches_etc.htm.

Setting Up Your Clutch Linkage

Assuming that you are using the correct components and have properly installed them as discussed above, you are now ready to set up your clutch linkage system. The first step is to achieve the proper clutch fork angle. This step involves installing the clutch fork, clutch fork ball stud, and throw out bearing.

Note: If you are using all stock components (flywheel, clutch, bellhousing, clutch fork, and mechanical linkage, etc.) it is likely that you can simply re-install these parts without going through any extra steps as these parts were designed by GM to work together properly. However, it is always good practice to go through the following procedures to be sure that everything is done correctly.

With that said, most of us are using at least some aftermarket components whether it be a scattershield, a billet flywheel, a high performance clutch, or a hydraulic clutch linkage system – all of which can, or will, effect your clutch linkage geometry in one way or another and will require you to carefully check your clutch installation process at each step.

In many occasions, the use of high performance, aftermarket components is either required due to high horsepower or special use applications or it is simply more fun to incorporate the latest and greatest aftermarket components as you build your dream car. It is in these instances where most of the clutch installation problems arise. *When applicable, there is a lot to be said for using stock replacement GM components. They are proven to work together and installation becomes much easier! If you have a base level motor or only a slightly modified motor and you use your car mainly for casual street cruising and general transportation purposes, we* ***strongly recommend*** *using stock GM, or stock replacement, clutch components including your stock mechanical linkage. In the end, using stock components will typically be the least expensive and easiest clutch system to install. Although it is not as impressive to say that you are using stock clutch components in your muscle car, from a practical standpoint these components simply work correctly and will give you thousands of miles of hassle free performance.*

Mechanical clutch linkage

Hydraulic TO bearing kit

Step 1: Creating the proper clutch fork angle

This is possibly the most important step in the clutch linkage installation process. Be sure to take your time!!

With the flywheel, pilot bearing, clutch disc, pressure plate and bellhousing all properly installed, the following steps will guide you through the clutch fork aligning process (these steps take place before the transmission is installed).

1. Install the clutch fork ball stud into the bellhousing.
   Note: If you are using an adjustable ball stud there will be excess stud protruding through the back of the bellhousing towards the transmission – this is to be expected at this stage of the process. At the end of the clutch fork aligning process you will be cutting off any excess stud to finalize this portion of the process. Using an adjustable ball stud is one method of helping you to achieve a proper clutch fork angle.

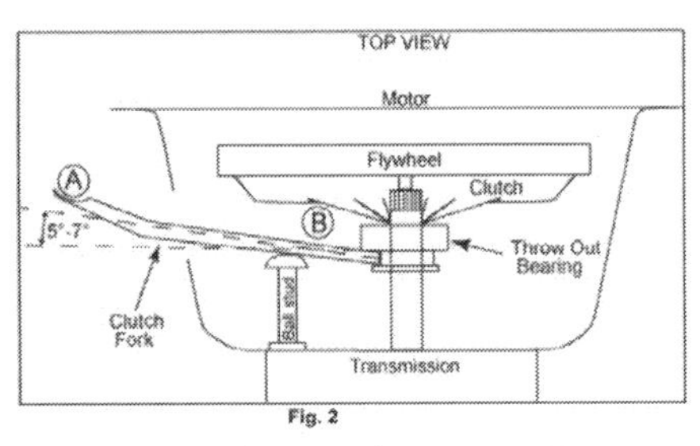

Fig. 2

4. Once you have achieved the proper angle, mark the ball stud where it is protruding through the bellhousing towards the transmission, remove the ball stud, and cut off the excess at the mark.

5. Re-install the ball stud and secure with provided locking nut. Place a small amount of grease on the head of the ball stud and re-attach the clutch fork to ball stud.

6. With the clutch fork properly aligned, you are now ready to install the transmission. Refer to the instructions provided with your transmission kit to properly install your transmission to the bellhousing.

7. With the transmission installed, the TO bearing needs be able to move away from the fingers of the pressure plate by approximately 1/16" to 1/8" This is what is know as "free play" and is measurable as 1" – 1 ½" of clutch pedal travel from the top, or end of travel, down to the point where you feel the throw out bearing contact the pressure plate.
   At this point you should be able to move the TO bearing back and forth by pushing and pulling the clutch fork. As described in step 3 above, when the TO bearing is against the pressure plate, the clutch fork should be angled at approximately 5°-7° towards the motor. If this condition does not exist, you will need to remove the transmission and re-set the clutch fork angle properly. It is possible that you may have an in-correct clutch fork, throw out bearing, or ball stud or you did not properly follow the instructions.
   Note: Each of the Classic Motorsports Group clutch kit components (that are part of our complete transmission kits) have been proven to work together as long as you follow the proper installation procedures. If you are using all CMG provided clutch parts, you are 100% certain that you have not made any errors during the installation process, and your clutch is still not operating properly, the only explanation is a defective part, a mis-boxed part by the manufacturer, or we sent the wrong part by mistake. If this is the case call us and we will correct the error.

Step 2: Installing the remainder of your clutch linkage

If you are using stock mechanical linkage, simply re-install it per your factory service manual and other than slight adjustments to the clutch fork push rod length, everything should work just fine. This is the main benefit to using good old fashioned mechanical linkage as opposed to using hydraulic linkage. Properly installed mechanical clutch linkage is the least expensive type of clutch linkage, is highly dependable, and easy to service. With this in mind, the following information will cover the issues associated with installing hydraulic linkage.

If you decide for fitment reasons or for "cool factor" reasons to use hydraulic clutch linkage, installing hydraulics will almost always be more challenging, more expensive, and will often times require some fabrication and/or modification.

If you are using the CMG internal hydraulic throw out bearing kit refer to the detailed instructions provided with the kit.

Note: Each of the Classic Motorsports Group hydraulic clutch kit have been proven to work together as long as you follow the proper installation procedures.

Important hydraulic clutch linkage concepts:

- **Master cylinder mounting**
  Achieving proper geometry when installing the master cylinder is critical to a properly functioning hydraulic clutch system. It is important to make sure that master is mounted securely to the firewall and at the correct angle. Proper placement of the master cylinder push rod on the clutch pedal is also critical. If positioned too high on the pedal, there will not be enough push rod travel which will not allow the clutch disc to disengage when the pedal is depressed. If positioned too low on the pedal, the pedal will become hard to depress.
  Note: The custom firewall mounting bracket and the modified master cylinder in the CMG hydraulic kits create the proper geometry for a correct installation.

- **Bleeding the hydraulic clutch system**
  Bleeding a hydraulic clutch system tends to be more difficult than bleeding a brake system. To help make bleeding as easy as possible, make sure that the fluid line running from your master cylinder down to your slave cylinder or hydraulic TO bearing does not have a loop in it. A loop in the line tends to trap air at the top of the loop making it difficult to bleed. Additionally, a pressure bleeder is recommended as opposed to using the "pump the clutch pedal" method.

- **Using a pedal stop with a hydraulic TO bearing system**
  Failure to use a positive pedal stop can cause bearing "O" ring failure if the clutch pedal is depressed too far. A failed "O" ring requires removal of the transmission to replace it.

2. Properly secure the throw out bearing onto the clutch fork **(Fig. 1)** and secure the clutch fork onto the ball stud.

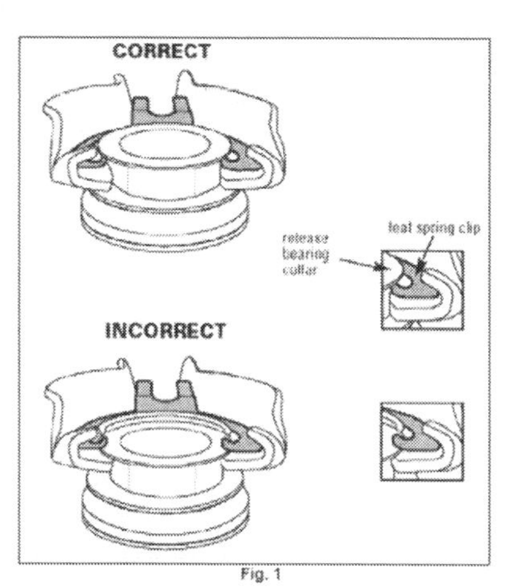

Fig. 1

3. Referring to **figure 2** below, with the clutch fork and throw out bearing installed on the ball stud, simulate the function of the clutch fork push rod by positioning your finger in the dimple of the clutch fork **(location A on diagram)** and pushing the clutch fork rearward until the throw out bearing moves forward and comes into contact with the fingers of the pressure plate. At this point check the angle of the clutch fork between the throw out bearing and the ball stud ***(location B on diagram)***. The clutch fork should be at an angle of approximately 5°-7° forward of parallel (angled towards the motor).
To achieve the proper clutch fork angle, use the adjustability feature of the adjustable ball stud to achieve the required angle. Simply screw in or screw out the ball stud to achieve the proper clutch fork angle.

Hydraulic Master Cylinder and Clutch Pedal Adjustment

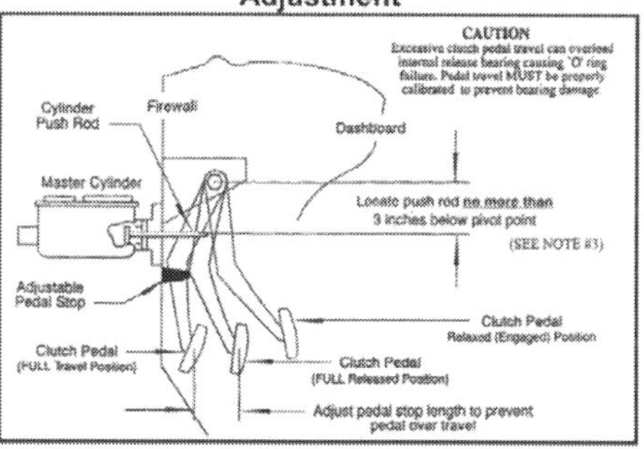

1. Park vehicle on slight incline so that when the clutch is fully released, vehicle will start to roll.
2. Depress clutch pedal slowly until vehicle starts to roll, indicating that the clutch is disengaged. At that point, set the brakes.
3. ***IMPORTANT*** Accurately measure the distance between the pedal and the firewall, and adjust travel stop so pedal does not exceed the distance of full clutch release. If your vehicle does not have an adjustment for pedal travel, then you will have to fabricate a pedal stop. ***Excess pedal travel after clutch disengagement can cause the master cylinder or slave cylinder to fail.***

NOTES

1. A pedal stop may be attached to the pedal or the firewall. A bracket with a bolt and a jam nut work nicely so that the stop is adjustable for more or less travel.
2. A 6 to 1 ratio is recommended with a 3/4" or 13/16" bore master cylinder. Example: If your pedal measures 12" from the pivot point to the pedal foot pad, you should NOT connect your push rod to the pedal any further than 2" down from the pivot point of the pedal.

These installation notes are provided to help you with the installation process. To the best of our knowledge, this information is accurate; however it is in no way guaranteed. Every car is unique and will represent unique challenges. There is no guarantee of proper fitment in your particular vehicle and you need to take responsibility for your own installation. When installing your transmission, be sure to follow proper torque & alignment specifications. Also, it is important to follow proper break-in procedures. Classic Motorsports Group is not responsible, in any way, for any damage, financial or otherwise, to you or your vehicle.

Classic Motorsports Group

Careful TIG welding results in the brackets being securely attached without warping the housing in the process.

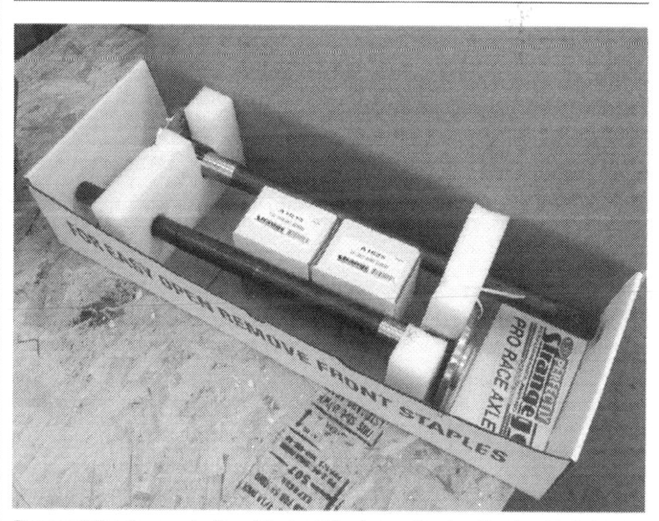

Strange S/S axles are designed to meet the demanding bending loads of street use. Manufactured from modified 1550 steel, they are induction-hardened. With high performance engines such as our Boss, Strange recommends upgrading to 31-spline axles as they are 38-percent torsionally stronger than a 28-spline.

When measuring for a driveshaft, the car must be at ride height—jacking the car up will change the distance between the transmission's output shaft and the rear end's pinion flange because of the suspension's movement. Most driveshaft suppliers will ask for the distance from the tip of the transmission output shaft to the centerline of U-joint at the third member and how far the output protrudes from the rear seal. Others will ask for center-to-center measurements (with the transmission yoke in place) between the output shaft and the pinion flange. The best plan is to check with the driveshaft supplier and follow their instructions.

There are a variety of factors that determine the strength of a driveshaft starting with the size of the tubing, which for performance applications will range from 3 to 3 1/2-inches with wall thicknesses of .083-inch. The material may be mild steel (the

GM and Mopar fans aren't left out; Strange makes rear ends for them as well. These Salisbury-style rearends don't have a removable center section—the gears are installed directly in the housing.

The Strange S-Series case is perfect for street and street/strip performance vehicles. This newly designed case features radial ribs for increased strength.

A common modification for drag racing rear ends is a back brace. While they look impressive, they're not necessary for street cars.

DRIVELINE VIBRATIONS AND HOW TO ELIMINATE THEM FROM THE CLASSIC MOTORSPORTS GROUP

Achieving front and rear ujoint alignment angles within the acceptable operating angle range is necessary to avoid driveline vibration and to allow the ujoints to last a long time.

Universal joints in most passenger cars have a minimum and maximum operating angle. The front ujoint when compared to the transmission output shaft and driveshaft should have an operating angle no less than ½° and no more than 3-1/2°. The rear ujoint, when compared to the pinion and drive shaft, should have an operating angle of no less than ½° and no more than 3-1/2°. The reason that at least ½° of operating angle is required is because the ujoints will not last without at least some angle or movement. The lack of this movement will cause too much wear on the needle bearings leading to bearing damage (called "brinelling").

It is possible to have an operating angle that is greater than 3-1/2° and still not have a vibration that you can feel but ujoint life will be shortened. It is difficult to determine exactly how much the ujoint life will be shortened - it will depend on how far past 3-1/2° you are. At optimum operating angles, ujoints can last more than 100,000 miles so even if their life were shortened by ½, you would still be happy as most of the muscle cars and trucks we are talking about only accumulate 3000 miles +/- per year. For example, ½ the life of a ujoint would be 50,000 miles divided by 3000 miles driven per year = 16.666 years! Not bad for a $20.00 ujoint. I have seen ujoints operating at more than 3-1/2° that have not had any problems but these were in daily grocery getters or rock climbing Jeeps. Our muscle cars have driveshafts that turn faster and are subjected to much more power so keeping as close as possible to optimum operating angles is advisable.

Front and rear ujoints should not be allowed to have operating angles of more than ½° apart from each other. An example would be the front joint being 2° down while the rear ujoint is 2-1/2° up. A greater angle than this will cause some harmonic vibration.

2. If the angles are not the same, make adjustments by raising or lowering the transmission and/or turning the rear end (if adjustable) to get the angles the same. If you have modified your car's suspension and you have leaf springs, you may need to use shims to change the pinion angle. Shims are available at most spring shops.
3. Measure each ujoint separately. First rotate the driveshaft so that the slip yolk and pinion yolks are at the 12:00 and 6:00 positions **(Fig. 4)**. These angles should be equal to each other.
4. Rotate the driveshaft 90°, or ¼ turn, so that the driveshaft yolks are at the 12:00 and 6:00 positions **(Fig. 5)** and then measure the angles.
5. Subtract the first measurements obtained in step 4 from the measurements in step 3. The results are your operating angles.

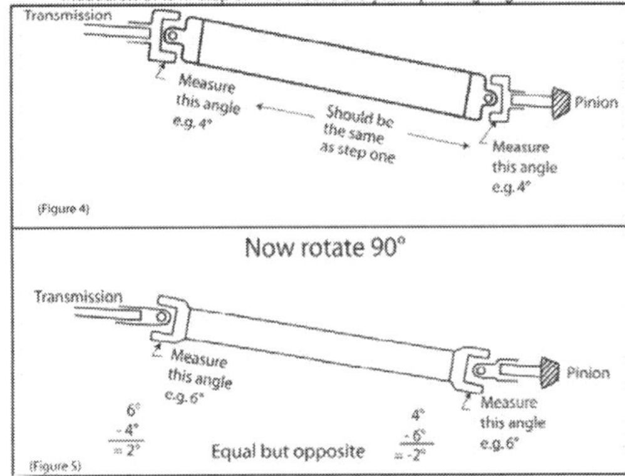

In this example we have +2 degrees on the front and –2 degrees on the back. Don't let the plus and minus thing confuse you. These plus and minus values are applied to the measurements because they are opposite. You can call it what you want as long as they (the angles) are opposite. In this example, the correct operating angles exist, equal but opposite, or -2 and +2.

U-joints do not turn at an even speed. The greater the angle, the greater the speed or velocity changes as the driveshaft turns. In other words, as the ujoint travels around to the outside of its angle it slows down. When traveling through the inside of the angle it speeds up. The greater the operating angle is, the greater the speed difference is. Having the opposite ujoint at the same, *but opposite*, operating angle cancels out this speed difference and keeps harmonics to a minimum. If your operating angles are more than ½° apart from each other, these velocity induced harmonics will resonate through the driveline. This is why you see constant velocity (CV) joints used in newer cars. CV joints are found in front wheel drive cars and they are common in BMW and Mercedes Benz driveshafts. CV joints are more expensive to replace but they do not live by the same rules as a u joint.

To measure your ujoint angles you will need an angle gauge **(Fig. 1)** or an inclinometer **(Fig. 2)**. The best place to obtain accurate measurements is from the top of the u joint cap. When taking measurements from the caps it is necessary to temporarily remove the retaining clips (if equipped) temporarily from the yolk. By placing a short socket from your tool box **(Fig. 1)** on the end of the cap, you will be able to maintain the correct level without allowing interference from the surrounding material of the yolk.

(Fig. 1)

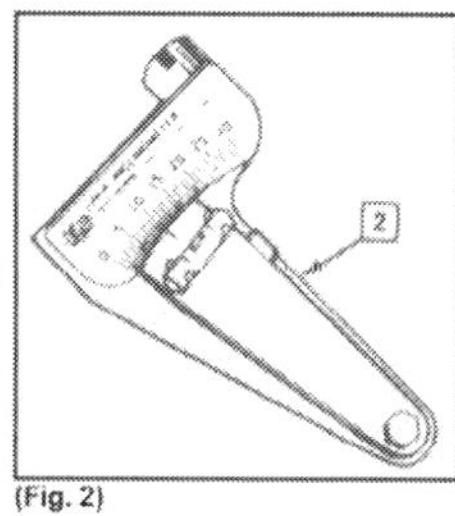

(Fig. 2)

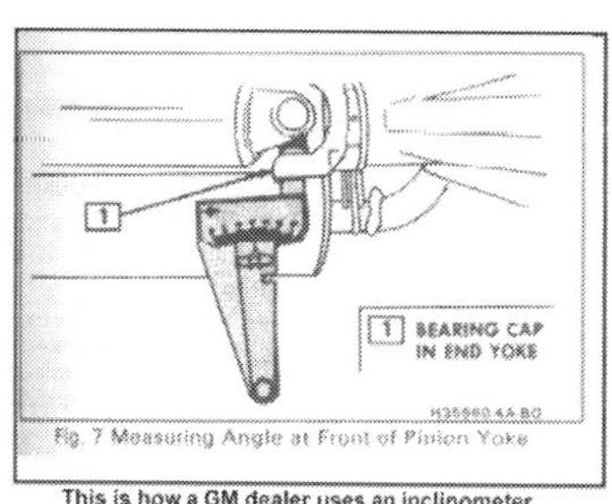

Fig. 7 Measuring Angle at Front of Pinion Yoke

This is how a GM dealer uses an inclinometer to measure drive line angles.

How to Measure U-joint Angles

1. **Establishing starting angles.**
   Measure the transmission and pinion angles as shown below **(Fig. 3)**.
   Note that the car does not need to be level; however the car's weight must be on its suspension.

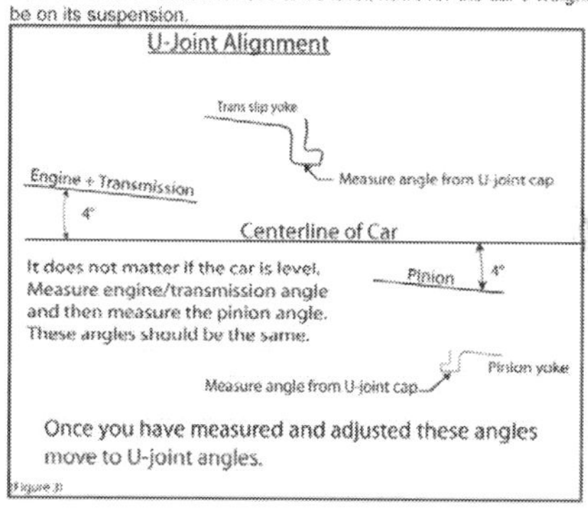

Trans slip yoke

Measure angle from U-joint cap

(Figure 3)

The diagram below shows gives an exaggerated example for clarity purposes.

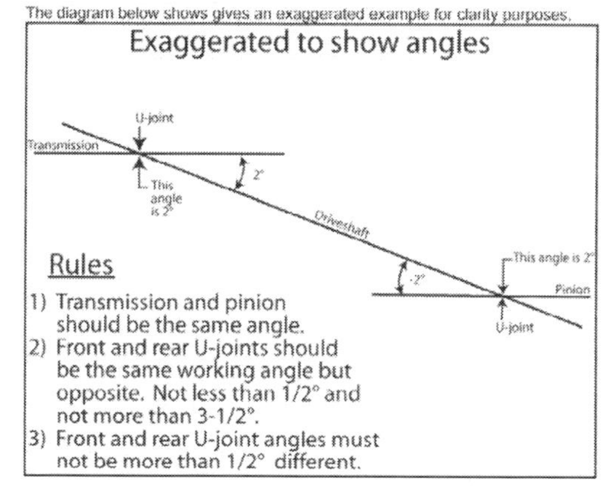

Exaggerated to show angles
U-joint
Transmission
This angle is 2°
2°
Driveshaft
This angle is 2°
-2°
It does not matter if the car is level.
Pinion
Measure angle from U-joint cap
Once you have measured and adjusted these angles
U-joint
Rules
1) Transmission and pinion should be the same angle.
2) Front and rear U-joints should be the same working angle but opposite. Not less than 1/2° and not more than 3-1/2°.
3) Front and rear U-joint angles must not be more than 1/2° different.

Rules:

1. **Transmission and pinion angle should be the same angle.**
2. **Front and rear ujoints should be the same working angle as each other, but opposite. Not less than ½° but not more than 3 ½°.**
3. **Front and rear ujoint angles must not be more than ½° different.**

If you require any more assistance on this subject or have any questions, please give us a call.

As an additional note, I do not subscribe to the practice of adjusting pinion angles to compensate for spring wrap or torque twist. If you have enough power to twist the axle housing far enough to change driveline angles to the extent they are going to cause problems then you have a RACE CAR! Race cars have different rules than street cars. Street cars spend the majority of their time on the street and the angles should be set up for the street. If you have a race car, you probably know all this stuff (or at least you should know it) and you will adjust angles for optimum performance at the track. Just remember - as in life, everything is a compromise!

GMJim

Strange can supply 28, 31, 33 and 35-spline axles for 9-inch rears. Of course with drivelines, the weakest part is vulnerable to breakage. A vehicle that requires a 35-spline shaft is bound to break an OEM gearcase so all the components must be matched to the application.

Strange can supply housings with all the necessary brackets in place, and they will install custom brackets on request.

most common), aluminum, or composite. While aluminum driveshafts are becoming popular, be aware that there can be a problem of galvanic corrosion between the steel U-joint caps and the yokes of the driveshaft due to the dissimilar metals. To prevent damage, special U-joints with protective coatings on the caps are available.

Another key to driveshaft strength is U-joint size. Its dimensions determine the "series" of a universal joint. For most street rods, a 1310- or 1330-series will be used. The 1350-series, a racer favorite because of its strength, has larger caps and the body and journals are bigger than the 1310 or 1330. A variation on the preceding series is called a conversion U-joint, one that has two different dimensions. As an example, a Spicer DC5-134X, is half 1310, and half 1330. Conversion U-joints are used

Strange Engineering builds tough stuff; they supply these top loader rearends with a 12-inch ring gears to leading Top Fuel and Funny Car teams.

These are raw center section castings prior to any machine work. Exceptional-grade nodular iron is used to make the cases and bearing caps, making them superior to OEM units

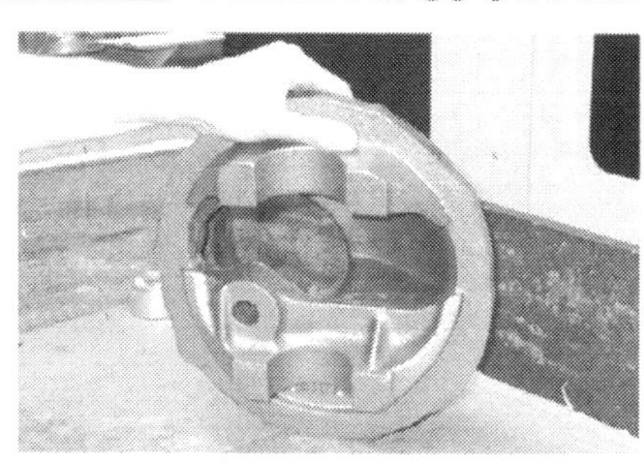

A raw housing seen from the gear side. The small hole is for the pinion support bearing, it will be accurately aligned with the pinion bearings during machining. The cases are clearanced for easy installation of posi units.

Speaking of tough, this is an axle shaft for a fueler.

The splines found on Strange S/S axles are hobbed to the proper involute spline form and then heat treated before heat treatment.

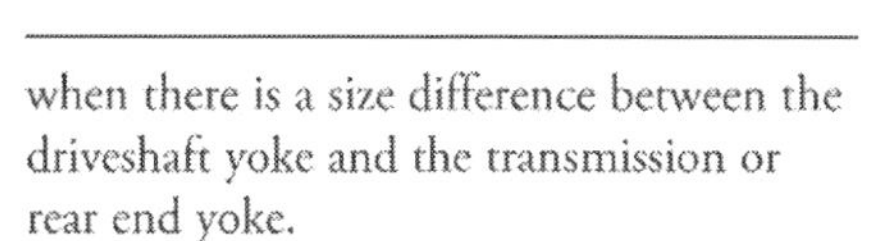

when there is a size difference between the driveshaft yoke and the transmission or rear end yoke.

While the front and rear U-joints can be different series, just like the weakest link in a chain, the shaft is only as strong as the smaller of the two.

Common U-joint sizes:

	1310	1330	1350
Cross length	3 7/32 inch	3 5/8 inch	3 5/8 inch
Cap Diameter	1 1/16 inch	1 1/16 inch	1 3/16 inch

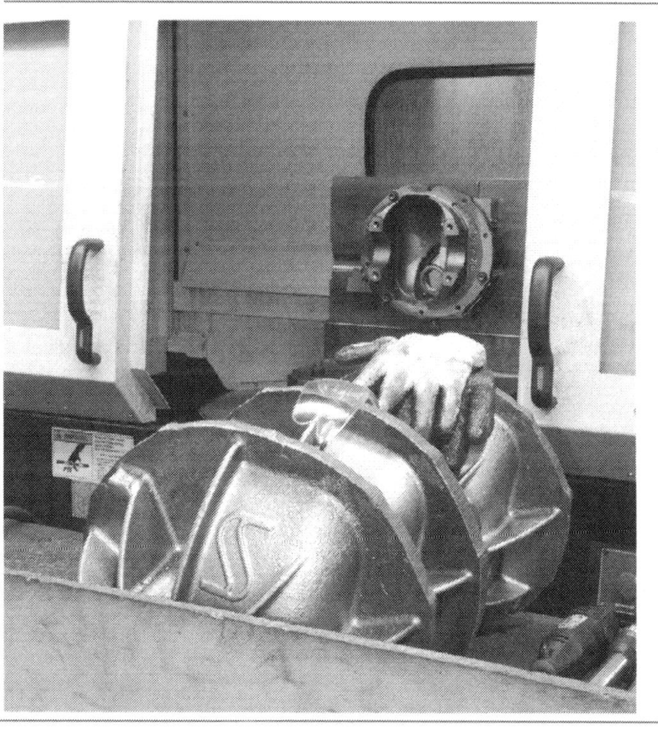

Thanks to the latest CNC machines, bearing bores are finished and attachment holes are drilled and tapped with the utmost in accuracy.

Chapter 7
BRAKES, FUEL SYSTEM, AND PLUMBING

By Ron Ceridono

The '08 Road Tour Speed33 has more-than-adequate stopping power, thanks to Wilwood's forged-billet Dynalite four-piston calipers. Square faced O-rings provide long service and decreased drag from positive piston retraction, and the top loaded brake pads can be easily serviced without caliper removal.

We've made a number of comparisons between the original equipment found on Model 40s a the contemporary components used on th '08 Road Tour Speed33. In virtually ever area, advancements in technology have allowed the Roadster Shop to construct a much more refined vehicle than was mass produced in a factory all those years ago. But with all the forward strides that the automobile has taken, from a functional standpoint, perhaps the most important is the increased safety factor provided by dramatically improved brakes.

Henry Ford didn't trust hydraulic brakes, but he did have a complete understanding of mechanical leverage—a evidently lots of faith in the leg strength o the average driver. Model Ts were equipp with mechanical brakes, or more accurate a brake, as stopping power consisted of a single external contracting band wrapped around a drum inside the transmission. A panic stop in a T usually involved stompi on the brake pedal and pulling on the aptly named emergency brake handle that activated mechanical drum brakes on the rear wheels. With the introduction of the Model A, Fords were fitted with four-wheel brakes, but they were still activated mechanically; the same basic system was used until the company converted to hydraulic brakes in 1939.

In the formative years of hot rodding, the emphasis was certainly on increasing the speed, but stopping power was also a concern. Fords with mechanical brakes w routinely retrofitted with hydraulics from '39 and later models (although due to the '39s "wide five" hub pattern, '40 and late brakes that mounted conventional wheels were preferred). Other later swaps for better stopping included adapting Lincol

Three pieces make up the front rotors: the disc, hat, and hub.

Chrysler, F-100, and Buick brakes, among others. And in the 1970s, the introduction of disc-brake kits was a giant step forward in street rod safety.

Disc brakes have a number of inherent advantages over drums. And while drum brakes can generate significant stopping power, their shortcoming is they can't do it for extended periods. All brakes rely on friction between two surfaces to stop the car; basically that means they turn the energy of the moving vehicle into heat. However, heat is also the enemy of brakes. As the braking surfaces become hotter, the coefficient of friction between the two is reduced and effectiveness is reduced. (The term that is often used to describe this is brake fade.) Because the caliper only covers a small part of the disc brake's friction surface, a large portion of the rotor is exposed to air, which

The hat attaches to the hub with five high-strength button-head fasteners, the heads of which are drilled. Once installed, these are safety-wired for security.

It's crucial that the fasteners holding the rotor to the hub are safety wired. Wilwood includes instructions on the correct procedure. Note that when safety wiring is done properly, if one fasteners loosens, it tightens the other.

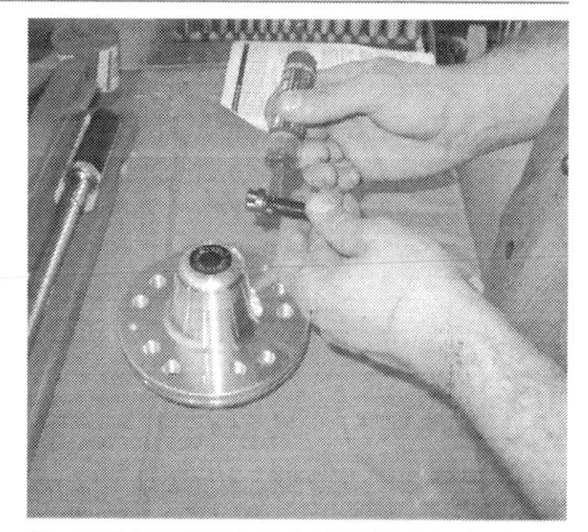
The studs install in the hubs from the rear. During installing the studs should be treated to thread locking compound.

The discs are attached to the hat with eight high-strength cap screws, also drilled for safety wire.

Wilwood hubs come with the bearings appropriate for the spindles being used. New bearings should be thoroughly cleaned before being packed with grease.

Once the rotors, hats, and hubs are assembled, and the greased bearings and the seals are installed, the assembly is slipped in place. Wilwood's hubs are drilled for late Ford and Chevy lug-bolt patterns.

Everyone seems to have their own way of adjusting wheel bearings. One is to tighten the nut to 10-12 lb-ft, while spinning the wheel, and then back off one flat or until the cotter pin fits. Another method is to tighten the nut as described, then loosen it, then tighten as much as possible with fingers—tighten or loosen the nut to the closet hole and insert the cotter pin.

In the rear, we used another pair of Dynalite calipers and Wilwood's parking brake system.

keeps it relatively cool. With a drum brake, most of the friction surface is in contact with the brake shoes, which leaves little surface area for cooling. Consequently, compared to discs, drum brakes get hotter faster and stay hot longer. During hard or continuous use, that reduces their efficiency dramatically.

Another factor that allows disc brakes to function more effectively than drums is the wiping action inherent in their design. In wet conditions, the friction pads of a disc brake caliper tend to wipe water off the rotor. With that, drums' moisture can become trapped between the shoes and drum, which lowers the coefficient of friction dramatically until the water is dispersed.

TYPES OF CALIPERS

Basically there are three types of calipers: fixed, sliding, and floating. Fixed calipers are mounted solidly to a mounting bracket with one, two, or more pistons per side to apply the pads. While fixed calipers work very well, they are very unforgiving of any runout in the rotor. If the rotor wobbles, it will tend to make the brake pedal pulsate on application.

Another caliper design is the sliding style. These have a single piston on just one side working like a C-clamp, as the piston pushes the inside brake pad against the rotor. Once it makes contact, the caliper slides in its bracket and pulls the outside pad against the rotor.

Similar to the sliding caliper is the floating design. Like the sliding caliper, floating calipers apply hydraulic pressure to one pad, then the caliper, which "floats" on a pair of mounting pins and pulls the other pad against the rotor. While the sliding and floating calipers work in a similar fashion, there is one major difference. With the sliding style, the braking force is transferred to the caliper, which means it must be a stout piece. With a floating caliper, the mounting bracket captures the pads. As a result, the caliper doesn't have to be as beefy.

REAR DISC BRAKES

One of the complications of using rear disc brakes is the inclusion of a parking brake. Generally, this can be accomplished in one of three ways. Some aftermarket designs utilize a separate set of calipers on the rear rotors, or an additional caliper and rotor on the pinion yoke for a parking brake. These parking brake calipers may be mechanically or hydraulically operated.

Another parking brake option is a small drum brake inside the disc brake rotor. In most cases, the caliper mounting bracket also acts as the backing plate for the parking brake, while the rotor has a small built-in brake drum.

One of the more recent ways of providing a parking brake with rear discs is by including a mechanism in the caliper that applies the pads manually. While it complicates caliper design, it simplifies the rotor and caliper mounting brackets.

TYPES OF ROTORS

Although disc brake rotors come in a wide variety of shapes and sizes, they can be

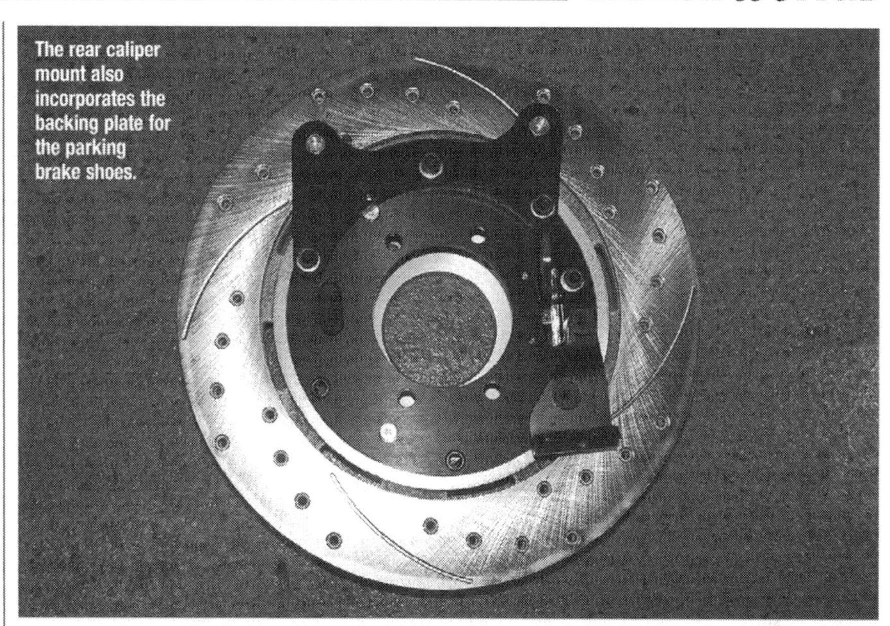

The rear caliper mount also incorporates the backing plate for the parking brake shoes.

Rear rotors are one piece with drums for the parking brake shoes inside the hats. Like the fronts, these rotors are drilled and slotted.

Obviously compact, the parking brake shoes are about the same diameter as the axle flanges, yet they supply plenty of holding power.

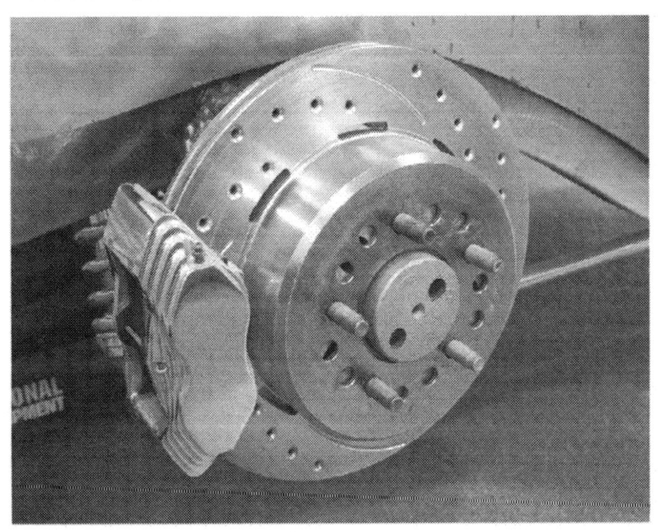

Compact but effective, this is the complete rear brake package.

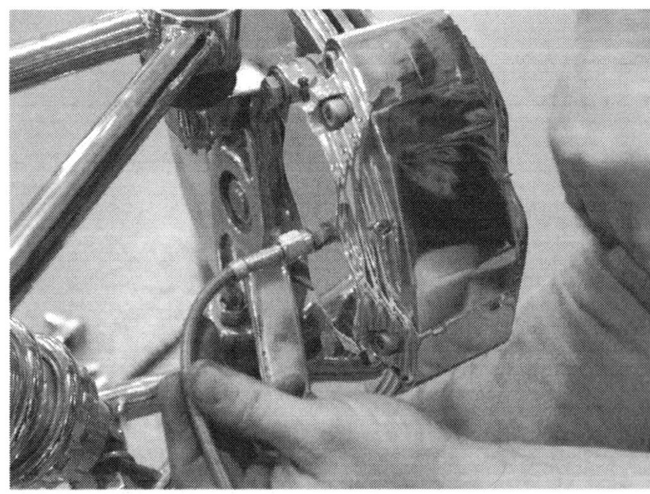

Thanks to four bleeder ports, the calipers can be mounted on either side of the car. Stainless steel braided lines connect the calipers to the chassis fittings.

Wilwood supplied the cool-looking, dual-chamber aluminum master cylinder. Outlets on both sides, slotted mounting holes in the flange, and through boltholes provide mounting flexibility.

As the Speed33 is equipped with a manual five-speed and a hydraulic throwout bearing, a Wilwood clutch master cylinder was mounted to the Roadster Shop pedal assembly.

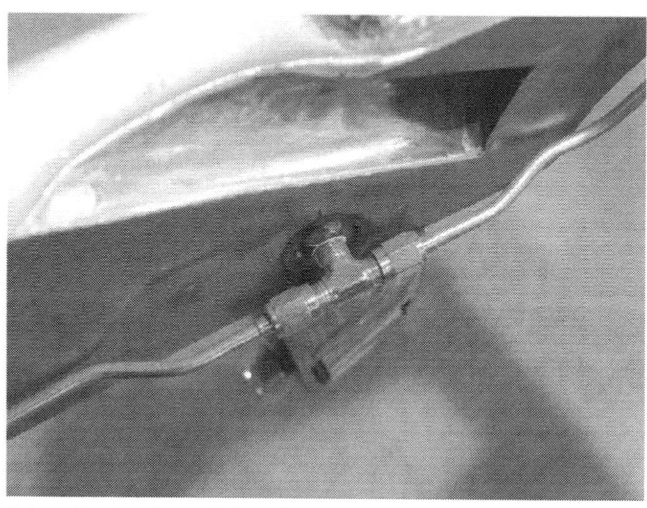

To keep the plumbing partially hidden, through-the-frame brake line fittings were used. Lines are stainless steel with AN fittings.

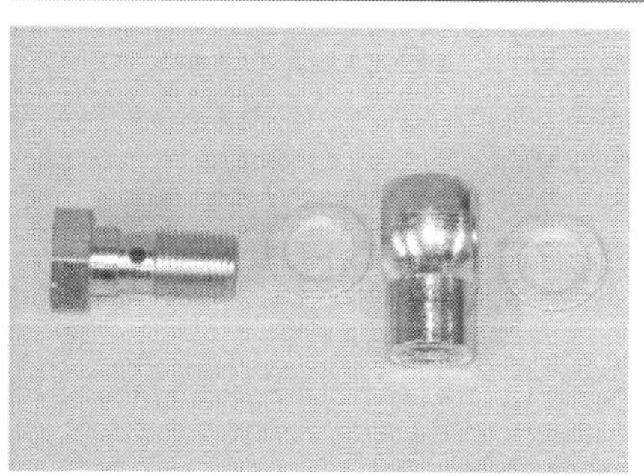

Banjo fittings are often found on brake systems. Sealing washers are used on both sides of the body.

Banjo fittings are clean-looking but they must be installed in applications that don't pull on the fittings, which could loosen them and cause leaks.

This is a 45-degree double-flare on steel tubing. The thicker flare makes it more resistant to cracking from fatigue, and a ferrule isn't required.

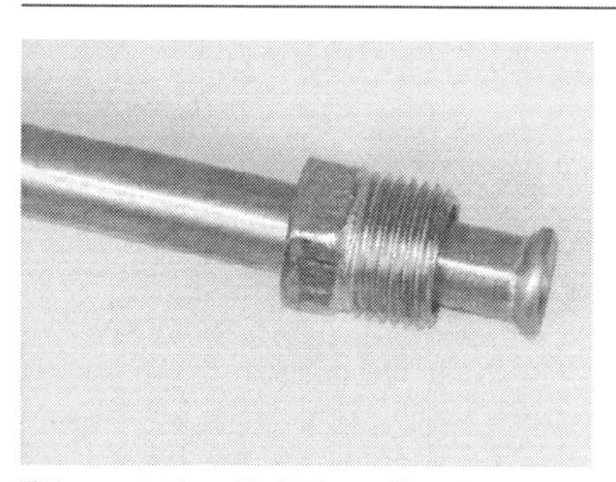

Fittings on tubing with 45-degree flares have male threads and a 45-degree seat that pushes against the flare.

Female fittings for 45-degree fittings have a seat that the flare seals against. As well as increasing strength, the double-flare also takes up the space between the two fittings.

This is a single 37-degree flare on stainless tubing for an AN fitting.

broken down into just two categories: solid and vented. Solid rotors are just that—a simple flat rotor. Simple and inexpensive, the disadvantage to solid rotors is that they do not dissipate heat well. While solid rotors are adequate for lightweight cars, particularly on the rear, a better disc brake rotor option for heavier vehicles is the ventilated style. This design separates the two friction surfaces with air passages to aid in cooling.

DISCS ALL AROUND FOR THE SPEED33

One of the leaders in aftermarket brakes is Wilwood Engineering. Its doors opened in 1977 when it began manufacturing disc brakes for Grand National racecars. Owner Bill Wood's original designs of high-performance disc brakes proved to be so popular that they soon found their way onto many racecars across the country, and today are the standard that all others are judged by. Wilwood's entrance into the aftermarket with replacement brake kits for

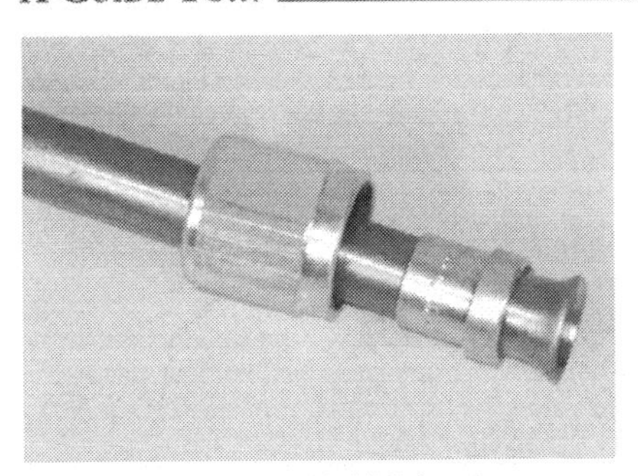
Fittings on tubing used with AN fittings have internal threads.

Here is a single 37-degree flare with the ferrule in place.

This is a fitting commonly used to connect AN flex lines to calipers—to the left is the 37-degree AN portion, on the right is 1/8-inch pipe.

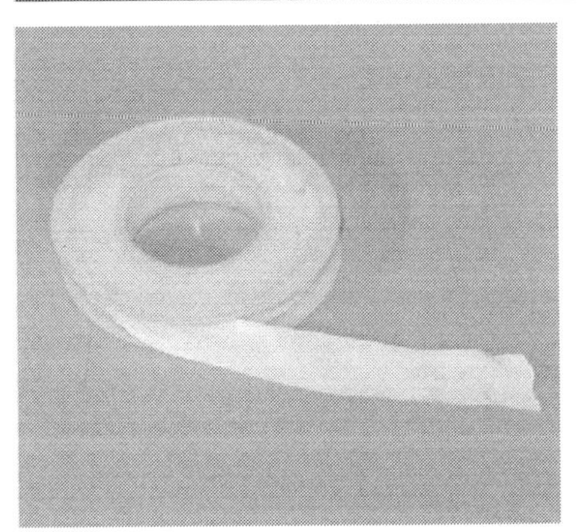
Teflon tape is not necessary on fittings with flared fittings; it can be beneficial with pipe fittings.

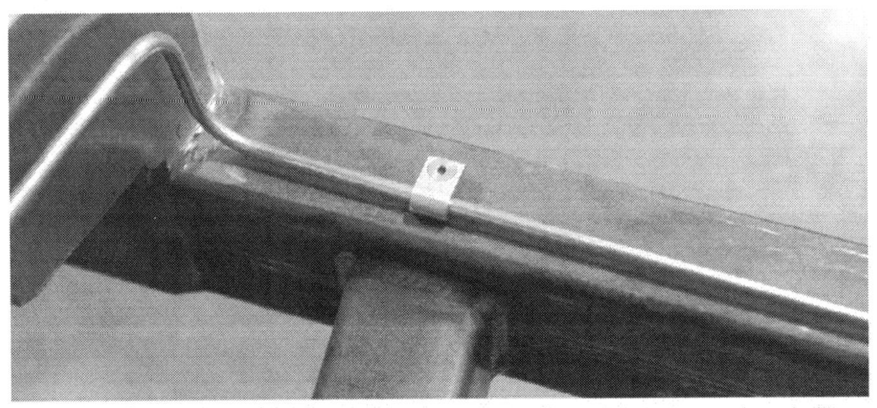
It's hard to make smooth, consistent turns in brake lines without a bender. They're inexpensive and will usually pay for themselves when compared to the tubing that's ruined trying to bend it by hand.

production cars, as well as street rods, has given enthusiasts access to the latest in race-bred brake technology.

CALIPERS

For the '08 Road Tour car, we settled on a proven combination we've used in the past. We equipped the Speed33 with Wilwood Billet Dynalite calipers all the way around. A four-piston, fixed design, they're powerful, compact, and very lightweight. Internal fluid crossovers eliminate external tubes and the four position; two-piece bleed screws allow for convenient mounting and easy bleeding. The Billet Dynalite uses standard, quick-change Dynalite pads, deep- cup stainless steel pistons, and high-temperature seals. Along with being effective, these polished calipers are good-looking, too, and the result is CNC sculpting around the edges and mirror-like polishing. The Billet Styled Dynalite calipers are available for .38-, .50-, .81-, 1.00-, and 1.25-inch rotor applications.

BRAKE PADS

Our calipers came equipped with Wilwood's PolyMatrix brake pads with the new "T" compound pads that are a low-dust, low-noise, improved-friction formula. These pads are highly resistant to fade and have long wear and low rotor-abrasion characteristics.

FRONT HUBS

Made from premium-grade billets, Willwood's forged aluminum hubs are unmatched for strength and lightweight. Hubs are drilled for 5 on 4.50-inch and 5 on 4.75-inch wheel lug patterns. The hubs are shipped complete with bearing races installed, new bearings, grease seals, screw-on billet aluminum hubcaps, and 1/2-20 RH grade 8 wheel lug studs. Aluminum backside mounting plates are supplied for solid rotor mounting directly to the hub.

CALIPER BRACKETS, AND HARDWARE

Wilwood furnished the front aluminum caliper mounting brackets with steel threaded bolt hole inserts. These mounts are CNC-machined for precise fit and come with grade 8 strength or higher nuts, bolts, washers, and alignment shims.

ROTORS

When it came to rotors, we had the option of the vented, drilled and slotted SRP or HP Series rotors. Both are manufactured from premium-grade, long-grain carbon iron to provide long wear with high thermal stability and resistance to distortion. We chose the SRP because of the venting and cleaning action of the holes, and the slots will reduce pad glaze and minimize irregular friction compound buildup on the rotor faces. The results are smoother engagement with an overall improvement in consistency and response from the pads. SRP rotors are silver zinc washed to prevent rust on the areas of the rotor not kept clean by pad contact.

REAR BRAKES

As in the front, polished-billet, Dynalite four-piston calipers were used

UNDERSTANDING FITTINGS

AN VS. NPT: UNDERSTANDING PORT THREADS, ADAPTER FITTINGS, AND LINE SIZES

The designation AN stands for Army/Navy and calls out mil/spec (military specifications) for dimensional standards of hydraulic lines, hose-end connectors, and port adapter fittings. AN specifications are a popular standard met by all companies that manufacture AN-style performance fuel hose and accessories. For many there has been much confusion about the subject of AN lines, NPT and ORB ports, and how all of this works together. Here are the answers for those who want to know.

The flare angle used to seal AN connections is required to be SAE, 37 degree, as apposed to the 45 degree flare commonly found on household plumbing adapters. This angle can be found on the male point of the port adapter fitting and on the female inside the hose-end nut. AN port threads are not NPT or "pipe thread," but instead utilize straight threads (like any normal fastener) and SAE O-Ring Boss (ORB) technology for sealing. AN lines, ORB ports, and the appropriate port adapter fittings are measured in inch/fractional sizes.

A dash (–) size in AN "speak" refers to the I.D. of a standard, thin wall, hard line as the basis to construct a comparable flexible hose that may be used in its place. A 1/2-inch, thin-wall hard line measures .50-inch on the outside diameter (O.D.), has an inside diameter (I.D.) of 0.440-inch, and a wall thickness of 0.030-inch. An appropriate, flexible replacement line would be -8 AN, with a minimum 0.44-inch I.D. Depending on line construction, rubber with stainless steel or nylon braid, or Teflon with stainless steel braid, the line's wall thickness and O.D. may vary.

AN line sizes will have a dash (-) preceding the line size. The number after the dash refers to the number of 1/16 of an inch O.D., thin wall, hard line to which the flexible line will compare. For example, calling for a –8 AN line would mean the engineer or system designer requires a flexible line made of certain materials suitable for the application that would have the minimum I.D. of an 8/16-inch (1/2-inch) O.D. hard line. The actual line construction is dictated by the application with regard to line flexibility, vacuum and pressure capability, abrasion resistance and chemical compatibility, etc. Regardless, the engineer knows a -8 line of any construction will have a minimum I.D. equal to 1/2-inch hard line (.0440-inch), and be able to support similar flow rates.

Here are some of the common Army/Navy (AN) line and thread specifications: -04 AN line = 4/16-inch = 1/4-inch hard line. –04 AN Port and Fitting thread is: 7/1-inch" -20 TPI. -06 AN line = 6/16-inch = 3/8-inch hard line. –06 AN Port and Fitting thread is: 9/16-inch -18 TPI. -08 AN line = 8/16-inch = 1/2-inch hard line. –08 AN Port and Fitting thread is: 3/4-inch -16 TPI. -10 AN line = 10/16-inch = 5/8-inch hard line. –10 AN Port and Fitting thread is: 7/8-inch -14 TPI. -12 AN line = 12/16-inch = 3/4-inch hard line. –12 AN Port and Fitting thread is: 1-1/16-inch-12 TPI.

Modern, high-performance fuel systems are predominately fitted with safer, better-sealing, higher-flowing, AN-ORB ports. These ports require a straight thread adapter fitting with a sealing O-ring installed over the threads up to the hex that disappears into the port when properly installed. No additional thread sealer is required or recommended.

NATIONAL PIPE THREAD (NPT) PORTS, AN PORTS, AND PORT ADAPTER FITTINGS

Over the years, in low-pressure hydraulics, NPT has been a popular thread for ports and adapter fittings. When NPT ports are used in a fuel system with AN line, an adapter fitting to convert from NPT to AN is required. NPT was designed for use with thick-walled pipe, typically black pipe used in fixed structures like buildings, to handle distribution of water and natural gas. Black pipe isn't particularly bendable, flexible, or lightweight, and is hardly desirable for plumbing a high-performance fuel system. As a result fittings that adapt NPT ports to AN line are common to allow flexible AN lines to be utilized in performance automotive fuel systems.

Unlike AN thread, which is straight, NPT ports and fittings are both tapered. NPT male to female adapters start loose, threading easily, but get tight and harder to turn well before the hex touches the port. When threaded together, the NPT design creates a wedging effect, binding the thread in order to seal. The use of a thread sealant is common and required with NPT, as it does not consistently create a positive seal on its own, like an O-ring configuration. It's common to see a number of threads showing on the adapter fitting when NPT is sufficiently tight, making NPT assemblies bulkier and less clean-appearing than a similar AN assembly.

NPT ports are commonly adapted to AN lines, but the NPT size designation is confusing, identifying the pipe I.D. rather than the O.D. Black pipe has a much thicker wall than hard line, so the pipe/port O.D. is much larger than the NPT size would seem to indicate. For example, a 3/8-inch NPT port will have an outside diameter of 5/8-inch, allowing for a wall thickness of 1/8-inch (0.125-inch). As a result, NPT port sizes allow the use of a one step larger AN line than their indicated size would seem to support. As long as the wall of the adapter fitting is not overly thick, the following NPT Port to AN adapters will provide a common I.D. through-hole:

Maximum AN line for NPT port size: 1/4-inch NPT is compatible with up to -6 AN (3/8-inch hard line) 3/8-inch NPT is compatible with up to –8 AN (1/2-inch hard line) 1/2-inch NPT is compatible with up to –10 AN (5/8-inch hard line) 3/4-inch NPT is compatible with up to -16 AN (1-inch hard line).

Adapter fittings are available for connecting larger than recommended AN lines to the above NPT ports. Beware, the inside diameter of the adapter fitting will necessarily be smaller on the NPT side, creating a flow restriction that many racers and hotrod enthusiasts overlook. This is a poor practice and should be avoided, but when no alternative is available, consider sourcing a steel NPT to AN adapter from a good hydraulic supplier. Steel adapters will have a thinner wall than aluminum, due to the increase in material strength, leaving a larger I.D. to support higher flow on the too small, NPT side of the adapter.

FUEL SYSTEM INSTALLATION TIPS FROM AEROMOTIVE

RETURN SYSTEMS

Something we are big believers in is the return-style system. The benefits of a dynamic, return-style fuel system are numerous, including longer pump life, a marked increase in pump to horsepower ratings (allowing smaller, lighter pumps to fuel more hp), even quieter pump operation is common. Two things are very important. First, the return line needs to be properly sized. Our goal is to ensure that the return line is not a greater restriction than the regulator itself. The second is that the fuel must return to the top of the tank, or as near the top as possible, preferably in a location that will not create turbulence around the pick-up point for the suction side of the fuel system. The easiest way to verify proper return side plumbing is to start the car and adjust the regulator to a couple psi below the intended set point. For example, if you want to hold 7 psi at the carburetor, verify that you can adjust the regulator down to 5 psi. This will confirm that the regulator and not the return line is actually determining the fuel pressure. This simple test will minimize the potential to experience pressure drop when the system goes from low demand to high demand, idle to WOT.

FUEL LINES

Routing fuel lines is mostly common sense. If you find yourself questioning your placement, chances are it shouldn't be there. Follow these simple rules.

- Stay way from heat (exhaust pipes/turbos)
- Any and all moving parts (driveshafts/ axles)
- Keep the fuel line(s) as high as you can, but still allow the pump to be gravity-fed on the suction side (do not route under frames or sub frame connectors)

If you stick with the native port size of the component, you should be safe. Aeromotive makes specific recommendations regarding line size in our instructions (also available on our Web site) and in the Power Planner of our catalog. In order of importance, the suction line needs to be at least as large as the inlet port on the pump. The return line can't be too large, but at least as large as the return port on the regulator. EFI systems can usually return with a -6 AN, whereas carbureted systems will typically require a -8AN return, and some carbureted racing applications may even require a -10 AN return.

USING FLEX LINE

The use of hose versus hard-line is really dictated by the builder's budget, style, and intended application. And by hose, we are only referring to stainless braided hose.

FUEL COMPATIBILITY

Most of the stainless braided hose available today is not a true Mil-spec hose, and does not seem to be as durable given the different additive packages common in pump gas today. Fuel vapor escaping from braided hose is the most common complaint. Some car builders are starting to use Teflon-lined hose to keep the vapor from permeating the rubber and stainless braid. It's harder to work with compared to steel braided rubber, but it does a better job of controlling vapors. Teflon line requires special fittings and some patience. Keep in mind that if you smell gas in your garage, you may not have a fuel leak, but rather a "vapor leak." Of course, most rods don't have vapor canisters like the other cars that may be sitting in the owner's garage, so the same gas in a different car will have a different effect on the olfactory senses.

on the rear of the Speed33. The big differences in the rear brakes are the rotors with integral hats and drum for the parking brake shoes and the caliper bracket that mounts the parking brake shoes.

MASTER CYLINDER

Wilwood's die-cast aluminum master cylinder is so pretty, it's too bad we hid it under the car. They are available in 7/8, 1, or 1-1/8 bore sizes to match the volume and pressure requirements of nearly any application. The mounting flange is slotted to accommodate bolt centers from 3.22-3.40 inches, so they can easily replace Chrysler, Corvette, GM, or Ford Mustang master cylinders. The body also features two through-hole mounts on 6.40-inch centers for easy side mounting to the frame. For ease in plumbing, there are pressure outlets on both sides.

PROPORTIONING VALVE

Pressure adjustments with the Wilwood proportioning valve range from 100-1,000 psi, and provide for a maximum decrease of 57 percent inline pressure. This adjustment will allow us to fine-tune the front to rear braking balance by proportionately decreasing the rear brake line pressure.

RESIDUAL PRESSURE VALVES

Necessary when the master cylinder is located lower than the calipers, two residual pressure valves prevent fluid drain back that occurs from gravity and vibration that results in excessive caliper piston retraction and a longer brake pedal stroke without causing the brakes to drag. With drum brakes, a 10-pound valve is used to compensate for return spring tension in the drums. Wilwood residual pressure valves are made from billet aluminum and color coded for easy identification—blue are 10-pound, red are 2-pound.

FUEL SYSTEM

Again we've stayed with components that have served us well over many Road Tour miles and have equipped the '08 car with an Aeromotive fuel pump, filters, regulator, and fuel log.

When it comes to pumps, Aeromotive has you covered whether you're running 200 hp or 2,000, carburetion or fuel injection, with pumps that can be submerged in the fuel tank or mounted to a framerail.

In a carbureted system Aeromotive may recommend stainless elements, before and after the fuel pump to take advantage of the ability to service the element rather than replacing it. They now offer

A 2-pound residual pressure valve was installed in the front brake line to keep fluid from draining out of the calipers.

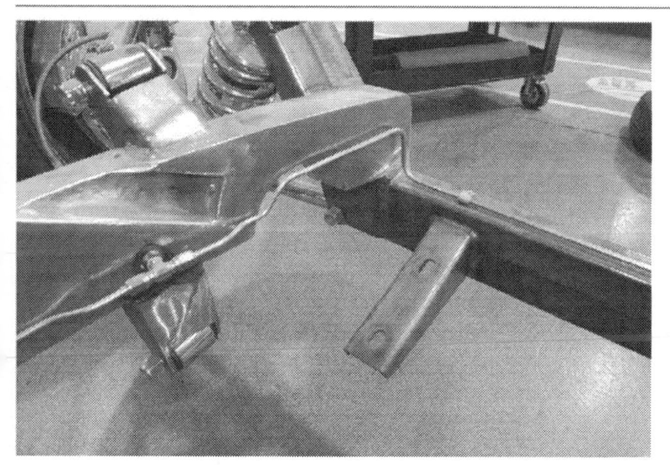

The Roadster Shop did a beautiful job of forming the 3/16-inch stainless steel brake lines to go over the steering and across the frame. The brackets on the front crossmember are for the Flaming River rack-and-pinion steering gear. Note the notch in the 'rail for steering clearance

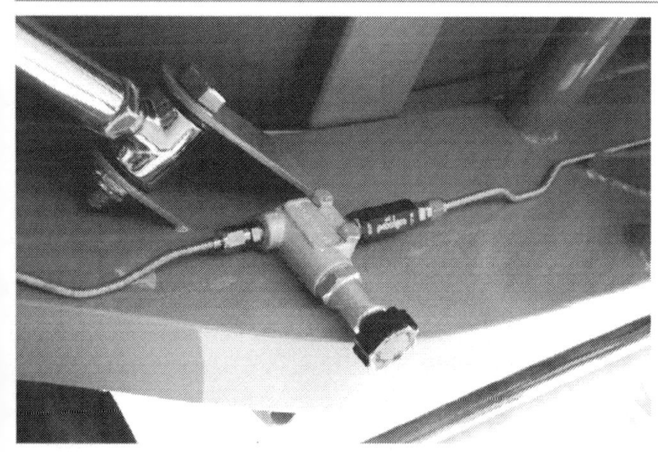

A Wilwood adjustable proportioning valve was installed in the rear brake line. Rotating the knob clockwise until it's all the way in delivers full pressure to the rear brakes. Turning the knob counterclockwise reduces pressure.

We opted for an inline hydraulic brake-light switch to activate the stoplights. A perfect place to install it was one of the unused ports in the master cylinder.

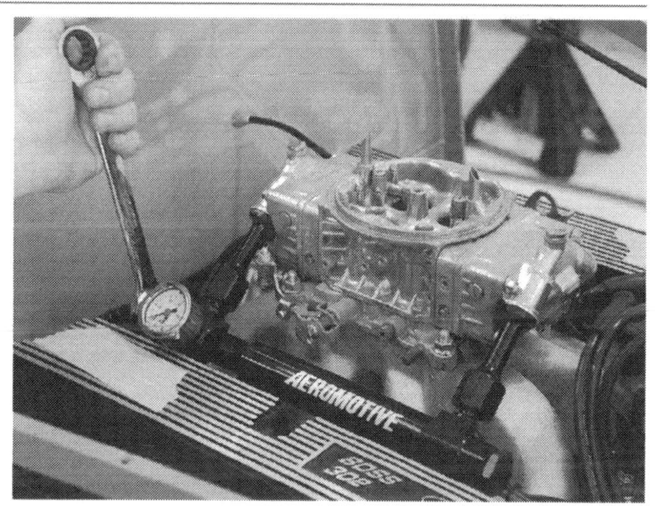

Aeromotive supplied the components to deliver fuel from the tank to the Holley carburetor. Note the fuel pressure gauge.

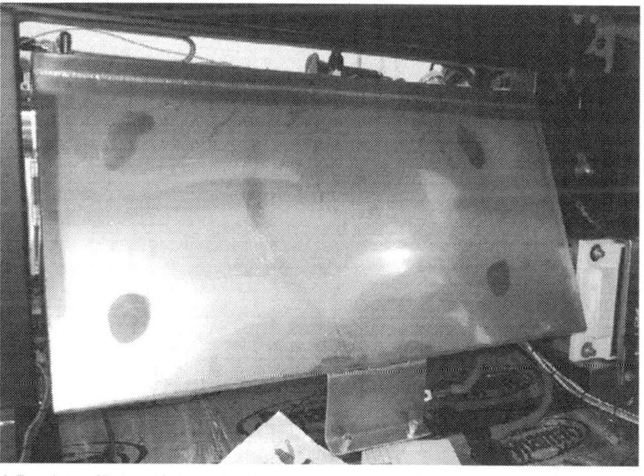

A Roadster Shop stainless steel gas tank resides in the trunk behind the seat.

The Aeromotive fuel log mount can be used with or with out a return or a "dead head" regulator. The type II bright-dip, black-anodized finish provides durability an great looks, while dual 1/8-inch NPT ports provide access for gauges or pressure transducers. These innovative fuel log telescopes and also uses a ball and socket assembly that swivels +/- 20 degrees to avoid obstructions.

Aeromotive's dry inline pressure gauges supply accurate readings even when exposed to underhood heat, unlike many of the liquid filled variety.

a 40-micron SS element in adition to the 100, so a 40 would take place of a number 10 fabric on the pressure side. Kyle Fickler of Aeromotive suggests using a fine filter in front of the pump when new gas tanks are installed or if contamination is suspected. (Keep in mind, new tanks and tanks that have been in cars under construction tend to collect grit along with various and sundry types of dirt and general junk.) Change the filter after the first tank of gas and install the recommended element.

Another feature found on many fuel systems today is a bypass. Due to the formulation of the gasoline currently being sold, vaporlock can easily occur. Return systems prevent the pump from "dead-heading," which creates heat; as fuel is constantly being returned to the tank, any heat absorbed by the fuel lines from any source (such as the exhaust system) is dissipated.

Depending on the needs of the engine, the tech experts at Aeromotive will advise what components should be used (the information is also on the Web site).

FUEL REGULATOR ADJUSTMENT TIPS FROM AEROMOTIVE

Regulators are a valuable accessory in any system as they allow precise adjustment of fuel pressure for optimum performance for carburetors or fuel injection. The may or may not include fuel tank return lines.

Once the regulator is installed, attach a suitable fuel pressure gauge to the 1/8 NPT port on the fuel pressure regulator.

Ensure that any spilled gasoline and any gasoline soaked shop towels are cleaned up and removed from the vicinity of the vehicle

Reconnect the battery and turn the fue pump on without starting the car. After several seconds, check the fuel pressure. If there is no fuel pressure, turn the fuel pum off, wait one minute, turn the fuel pump on, and recheck the fuel pressure. Repeat this off and on procedure until the fuel pressure gauge registers fuel pressure.

With the fuel pressure gauge registerin fuel system pressure, check for fuel leaks from and around the Aeromotive regulator and all fuel lines and connections near the regulator. If any fuel leaks are found, turn the fuel pump off, remove any spilled fuel, and repair the leak before proceeding.

Once the fuel pressure gauge registers fuel system pressure and there are no fuel leaks, start the engine and adjust the regulator to the desired fuel pressure (regulator is adjustable from 3-15 psi). Turning the adjustment screw clockwise wi increase fuel pressure.

Once the desired fuel pressure is achieved, tighten the regulator adjustment jam nut.

If you do not want to keep the fuel pressure gauge on the vehicle, relieve the fue

A TYPICAL AEROMOTIVE FUEL SYSTEM FOR A CARBURETED FUEL SYSTEM WILL BE ONE OF THE FOLLOWING:

Approved for Street Duty — Approved for Racing Duty

R/D SERIES 7 PSI CARBURETED SYSTEM - 200 to 800 HP

AN-08 Line — AN-08 Line — AN-08 Line — AN-06 Line — Carb

SS SERIES CARBURETED SYSTEM - 200 to 750 HP

SS Ads Regulator P/N 13201,13309

AN-06 Line — AN-08 Line — AN-08 Line — AN-08 Line — AN-06 Line — Carb — AN-06 Line — Carb

AN-06 Return Line

A2000 CARBURETED SYSTEM - Up to 2500 HP, drag race only

AN-12 Line — AN-10 Line — AN-10 Line — AN-10 Line — AN-10 Line — AN-06 Line — Carb(s) — AN-06 Line — Carb(s)

AN-10 Return Line from Regulator

MECHANICAL CARBURETED SYSTEM - 200 to 500 HP

SS Ads Regulator P/N 13201,13309

AN-10 Line — AN-10 Line — AN-08 Line — AN-08 Line — AN-06 Line — Carb — AN-06 Line — Carb

AN-08 Return Line

BILLET PULSE PUMP SYSTEM - For all pulse pump engine applications.

AN-04 Line — AN-04 Line — AN-04 Line — Carb

A1000 CARBURETED SYSTEM - 1200 HP forced induction, 1500 HP naturally aspirated.

AN-10 Line — AN-10 Line — AN-10 Line — AN-10 Line — AN-08 Line — Carb

AN-08 Return Line

ELIMINATOR CARBURETED SYSTEM - 1700 HP forced induction, 2300 HP naturally aspirated.

AN-12 Line — AN-12 Line — AN-10 Line — AN-10 Line — AN-06 Line — Carb(s)

AN-10 Return Line

PRO-SERIES CARBURETED SYSTEM - 2000 HP forced induction, 2600 HP naturally aspirated.

AN-12 Line — AN-12 Line — AN-10 Line — AN-10 Line — AN-06 Line — Carb(s)

AN-10 Return Line

BELT OR HEX DRIVE CARBURETED SYSTEM - Gasoline 3000 HP forced induction, 4000 naturally aspirated. Alcohol 1800 HP forced induction, 2000 naturally aspirated.

AN-12 Line — AN-12 Line — AN-10 Line — AN-10 Line — AN-08 Line — Carb(s)

AN-10 Return Line

A TYPICAL AEROMOTIVE FUEL SYSTEM FOR A FUEL-INJECTION SYSTEM WILL BE ONE OF THE FOLLOWING:

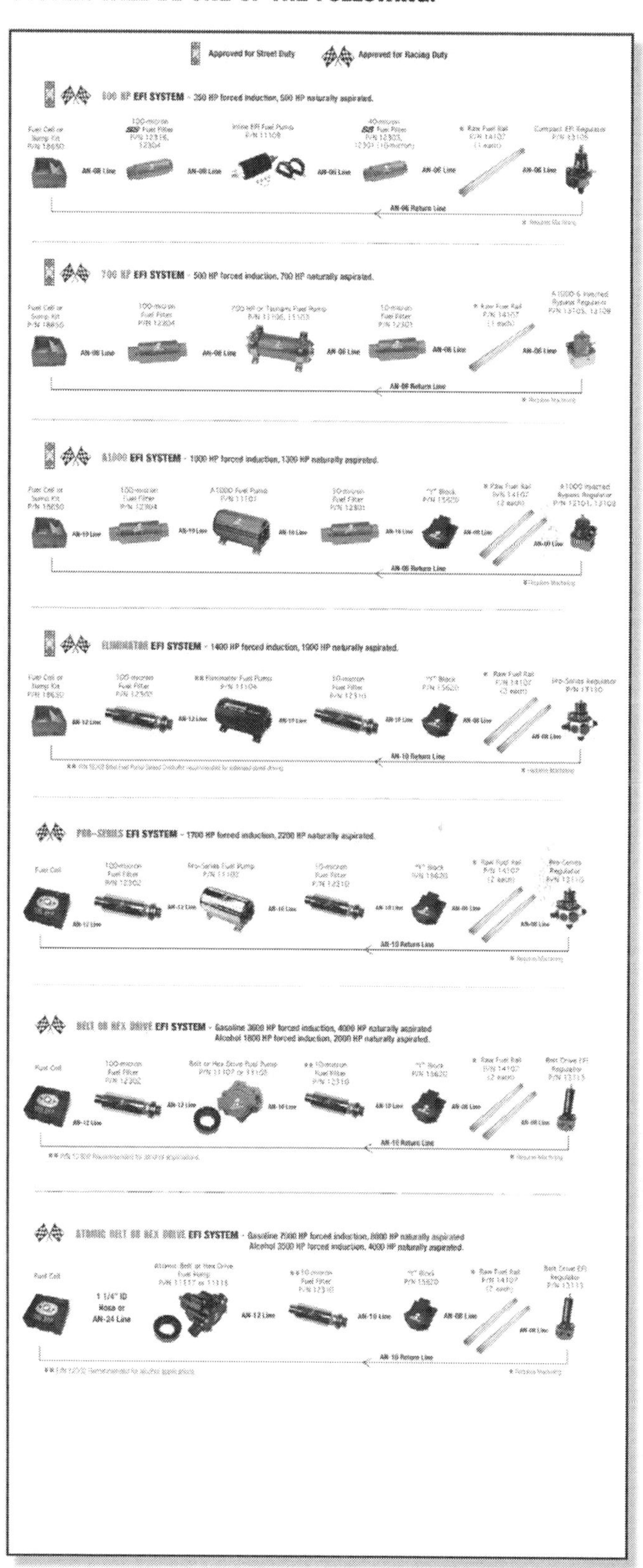

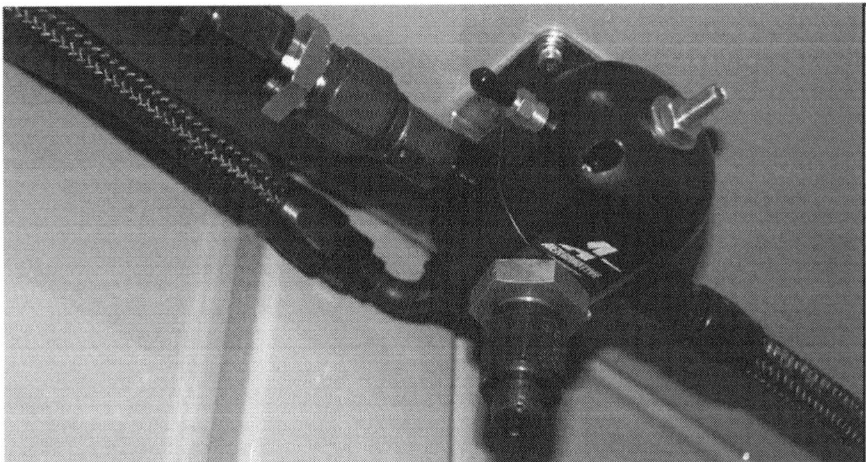

We used an Aeromotive bypass regulator. The barbed fitting is for boost referencing, used in blown applications to increase fuel pressure under boost. Typically, the fuel will enter the front of the regulator, and then feed the carb out of the 2-6AN outlets on either side, rather than flowing through the bottom as shown in the photo. This regulator could also have been screwed directly to the log using P/N 15640 which is an AN-10/AN-10 Swivel Union.

The filter and pump were mounted to the rear crossmember.

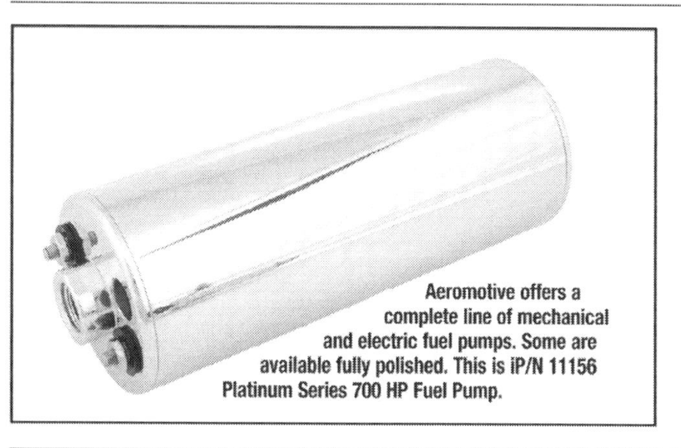

Aeromotive offers a complete line of mechanical and electric fuel pumps. Some are available fully polished. This is iP/N 11156 Platinum Series 700 HP Fuel Pump.

Aeromotive offers a variety of fuel filters; in black as P/Ns 12321 (10 micron) and 12324 (100 micron), or Platinum as P/N 12351 (10) and P/N 12354 (100).

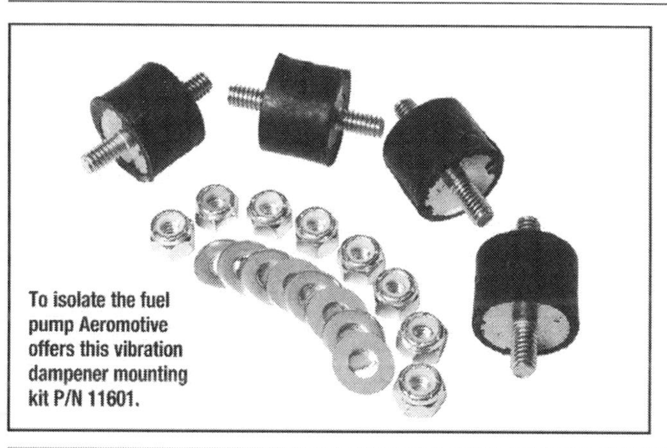

To isolate the fuel pump Aeromotive offers this vibration dampener mounting kit P/N 11601.

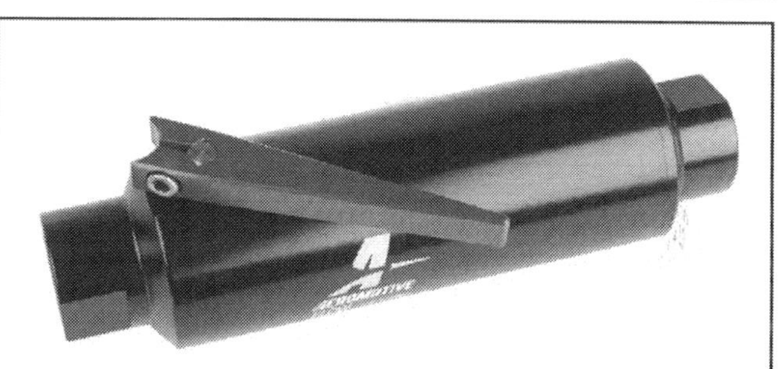

Cleaning and replacing the filter element is a lot easier and less messy with Aeromotive's shutoff valve-equipped fuel filters. They feature 100-micron stainless steel elements and are recommended for use between the fuel tank and fuel pump inlet.

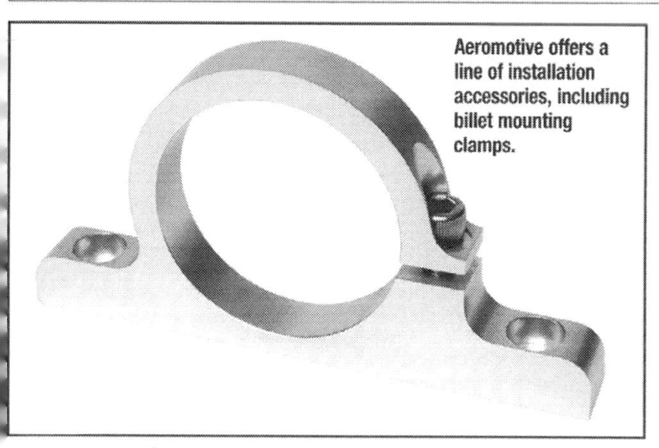

Aeromotive offers a line of installation accessories, including billet mounting clamps.

system pressure as instructed in the appropriate vehicle service manual. Remove the fuel pressure gauge and reinstall the 1/8 NPT pipe plug into the regulator gauge port using thread sealant.

Test-drive the car to insure proper operation and recheck the fuel system for leaks.

PLUMBING THE CHASSIS

Brake and fuel lines should only be made of steel or stainless steel, fittings for either may be standard automotive 45-degree or 37-degree AN. When using 45-degree fittings, the ends of the tubing have to be double-flared. Flared lines with fittings in place are available at parts houses in various lengths; when building a street rod, odds are custom lines will be required, so a special double-double flaring tool is needed for the two-step operation. When double flaring, stainless fully annealed tubing is required.

The popular AN (for Army/Navy) fittings found on aircraft and race cars require single flares with a reinforcement ferrule. Another difference is standard automotive fittings have male threads on the tubing and female on the fittings, while AN connections have female on the tubing and male on the fittings.

One of the common misconceptions is that the size of brake tubing affects system pressure—it doesn't. Brake lines are generally 3/16 or 1/4 inch, and there will be no system pressure difference between the two. On the other hand, fuel line size can be critical because of the volume required. As can be seen in the Aeromotive charts, most performance engines will require at least a 3/8- to 1/2-inch fuel line (AN lines are measured in dash numbers in 1/16-inch increments, so a 3/8-inch line is a -6).

LAST, BUT NOT LEAST

A Wilwood adjustable proportioning valve was installed in the rear brake line. Rotating the knob clockwise until it's all the way in delivers full pressure to the rear brakes. Turning the knob counterclockwise reduces pressure. ■

Chapter 8
EXHAUST SYSTEM

By Ron Ceridono

The completed exhaust system on the '08 Road Tour Speed33 was built in-house at the Roadster Shop. It looks good, doesn't rattle, and sounds great.

Many, many years ago, a friend was pulled over for the umpteenth time for loud pipes. When the officer, who had stopped him several times before for the same infraction, asked in frustration why it was necessary to make noise that would, as he described it, "wake the dead," my pal responded with typical teenage logic: "What's the sense of having a hot rod if it ain't loud?"

Back in those days, the fix for loud pipes was simple: pull the gutted glasspacks off, stuff them full of steel wool, and put pieces of screen over the outlets to hold it in place. That would usually make the offending system quiet enough to be acceptable to the constabulary. Then, shortly after having the fix-it ticket signed off, the screen would burn up, all your mom's used scrub pads would blow out the tailpipes, and you'd be cool again. That was until the next run-in with the law.

Thankfully, since those days we've all discovered that ear-piercing sound and performance aren't synonymous, but for most of us, nothing will ever take the place of a healthy V-8's rumble. And that's exactly what the'08 Road Tour Speed33 has, thanks to its Sanderson Headers anc Hushpower mufflers.

THE ADVANTAGE TO HEADERS THOUGHTS FROM SANDERSON'S TONY GARISTO

While stock manifolds can often be usec on a street rod, they are at best a compromi used by manufacturers because they are relatively inexpensive. Stock exhaust systems are intended to work in a wide range of driving conditions and generally are not very efficient, often sacrificing performance and efficiency for ease of production and reduced costs.

Typically, production engines use a log-type manifold on each cylinder bank connecting through a "Y" pipe into a single catalytic converter and muffler, all with pipes of 2 inches in diameter or less. While this may be OK for your grocery-getter, if you're looking for low-end power, midrange acceleration, top-speed potential, and yes, even better fuel economy from your street rod, this isn't the way to get it. Anything that causes turbulence or backpressure in the exhaust system reduces the power the engine can produce. Stock manifolds contribute heavily to turbulence because all the exhaust dumps directly into a single tube. Tubular designs separate each cylinder's exhaust pulse, reducing the possibility that spent gases will flow back into an adjacent cylinder and contaminate the incoming fuel and air mixture. This is especially crucial when you're running a cam with more overlap. Simultaneously, tubular headers reduce backpressure, allowing more fuel and air to enter the cylinder's intake stroke. Both these factors add up to more combustion efficiency, i.e., more power to the wheels.

While just about everyone realizes tubular headers work better than OEM exhaust manifolds, there are some common misconceptions. First is the size of the headers' primary tubes. It's easy to assume the bigger the tube, the better, but that's not the case.

The fact is primaries that are too large actually cost you torque and horsepower by slowing down the rate at which the exhaust travels through the system. Think of your engine as an air pump. Every time the exhaust leaves the combustion chamber, it's being forced into the primary tube for that cylinder. Smaller diameter pipes flow less volume than large ones, but the exhaust in the smaller pipe flows faster. Until you reach the rpm level where the sheer volume of exhaust gases require bigger primaries. Smaller tubes scavenge far more efficiently. If you're using the engine in the 1,500-3,500-rpm range, which is typical for a street driven car, you definitely want 1 1/2- to 1 5/8-inch primary tubes for a small-block and 1 3/4- to 1 7/8-

HEADER INSTALLATION TIPS

Besides a few common tools, what's really required is the patience to do it right. Sanderson headers are built by hand from the finest materials. Properly installed, their products will give you years of trouble-free performance.

Be sure your engine is in tune. Timing and the fuel/air mixture need to be right on to avoid heat-related gasket problems.

The heads must be perfectly clean. Remove all traces of carbon, old gasket material, and other debris, starting with a scraper and a single-edge razor blade. Finish with a wire brush and a final polish with a Scotch-Brite or similar abrasive pad. Wipe all mounting surfaces with acetone (use care, as it is flammable). Install two studs, one in each end of the head, to align the flange.

Coat the contact surfaces of the built-up weld rings on the back of the header flange with Permatex Ultra Black RTV, then slide the header over the studs. Starting with the ones that are hardest to reach, install all the header bolts finger-tight. Remove the studs and install the end bolts. Working from the center, alternating left to right, snug up the bolts to 10–12 lb-ft torque with a short box-end wrench. They sell a special thin-wall Snap-On™ wrench that's really handy for the job.

FIRE UP THE MOTOR, RUN IT FOR FIVE MINUTES, AND LET IT COOL COMPLETELY

Re-tighten the bolts, being careful not to over-tighten them. Drive the car 10 to 20 minutes—not hard or at freeway speeds. Let the motor cool, and then tighten the bolts again. Take the car out for 20 to 30 minutes, this time at speeds between 50 and 60 mph. When the motor is completely cool, check the bolts for tightness. Drive 75 to 100 miles, cool down, and then recheck. Repeat this procedure until the bolts stay tight.

SPECIAL INSTRUCTIONS FOR NEW OR REBUILT ENGINES

Out-of-tune motors can permanently damage chrome, stainless, and ceramic-coated headers. Exhaust gas temperatures in fresh engines can easily exceed the limits of these materials. For first-time fire-up, follow these additional steps.

Install an old pair of headers or your stock exhaust manifolds without gaskets. Start the motor and adjust the timing, carburetor settings, and valves, and check carefully for vacuum leaks. Run it 10 to 20 minutes to burn out all traces of assembly lube. Check for soot at the end of the tailpipe, caused by a too-rich fuel mixture. Correct this before you bolt on your new headers. Let the motor cool completely, unbolt the old exhaust manifolds, and follow the procedure above to install your new headers.

We used coated, tight-tuck Sanderson headers on our Boss Ford. They have thick flanges for excellent sealing, and spark plug and fastener access is excellent.

This overhead view of the right side shows how smooth and tight Sanderson bends the primary pipes.

Planning is a big part of making 50 pounds of street rod parts fit in a 2-pound engine compartment. The Roadster Shop crew mocked up the steering and exhaust using a plastic block

inch for a big-block. Any bigger and you'll lose low-end torque. Beyond 3,500 rpm, it's a question of where you want the power peaks. Small tubes don't lose their edge in horsepower or torque until you get above 5,500 rpm. So, even if you're running a radical cam and blower, you're better off sizing your headers smaller rather than larger, unless you plan to do most of your driving at full throttle. Sanderson headers are sized correctly for even the most heavily modified street motors.

MUFFLERS

Flowmaster mufflers produce one of the most identifiable sounds in the automotive world. Many different tones are available depending upon the muffler series ranging from the deep, aggressive tone of the Super 44 to the quiet and subtle but unmistakable tone of the 70 Series. Rather than packing like most inline mufflers, Flowmasters use a series of deflectors that are part of their sound energy cancellation technology, so there's no problem with packing material deteriorating and the muffler getting louder over time.

In addition, the deflector in a Flowmaster muffler acts as a one-way check valve, eliminating reversion back to the engine, and creates a low-pressure area to help scavenge exhaust.

Another offering from Flowmaster is the Delta Flow series. They offer superior scavenging of exhaust gases even moreso than a comparable (standard) Flowmaster muffler by using multiple deflectors compared to single a deflector. Delta Flow technology provides a cleaner, faster scavenging path by eliminating the chance of turbulence commonly found behind a single deflector model.

FLOWMASTER VARIATIONS

Flowmaster mufflers come in a variety of configurations. The Super 44 Two Chamber uses the technology seen in the larger Super

HEADER FINISH AND UPKEEP TIPS FROM SANDERSON

PLAIN FINISH:

Wash headers with acetone (flammable). The headers should be heated to approximately 200 degrees by using either an oven or a torch.

Hang the headers using a coat hanger through the bolt holes.

Spray the headers with VHT paint while the headers are still hot. Spray inside and out.

This process bakes the paint on the header and will protect the headers from external and internal rust.

CHROME AND STAINLESS FINISH:

New and untuned motors have exhaust temperatures that exceed the intended use of the header's materials. These headers must only be used on properly tuned motors. This includes chrome, stainless steel, and ceramic-coated headers.

Headers should be cleaned with a mild detergent or soap, such as Windex. Spray VHT paint inside all the tubes and collector. This will prevent rust buildup (chrome only, not required for stainless steel).

Apply a heavy coat of paste wax, then let dry. When the wax is dry, buff—do not simply wipe off. Treat your new Sanderson Headers' finish with the same care that you would treat your car's paint job. Wax headers frequently, this will help prevent bluing.

After installing your Sanderson headers, re-polish them to be sure all finger prints and grease are removed.

It is very important to run a low-backpressure exhaust system with chrome and stainless headers. Too much backpressure creates excessive heat, which in turn will discolor your headers.

Discoloration can also result from improper air/fuel mixture, incorrect ignition timing, or oil blowing by valveguides or piston rings.

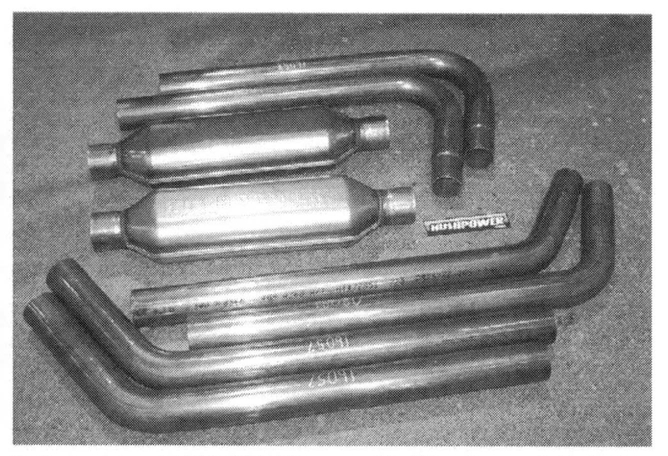

Hushpower's new U-Fit Dual Pipe Kit comes with all the pipes needed to build a custom exhaust system in 2.25, 2.50, and 3-inch pipe diameters. Kits include the front adapter pipes, intermediate pipes, H-pipe assembly, over-the-axle pipes, and optional tailpipe exits. Each piece has a slip-fit connection for easy assembly. These kits are designed for the professional installer or experienced do-it-yourselfers. Hardware is not included.

40 Series. The Super 44 is the most aggressive, deepest-sounding of the 4-inch–case street mufflers.

The Super 40 uses Gen II Delta Flow technology, which means it has the sound of the original 40 Series, but with low interior resonance.

The Super 40 Two Chamber increases scavenging for better performance and reduced interior resonance over the standard 40 Series with a nice growl outside the vehicle. Sounds great on late-model performance cars with catalytic converters.

The Series 80 Cross Flow Two Chamber is designed for applications where the muffler must be mounted transversely (crossflow) behind the rearend.

The 50 Series HD Three Chamber is primarily for today's higher-horsepower trucks such as the Dodge HEMI. This muffler will perform well on various vehicles when a deeper, more aggressive tone is desired.

The 50 Series Delta Flow Three Chamber is the latest design of the 50 Series muffler that utilizes Delta Flow technology along with a Helmholtz chamber to eliminate most all interior resonance and still have that famous Flowmaster sound outside the vehicle.

The 60 Series Delta Flow Three Chamber is for sport compacts cars and trucks.

The 50 Series Big Block Three Chamber is a larger version of Flowmasters 50 Series Delta Flow muffler and is specially designed for trucks, light SUVs and high-horsepower vehicles. The larger H-chamber reduces interior resonance to a minimum.

The 70 Series Big Block II Three Chamber uses a large case for increased volume and added sound reduction that will still fit many applications that our 50 Series "Big Block/HD" muffler won't.

INSIDE THE HUSHPOWER

Hushpower is a newly created and separate division of Flowmaster, Inc. based in Hayden, Idaho. The new series of mufflers utilizes a revolutionary patented design that is completely different from the original chambered design,

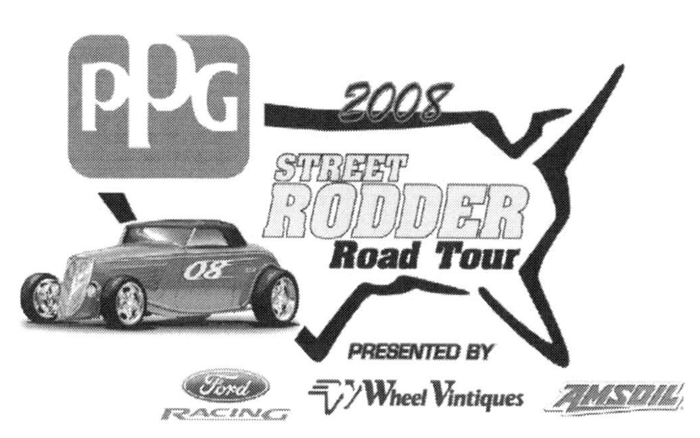

HUSHPOWER TEMPERATURE TESTING

Date: 1/7/2008
Test vehicle: 1993 Suburban 454
System: 2 1/4-inch dual

A Hushpower HP-2 #12418400 was placed on one side of the system; the OEM muffler on the other. Temperature sensors were placed directly to the case of each muffler, along with sensors attached to the floorboard 3 inches above the muffler case. The vehicle was strapped to the dyno for the test procedure.

After 5 min. idling, no load.
Hushpower case temp: 85° F — Floorboard temp: 64° F
OEM case temp: 157° F — Floorboard temp: 66° F

After 5 min. cruising at 55 mph under road load conditions.
Hushpower case temp: 141° F — Floorboard temp: 116° F
OEM case temp: 637° F — Floorboard temp: 147° F

After 10 min. cruising at 55 mph under road load conditions.
Hushpower case temp: 189° F — Floorboard temp: 134° F
OEM case temp: 704° F — Floorboard temp: 185° F

After 15 min. cruising at 55 mph under road load conditions.
Hushpower case temp: 249° F — Floorboard temp: 145° F
OEM case temp: 705° F — Floorboard temp: 187° F

Please note: We feel the floorboard temperatures would be significantly lower in on-road testing because of the massive increase in airflow associated with driving the vehicle at highway speed on the open road. We have yet to verify this data with on-road tests. This overall case temperatures should be nominally lower also. Lee Thompson, General Manager of Hushpower produced this data for you on 1/7/08.

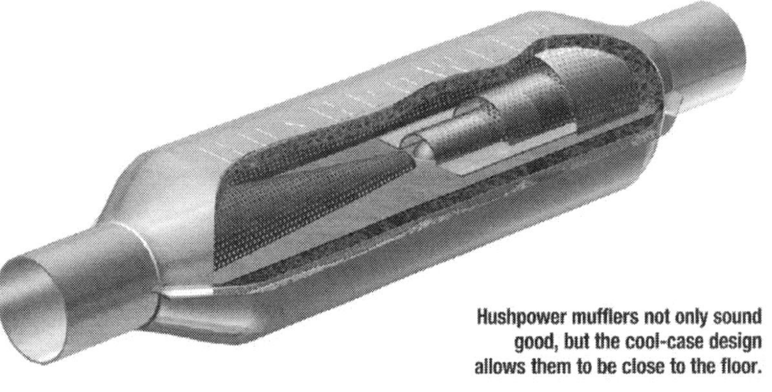

Hushpower mufflers not only sound good, but the cool-case design allows them to be close to the floor.

Thanks to the design of the Roadster Shop chassis, there's plenty of room to route the exhaust pipes. Always keep the pipes away from the master cylinder and brake and fuel lines.

When fitting pipes, accurate cuts are important. Mismatched cuts result in poorly fitting joints that are hard to weld.

and traditional glasspack products currently available.

ENTRY CONE

Hot exhaust gases entering the tapered inlet section are actually accelerated as they pass through the perforated cone into the outer core area. The perforation pattern and entry angle are specifically engineered into each product to provide optimum airflow characteristics. The sound energy is reflected and redirected back into itself as well as into the outer thermal core by the carefully selected taper angle of the entry cone.

LAMINAR FLOW AREA

The hot exhaust gases are released and allowed to expand into this section in multiple layers due to the tapered angle of

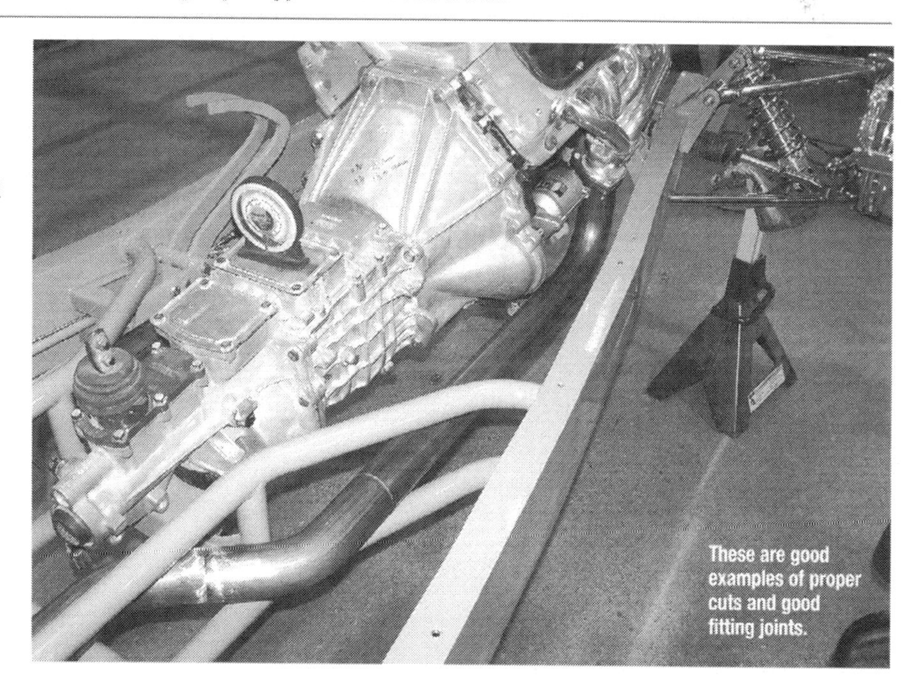

These are good examples of proper cuts and good fitting joints.

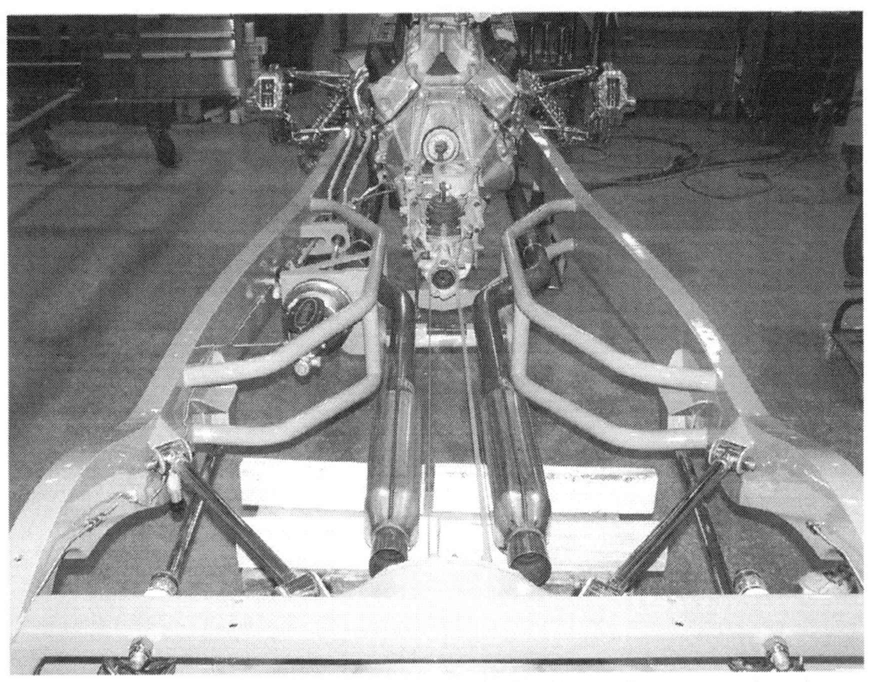

Seen from the rear, pipes and mufflers run adjacent to the driveshaft. The mufflers were turned on edge to increase clearance between the driveshaft and X-member.

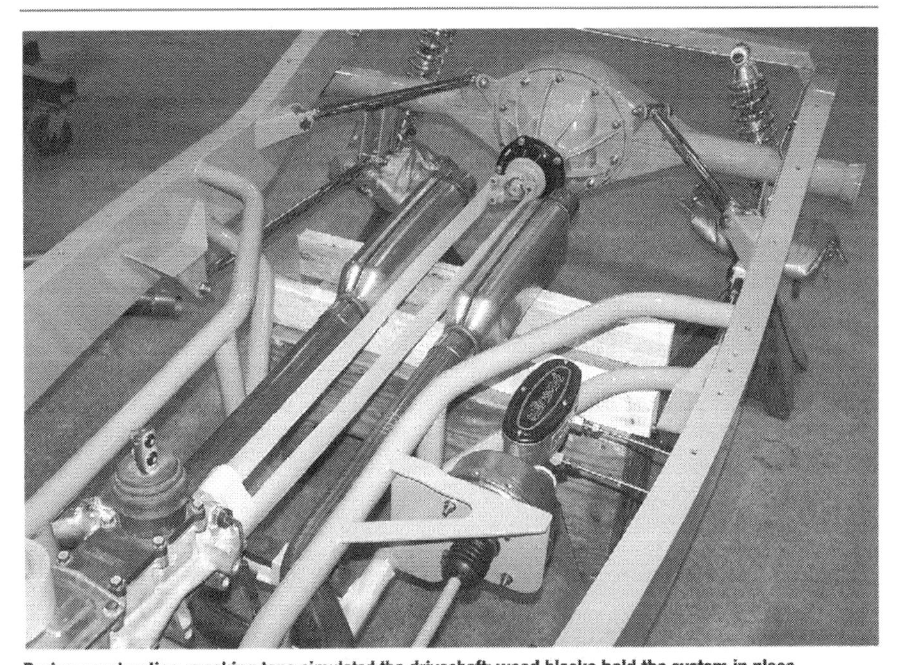

During construction, masking tape simulated the driveshaft; wood blocks hold the system in place.

the entry cone. This produces a controlled laminar flow pattern that reduces turbulence inside the muffler. Sound waves lose energy in this section through the expansion of the exhaust gases and reflective angles of the cones, which direct the waves into the thermal barrier material.

THERMAL BARRIER

The thermal barrier between the outer core section and muffler case provides a portion of the mufflers sound energy absorption characteristics. This thermal barrier is engineered to deliver much lower exterior case temperatures, allowing the muffler to be placed closer to heat-sensitive areas

EXIT CONE

The increased surface area and angle of the tapered exit cone provides an "easy exit" for the hot exhaust gases that encourages the flow out of the muffler. The carefully selected taper angle of the exit cone directs and focuses the sound energy back into itself. This convergence of sound waves reduces the sound level as it passes out of the muffler.

Hushpower mufflers come in a variety of configurations:

HP-2 Series Mufflers 409S: 18 inches long, painted 409S outer shell, and 409 internal components. Available in 2.00, 2.25, and 2.50-inch inlet/outlet sizes.

HP-2 Series Shorty 409S: 12 inches long, painted 409S outer shell, and 409 internal components. Available in 2.00, 2.25, and 2.50-inch inlet/outlet sizes.

HP-2 Series Muffler 304S: 18 inches long, polishible 304S outer shell, and 409S internal components. Available in 2.00, 2.25, and 2.50-inch inlet/outlet sizes.

HP-2 Series Shorty 304S: 12 inches long, polishible 304S outer shell, and 409S internal components. Available in 2.00, 2.25, and 2.50 inch inlet/outlet sizes.

PIPES

With the headers decided on, we turned to Flowmaster for the remainder of the exhaust system. Ray T. Flugger founded Flowmaster in 1983 with the goal of manufacturing and marketing performance exhaust products that created power, fuel efficiency, and controlled sound. To that end, Ray spent years researching the impact of header length, pipe diameter, H-pipe equalization, and backpressure on engine performance and how gas, heat, and sound were transmitted and dissipated throughout the exhaust system. The results of that research are mufflers that can deliver gains in fuel economy

Routing pipes up and over the rear axle can be a challenge. In this case, they go under the top triangulated four-bars and then over the housing.

and horsepower, not to mention that recognizable Flowmaster sound.

As with the headers, there were some questions about the rest of the exhaust system, so we went to our go-to guy on such matters, David Featherston of Flowmaster. Here are our questions and his answers.

HOW IS PIPE SIZE DETERMINED?

The size of pipe used in an exhaust system is a critical item to consider. Pipe diameter will affect the sound level and performance characteristics of the muffler, but keep in mind that bigger is not always better. Too large of a pipe can actually hinder exhaust scavenging by allowing atmospheric pressure to move back up the pipe. Smaller-diameter tubing flows exhaust faster than larger tubing, which results in better scavenging, i.e., flowing a larger volume of spent gases per minute.

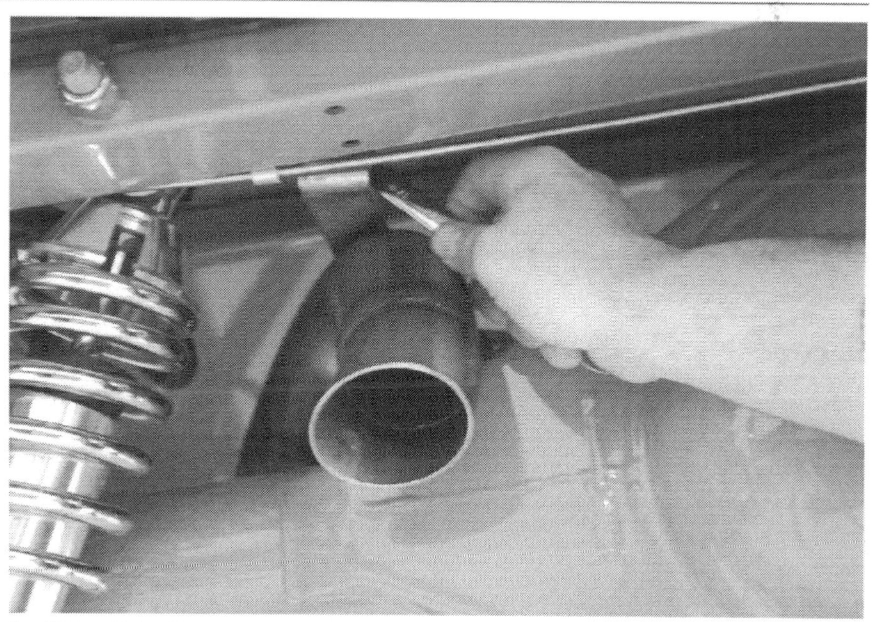

Small tabs with insulators are used to secure the tailpipe to the rear crossmember. The ends of the pipes are almost hidden by the rolled rear pan.

From this angle, the circuitous route of the tailpipes can be seen. The trick when working with tight clearances like this is to move the rear end through its range of travel to make sure there is interference between it and the pipes.

When building a performance exhaust system, it's important to size the pipe diameter from the header back to the displacement and horsepower of the engine, and to maintain consistent size from the collector to the end of the tailpipe. As we said, bigger is not always better.

As a general rule, most street applications use 2.00–2.50-inch pipe, while modified street applications will generally use 2.50- or 3.00-inch pipe.

WHAT PIPE MATERIAL DO YOU RECOMMEND?

Flowmaster uses aluminized steel almost exclusively in its manufacturing processes. From experience, we have found that aluminized steel does not suffer from the cracking often associated with welding stainless. For those looking for a clean, smooth look, our aluminized steel

The finished exhaust system is clean and simple with plenty of clearance between the pipes and temperature-sensitive items.

is easy to ceramic-coat for a fine color-matched finish.

WHAT ARE THE ADVANTAGES TO MANDREL BENDS?

All Flowmaster kits are manufactured with mandrel-bent tubing. This allows Flowmaster to create smooth high-flow bends that are not only aesthetically pleasing, but their smoothness speeds the exit of waste exhaust gases, unlike compression-bent tubing found from other manufacturers or muffler shops. A typical compression-bent tubing exhaust system can easily limit exhaust gas flow by 40 percent, which not only robs your engine of torque and horsepower, but also wastes fuel and creates unwanted tuning resonances in the exhaust system.

Thanks to their compact size, the Hushpower mufflers don't hang below the X-member, even when turned on edge.

DO YOU RECOMMEND BALANCE PIPES?

An "H" pipe, commonly referred to as an equalizer, balance, or crossover pipe, connects the two exhaust pipes. It will balance the pressure of the exhaust pulses in the system, thereby reducing interior and exterior sound while increasing power. In general, the "H" pipe should be installed as close as possible to the header collector. With manifolds, the "H" pipe is placed just past where the downpipes become horizontal. "H" pipes should be the same diameter as the main pipes or no more than 1/2-inch smaller. Flowmaster also offers a Universal Scavenger Cross-over Pipe that is a great application in any high-horsepower racing application. It uses D-Port Tuning technology, which helps with scavenging of waste exhaust gas and builds torque.

Band-style clamps were used to connect the slip-fit joints. They can be tightened without crushing the pipes like U-clamps can, which makes the pipes difficult to separate at a later date.

HOW DO FLOWMASTER MUFFLERS WORK?

The design of our mufflers may look simple, but it has taken years of research to develop our patented muffler technology. Our designs take the pressure and sound energy released from an engine's combustion chamber into the exhaust system and create a low-pressure area between exhaust pulses that scavenge or pull, spent gases out of each cylinder more efficiently than even an open pipe system. This improved removal of exhaust gases promotes a more efficient charge of unburned fuel and air to enter the cylinder for the next cycle. As a result, the engine has a purer mixture to burn, and now requires less fuel to achieve the same level of performance.

DO TAILPIPES AFFECT POWER?

Tailpipes aid in keeping atmospheric pressure from rushing back into the muffler. They can also improve performance and control sound. Tailpipes should be a minimum of 10 inches, and not longer than six feet. A tailpipe length of more than six feet may need a resonator.

WHERE SHOULD MUFFLERS BE POSITIONED?

The preferred muffler location is mid-ship approximately 18 inches back from the header collector. Another reason to put them midship is for improved interior resonance and sound control.

WHEN IS HEAT SHIELDING NECESSARY?

Heat shielding may be needed where exhaust pipes pass close by electrical, fuel, or brake lines, as temperatures in the exhaust system can exceed 1,200 degrees. For heat control, Flowmaster offers both tailpipe and muffler head shields and the unique Hushpower II muffler with an insulated case. This muffler works well under hot rods, customs, and modified trucks, where space is an issue and heat control is required. ■

Chapter 9
BODYWORK & PAINT

The Speed33 is one classy street rod. Bodywork and paint was done in-house at the Roadster Shop using all PPG materials.

It's been said that beauty is only skin deep; however, when it comes to the paint job on street rods much of the beauty comes from what is below the surface. While a smooth, glossy paint job is the ultimate goal, the final product is only as good as the surface it is applied to. Glossy paint over bad bodywork results in glossy lumps and bumps. On the other hand, perfect bodywork is wasted under dull, lifeless paint.

Keep in mind when it comes to the outward appearance of a street rod, two terms are often used together—fit and finish. And the fit comes first.

Although the Speed33 body has an extremely stiff substructure, it's conceivable that after bolting it to a frame the gaps and panel alignment change. In such cases, shims may be required to correct the problem. Available at most auto body supply outlets, shims come in a variety of thicknesses. In some cases different thickness shims might be required on one side of the body compared to the other; it happens on production line automobiles all the time.

The shimming process can be quite time-consuming, but the results are often worth it. There may be several rounds of shimming, or none at all, as was the case with our Roadster Shop chassis. The point is to make the gaps and panel alignment as close as possible before doing any hammering or filling.

Fitting the hood of a Model 40 is another chore that takes time and patience, but it has to be done, as the gaps are so obvious. To make adjustments the radiator can be moved up and down, again with shims (rubber pads are normally used between the frame mounts and the radiator to provide some cushioning). Support rod from the firewall to the radiator, or, as i the case of the Speed33 the hood hinge latch brackets, determine the distance between the radiator shell and cowl.

One of the subtle changes on the Speed33 is the grille shell has been dropped one inch to enhance the car's lines. For our car, the Roadster Shop b a one-off hood that was the prototype f production hoods that will be available. The one-piece top has modified charac lines and is mounted via a hinge and la kit from Yogi's that allows it to be oper from the driver's side or easily removed

Another modification that sets this car apart from most Model 40 highboy

With pinched rails and a lowered grille shell, lowering the Road Tour Speed33 required a custom hood. They are now available from the Roadster Shop.

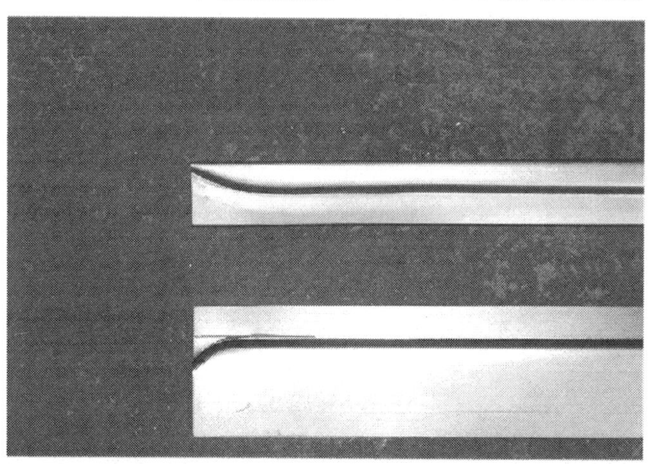

New character lines that matched the body were made. They will be added to the trimmed hood.

This first step in modifying the off-the-shelf hood was to trim the edges.

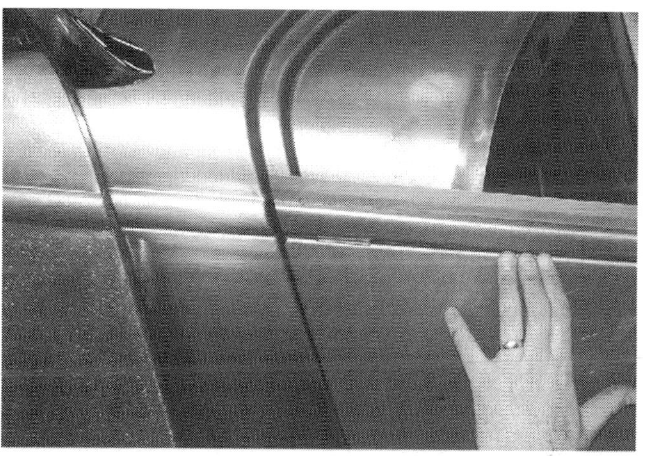

Here the hood's character lines are compared to the body.

are the custom panels that fit between the bottom of the hood sides and the frame rails. The stock pieces have large bulges that are normally hidden by the fenders, but on highboys these pieces hang out in the breeze; along with the pinched rails, the custom flat panels do a lot to clean up the front end of a fenderless Model 40.

BODY PREP

With the hood and side panels fabricated and put in place, the crew at the Roadster Shop began preparing all the sheetmetal for paint. While Speed33 bodies are extremely straight as delivered, there will probably be some imperfections that require minor massaging, and if you're working with the Roadster Shop, you can count on it. They settle for nothing less than perfection, and when they were done with the Road Tour car, that's what we had.

While we've all seen bare metal bodies that appeared to be flawless, the fact that virtually all of them still have imperfections that would show up with paint. Making a bare steel body perfect with metalworking techniques is impressive, but it's not only outrageously expensive, it's also unnecessary. The fact is that for curing minor imperfections there is absolutely nothing wrong with properly applied polyester body filler. The new lightweight materials adhere extremely well, sand and "featheredge" easily, and don't shrink. However, like most finishing products, they have to be applied correctly. The secret to using body filler is to follow the mixing ratios exactly, don't get creative with the hardener in an attempt to speed up or slow down the curing time, stick to the recommended ratios, and prepare the surface according to the manufacturer's directions.

Over the last few years there has been some great debate concerning the adhesion of body filler and if it should be applied to bare metal or over the top of certain types of sealers. According to our sources it has been found that a reaction between the compounds in the filler and most sealers will in time create problems. The best course of action is to apply filler to clean and sanded bare metal.

To prep the Speed33 for paint, some minor metalwork was done, primarily on the edges of the top cover. A skim coat of filler was applied in a few areas that were slightly low, but it didn't take much.

Satisfied with the shape and cut to length, the new sections were clamped to the trimmed hood.

To support the hood hinges and latch, a structure was fabricated that extends from the grille shell to the firewall with vertical supports that attach to the framerails.

The process of welding the hood sides called for patience and skill. When finished and painted, the seams couldn't be detected, inside or out.

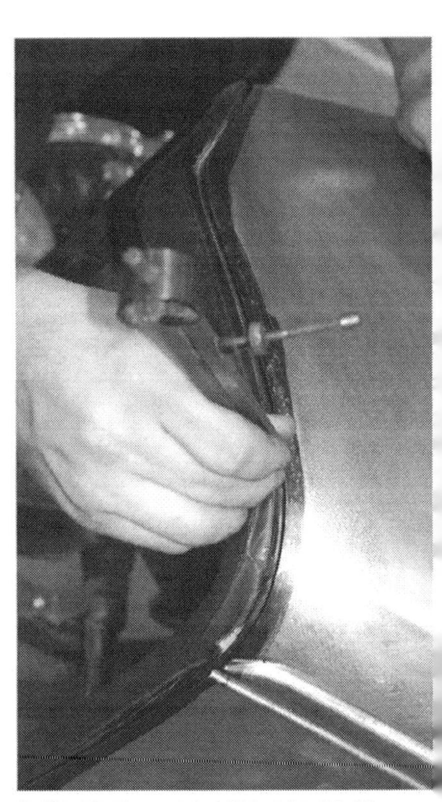

Scribing the top panel and trimming it to fit established the gap between the grille shell and hood.

The braces used to stiffen the hood top are Dan Fink Metalworks products from Yogi's.

With the bodywork concluded, the next step is paint, however; before the final color comes out of the spray gun there are a few other materials involved (PPG products were used exclusively from start to finish). There have been lots of changes since the days of hand-rubbed lacquer. Today there are rules that establish the amount of volatile organic compounds (VOCs) that can be contained in paint and refinish products. According to the Environmental Protection Agency, VOCs have been proven to be a public health hazard. As a result, automotive refinishing products have been reformulated. There are still those who resist change and insist that the old products are better, but modern urethanes are lacquers equal in appearance, will last longer, and the new lower VOC varieties are more environmentally friendly.

From start to finish, a variety of products are involved in producing a quality paint job, and the best procedure for selecting them is to use a system approach. All the various materials must be compatible and one way to do that is to work backwards—decide on the type of paint to be used, then choose products that are designed to work together. PPG products were used exclusively on the Road Tour Speed33. PPG Industries is a leader in its markets with manufacturing facilities and equity affiliates in more than 60 countries around the globe.

To understand what's involved in a start-to-finish paint job, here's a look at the products commonly used.

PRIMER

The function of any primer is to provide a surface for paint to adhere to. Primers by nature are thin and do little to fill imperfections. There is no advantage to heavy coats of primer; in fact, it should be avoided.

PRIMER/SURFACERS

These products are a foundation for the paint, plus they fill imperfections. Multiple coats of primer-surfacer will build a thick film quickly and allow for block sanding to get rid of surface irregularities

Satisfied with the fit of the top, Dean Ellis turned his attention to the hood sides.

Dan Fink Metalworks hinges and latches secure the hood; they're right out of Yogi's catalog.

DIFFERENT ABRASIVES - ROUGH STUFF
THE LOWDOWN ON ABRASIVES

By Jim Rizzo

We all have sandpaper, grinding discs, and cut-off wheels and use them regularly out in the shop, but they're items we take for granted and use without much thought. Recently, while reloading my grinder with a new disc, I happened to take a closer look at the one I was loading and wondered what the story was behind it (perhaps being a new fan of that cable TV show *How It's Made* has piqued my curiosity). I went ahead and finished what I was doing but also decided to do a little investigating regarding abrasives.

Abrasives, like sandpaper or grinding discs, operate pretty much like cutting tools. The rough particles on sandpaper and discs are a coating of sharp-edged materials that cut much the same way a file does. But, sandpaper is sandpaper, right? Well, not exactly. There are actually two different types-or grades, as they're called in the industry-of sandpaper on the market: commercial and industrial. The commercial grade is the stuff commonly available at hardware stores. The industrial grade is usually available only through industrial supply stores and/or autobody supply jobbers. The industrial-grade abrasives found in the latter outlets are made from higher-quality materials and are designed to be used in production or commercial situations. In other words, this type of abrasive is the heavy-duty version and the type we should be using.

Starting with a few simple explanations, let's go over what grit is. When talking about abrasives, "grit" is a reference to the number of abrasive particles per inch of sandpaper. The lower the grit designation or number, the rougher the sandpaper; conversely, the higher the grit number, the smoother the sandpaper. It makes sense if you realize that fine sandpaper, like 1,200-grit for example, would require 1,200 tiny particles of abrasive to fit within 1 square inch of surface-they'd be pretty darn small. At the other end of the spectrum might be 36-grit, which would only have 36 big (relatively speaking) chunks of abrasive per square inch-pretty rough compared to 1,200-grit.

The grit you use depends on the job you need it to do. For example, 16- to 24-grit sizes are generally reserved for hard-backed grinding discs and are primarily used for stripping heavy rust or multiple coats of paint off heavy or thick material-not sheetmetal or thin stuff, because they're so aggressive they'd cut right through it if you aren't extremely careful.

The 36- to 60-grits are considered coarse but are usually the starting point for sheets of sandpaper, though these grits are also available in hard-backed discs, as well. Still considered fairly aggressive, these grits can be used for heavy sanding and stripping of heavy material, but they can also be used on thin material. Just remember that one still has to be careful if these grits are used in conjunction with a sanding machine of any sort, versus by hand. Eighty- to 120-grits are considered medium and used primarily for smoothing of a

Sandpaper is sandpaper, right? Not so. Cheap, light-duty, dime-store sandpaper will often be better at pissing off the user than removing material. Pass up on the cheap stuff and stick with professional-type industrial-grade paper and discs like that offered by 3M, Norton, or Carborundum. There's nothing worse than abrasives that wear out in nothing flat.

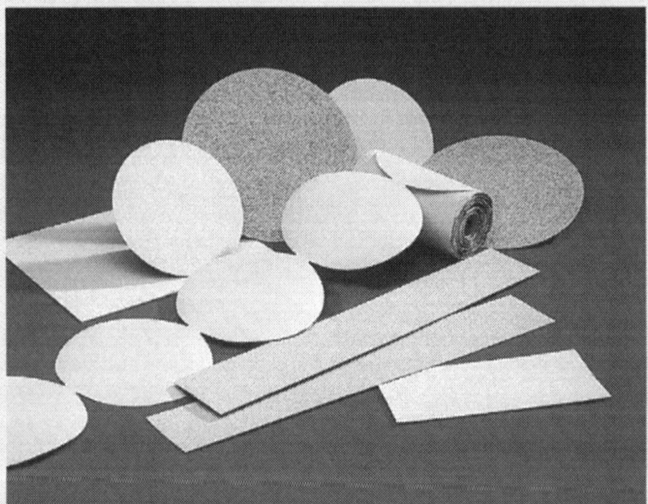

Abrasives come in a wide array of designs: 9x11 sheets; 5-, 6-, and 8-inch-diameter discs; 4x8 sheets; and 2-1/4x17-1/2-inch long-board paper being the most common in the autobody trade. All are available in a wide variety of grits, and the 9x11 is the standard for wet or dry paper.

surface and/or removing smaller imperfections and marks. Grits in the 150 to 180 range are considered fine and good for a final sanding pass before a primer coat, for example. The 220- to 240-grits are designated as very fine and are good for sanding between coats of primer or sealer. The 280- to 320-grits are labeled extra fine and are used for removing dust spots or fine scratches between finish coats. The 360- to 600-grits are considered super fine and are used for sanding a surface to remove some luster, surface blemishes, or finer scratches. Then, 800- to 2,000-grits are designated ultra fine and are usually reserved for final color sanding of paint or for final finishing of metal that's destined to remain uncoated.

So, now that we've covered the basics of grit, we'll look at the difference between commercial- and industrial-grade abrasives. There are three main components to sandpaper: the abrasive grit, the backing material, and the bonding agents that attach the grit to the backing, whether it be discs or paper. Industrial-grade sandpaper uses higher-quality (read that as heavy duty) components as well as tighter manufacturing tolerances (read that as harder and sharper grit that are less likely to break down or wear out, better bonding agents that hold the abrasive to the backing material, and heavier-duty backing that is less likely to tear or wear through).

Metalworkers and bodymen use a sanding procedure sometimes called "going through the grits." Not to be confused with a good old Southern breakfast, it refers to the process of sanding where one uses progressively finer pieces of sandpaper to get a smooth finish. By going through the grits, each progressive sanding step removes the scratches left over from the previous step. Skipping grits to save time is not necessarily a good idea, as you'll usually end up sanding longer just to remove the scratches left by the previous grit. You'll always want to start low with coarser grit, and then work your way up to a finer grit.

There are also different types of sandpaper, specifically, or more commonly, open-coat and closed-coat. Open-coat sandpaper has gaps and open spaces between the grits, which help prevent clogging by giving the removed material a space to separate or fall away from the paper or disc. Closed-coat is better for sanding metal finishes, as it's more aggressive but does clog a bit easier on softer materials like primer or some body fillers.

Though not a complete course on abrasives, hopefully this will give you a bit of a background on a common tool we all use without much thought, and a basic guide to sandpaper and sanding disc choices.

The new (at least, new to me) sanding blocks from Wet Wedge are ingenious products when it comes to wet sanding. They're designed to save time and sandpaper, plus they go a long way to ensure a perfectly straight finish-even for me, someone known for building the friendliest cars in town, cuz they wave to everyone as they go by.

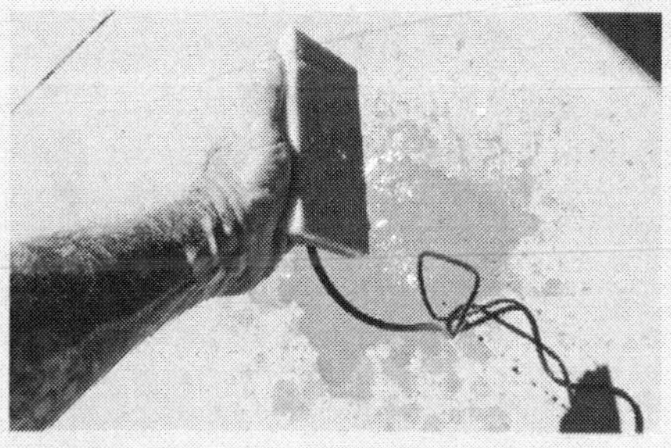

The Wet Wedge is a selection of assorted self-wetting sanding blocks. In other words, they're directly supplied with a constant stream of clean water emitted through the body of the block via tubing that connects to a garden hose. A built-in valve controls the amount of water needed, and their water-fed design saves you from constantly bending over. Plus, they continually flush the surface with fresh water to remove sharp particles and sanding sludge and help paper last longer with less clogging-a perfect tool for sanding primers, color, and clearcoats.

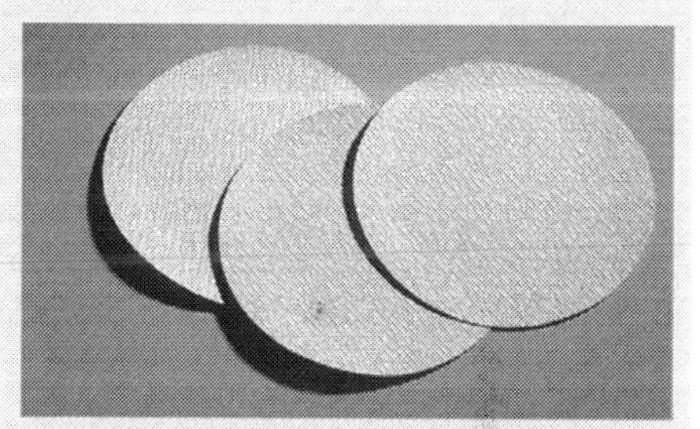

Some of the most widely used types of sandpaper in the autobody segment are 6- and 8-inch-diameter discs. These here are the plain-backed style that requires an adhesive, either spread from a tube or sprayed from an aerosol can, to attach them to a sanding disc.

Another version of the venerable DA disc-known by that name because of the dual-action sander on which they see the most use-are self-adhesive or pressure sensitive adhesive (PSA) discs most commonly sold on rolls, though they are available as individual peel-and-stick discs, as well.

PSA discs require special sanding pads with a smooth rubberized face that allow easy attachment and removal of the self-adhesive discs. These are available in 6- or 8-inch diameters, just like the sandpaper.

Abrasives are by no means restricted to sheets and discs. Almost all metal fabricators use belt sanders of one sort or another. The same rules apply to these as they do to sandpaper-buy the good stuff and stay away from the bargain-priced crap, because what you save in cash, you'll waste in time and energy.

Many of the unique parts fabricated for the Road Tour car are now readily available from the Roadster Shop. Here Sam Waltermire begins forming the lower hood panel.

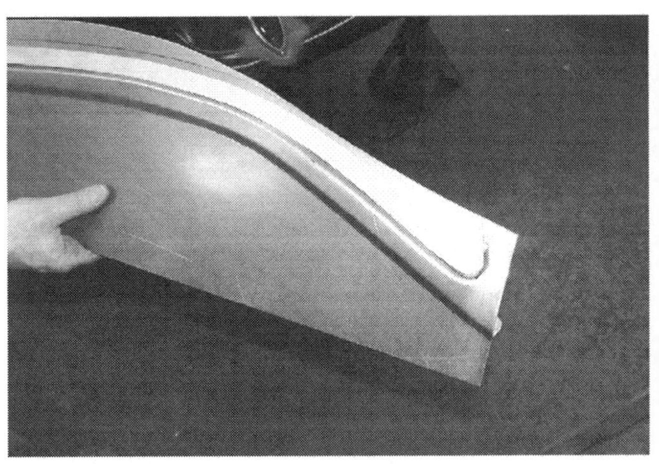

This is the panel that fits between the hood and the frame; it eliminates the big outward bulge the stockers have.

Jeremy Gerber transferred paper patterns into the main part of a new transmission tunnel.

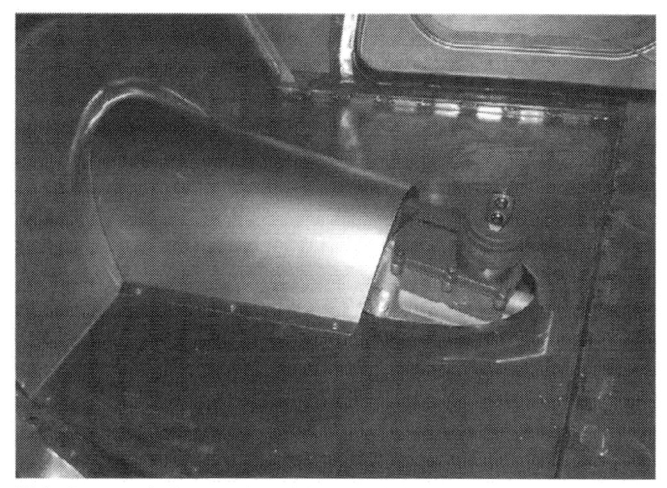

While the transmission tunnel won't be seen, the workmanship is first-rate, just like the rest of the car.

The final step in building the transmission tunnel was locating the hole for the five-speed's shift lever.

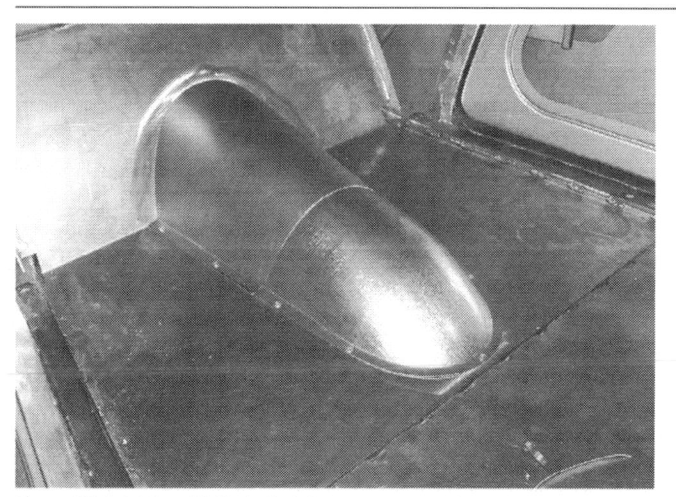

Along with being beautifully crafted, the new transmission tunnel fits the TREMEC tightly to preserve interior space.

The access holes in the door seemed like perfect locations for the Custom Autosound speakers, so filler panels were fabricated.

and provide a super-straight base for the topcoat. Always keep this in mind: if the car is not straight in primer, it won't get any better with paint. That's the reason bodies are often block-sanded several times.

Contemporary primer-surfacer, such as those available from PPG, are catalyzed, which eliminates shrinkage and the sand scratches that used to result from the solvent evaporating from lacquer-based products. Additionally, primer-surfacers provide excellent corrosion resistance and a chip-resistant base for color coats.

SEALERS

These products are intended to keep the solvents in the topcoat materials from

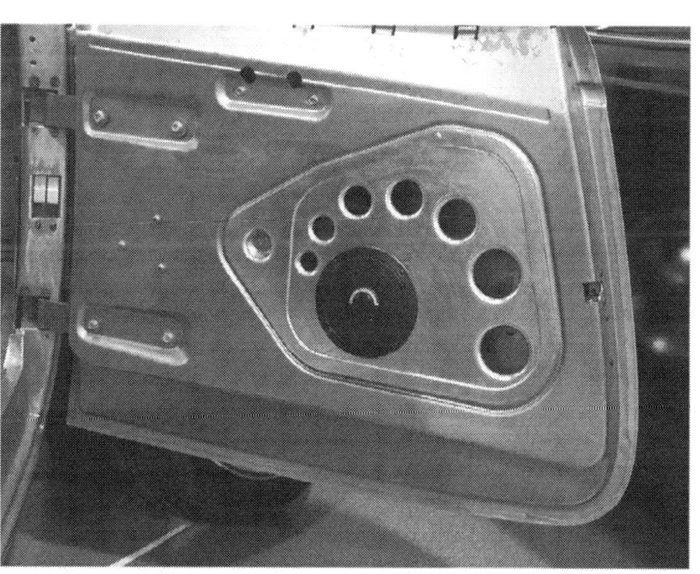

To add some style to the panels, various-sized dimpled holes were punched around the speakers.

The American Speed Company flat dash in the Speed33 is a blend of '32 and '33-34 styling. Ours uses a Lokar insert.

Every square inch of the body was checked with a critical eye. While the fit of all the panels was quite good, some minor massaging on the gaps of the top cover was required.

Careful work with a hammer and block squared the gaps between the top cover and trunk lid.

penetrating whatever is underneath as well as preventing undercoats from bleeding through. If you've ever shot lacquer over enamel and watched the surface wrinkle like a prune, you understand the need for a sealer.

PRIMER/SEALERS

PPG's epoxy sealers are unique in that they serve a dual function, acting as both a primer and a sealer; in some instances they will also take one step out of the finishing procedure.

Again, primer/sealers are not designed to fill imperfections, so heavy, multiple coats are a waste of material. One light coat is all that's necessary.

SINGLE STAGE/BASECOAT-CLEARCOAT

Modern paint materials are available in different packages. There are single-stage urethanes that are applied very much like the once-popular acrylic enamel—shoot on the color and you're done. PPG's Concept DCC is Deltron's direct gloss system, meaning no clearcoat is required.

Another option is PPG's Deltron 2000 (DBC) system. With these two-stage paints a highly pigmented base is applied that looks flat when cured. A second stage, or clearcoat, provides the gloss and a durable, chip-resistant surface; that's what's on the '08 Road Tour Speed33. The basecoat provides the color for the vehicle. The clear protects the basecoat and produces the glossy finish...

CLEARCOAT

There are a variety of clearcoats; we used PPG's VC5200 Custom Clear. It's a high-solid, easy-applying urethane clearcoat with excellent gloss.

BLOCK SANDING

Although just about everyone in the hobby has heard the term "block sanding" at one time or another, there are still do-it-yourselfers that confuse the process with hand sanding. And hand sanding, especially on large surfaces, should be avoided at all costs. To understand why, look at a handprint on a flat surface. It's obvious

Some careful touches from an abrasive disc was all it took to perfect the fit between the top cover and the quarter panels.

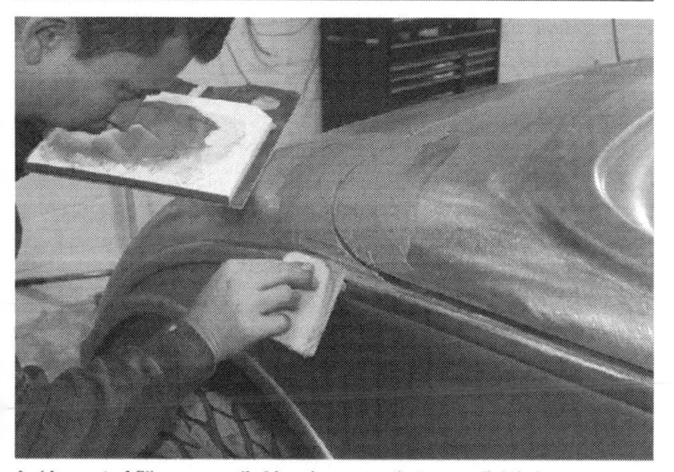

A skim coat of filler was applied in a few areas that were slightly low.

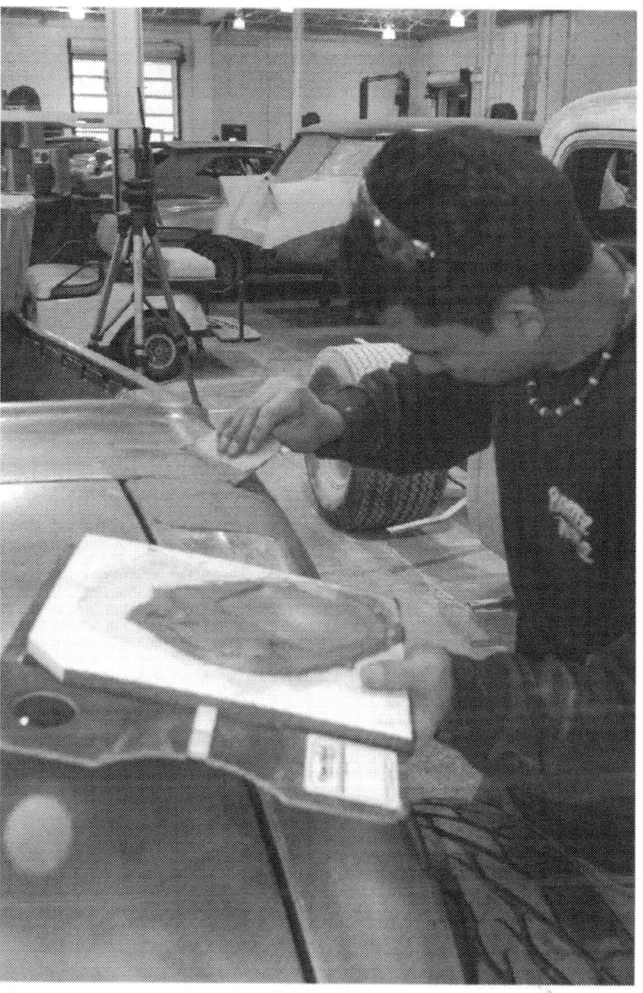

Filler can also be used to help perfect the fit between two adjacent panels.

Much of the filler is "knocked down" with an air-powered dual-action sander.

Long sanding blocks were used to get all the filler straight. Sanding across the gaps results in panels that align perfectly.

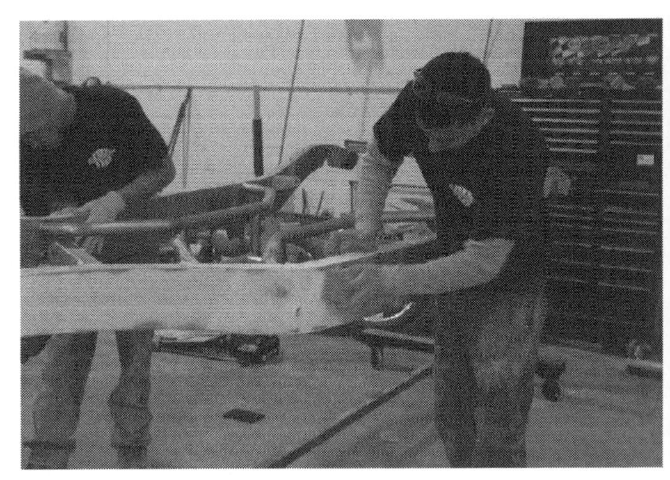

The frame was treated to the same finishing techniques used on the body.

A rotisserie makes it much easier to finish off the bottom of the body, which in this case is as nice as the top.

that more pressure is applied in some areas than others, and that's why a hand is a lousy tool for sanding. The uneven pressure applied to the sandpaper will result in an uneven surface, the very thing you're trying to get rid of. Just remember this: Fingers are for scratching, hands are for holding, and blocks are for sanding.

After the first application of primer/surfacer has been applied, the first round of block sanding is usually done with 320 grit paper. This process may be repeated if necessary, then a final application of primer surfacer followed by more block sanding by with 500 grit paper. In some

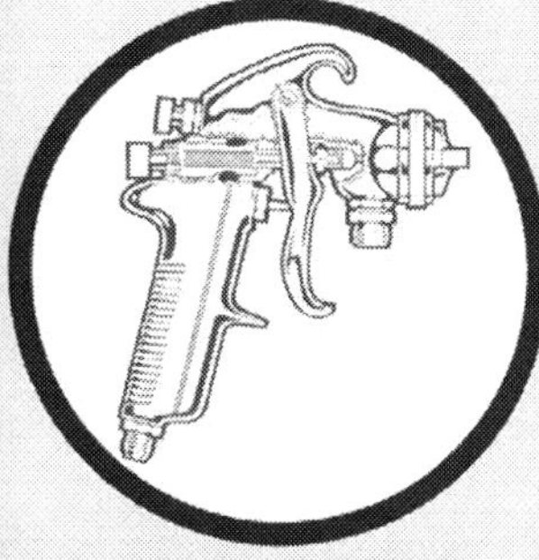

12 SPRAY GUN TIPS

A bit of useful knowledge for the novice painter: Believe it or not, doing your own paintwork is not something that should be out of the question for the accomplished street rod hobbyist. Sure, along with wiring and upholstery it is one of the few jobs that most rodders instinctively decide to farm out, but in many cases it really needn't be. It's just a learned skill—one that can be pretty well mastered by trial and error. With this in mind here's a dozen spray gun tips that'll hopefully give you a bit of insight on painting, and perhaps a move closer to convincing you to give it a try.

1) PRIMER & FINISH

Always designate one gun for primers and undercoats, and another to be used for your topcoat finishes only. Many primers, sealers, and undercoats contain huge amounts of solids that may not be easily cleaned from the gun internals and may end up suddenly spitting a few granules from the gun during your topcoat application—usually in the most obvious spot on the vehicle.

2) SUCTION VS. HVLP

Choose the correct type of equipment for the job. In this case we're talking about the traditional suction-feed high-pressure or the more modern High Volume Low Pressure (HVLP) type gun. OK, so what's the difference and what would be the advantage of one over the other, you ask?

HVLP spray guns were designed to reduce overspray and get more material to the surface and less into the air as overspray. There is an internal restrictor inside of an HVLP gun, which restricts the incoming air pressure in order to provide a reduced air pressure at the air cap. This differs from a conventional gun. A conventional gun does not have an internal restrictor, and therefore whatever the inlet pressure is set at, the air cap pressure will be the same.

With an HVLP gun you don't have clouds of overspray filling the air (or garage), but they use a large volume of air compared to a standard suction-type gun, making compressor capacity a deciding factor.

3) BECOME FAMILIAR WITH THE CONTROLS

Get to know your spray gun. Regardless of gun type, it's important to read the owner's manual provided with the equipment so you'll be familiar with its controls and adjustments.

4) KEEP IT CLEAN

Always strain your material, be it primer, sealer, or finish color. Contaminants will not only possibly exit the gun, marring your paint job, but may restrict an air or fluid passage, disrupting the spray pattern and causing a less-than-satisfactory finish.

5) MATCH THE EQUIPMENT TO THE MATERIAL

Always match your needle and nozzle sizes according to the material to be sprayed. All manufacturers have guidelines and requirements for their respective products—following them will greatly improve your finish result.

6) REDUCE AS REQUIRED

No matter what brand or type of finish you're planning on spraying, always thin or reduce the material in accordance with the manufacturer's instructions. Materials are much more complex these days and eyeballing the paint rolling off a paint paddle just won't cut it these days. Pick up and learn to use a viscosity cup; it's worth the extra minute or two. Refer to the paint manufacturer's product information sheet for specific details on the product.

7) HANDLE WITH CARE

Never use a metal object (like a torch tip cleaner or penknife) to clean your spray gun's air nozzle. A bristle brush or, if need be, a wooden toothpick should be used so the machining of the openings are not marred or damaged since these openings control correct paint atomization and spray pattern.

8) TECHNIQUE

Always move your spray gun parallel to the surface being sprayed. Spraying in an arc will produce an uneven coating.

9) CORRECT PRESSURE

Always spray using the paint manufacturers recommended pressure. An air regulator at the gun will ensure proper pressure at the gun – air pressure at the source is different as it is restricted depending on air hose diameter and length.

10) TRIGGER CONTROL

Release the trigger at the end of every pass and overlap passes 50 percent to ensure even coverage.

11) PROPER STORAGE

Storing your spray guns with a bit of clean solvent in the cup will keep the gun's needle packings from drying out and cracking, which could cause possible air and/or fluid leaks.

12) AIR FILTRATION

Clean air is a must for a successful paint job. Oil and/or water contamination is sure trouble for any paint job. A permanent air filter at a minimum is a requirement, and a separate disposable filter at the gun is added insurance.

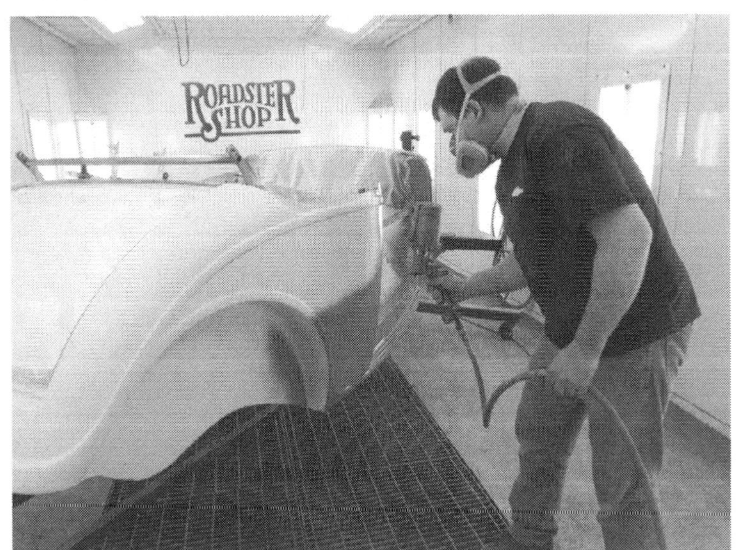

With the basic bodywork done, PPG DP series epoxy primer was applied, followed by primer surfacer.

After a thorough inspection, the body shell and parts were given an application of PPG NCS2002 Pre-Paint Sealer. They were then deemed ready for paint.

All the edges of the body were carefully sanded to make them smooth and even.

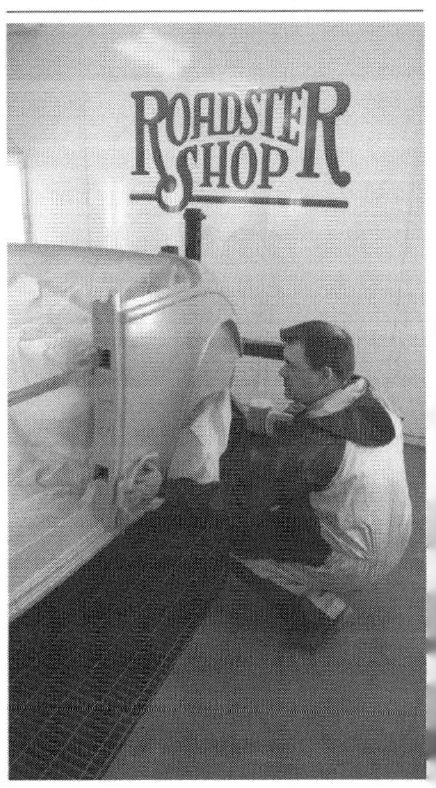

Before the color was applied the body was wiped down with a tack cloth to remove any dust.

Long sanding blocks were used to get the body super straight. This is the labor-intensive portion of a good paint job.

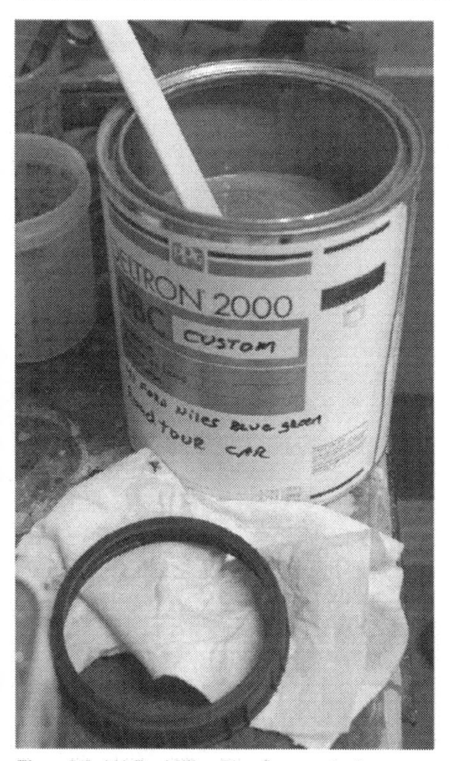

The subtle '41 Ford Niles-Blue Green color is a custom mix of Deltron 2000 DBC basecoat.

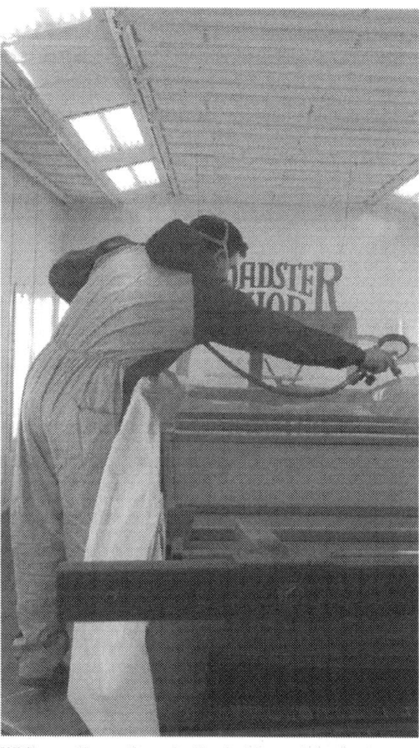

While on the rotisserie the bottom of the body was painted.

Part of the reason for the excellent results produced by the Roadster Shop is the state-of-the-art spray booth and equipment.

To ensure all the hard to get to surfaces were covered, color was applied to the body shell while the doors and other components were hung and painted individually.

With the application of Vibrance clear the color came alive, but the Roadster Shop wasn't done yet.

Before the graphics were applied, the area was sanded.

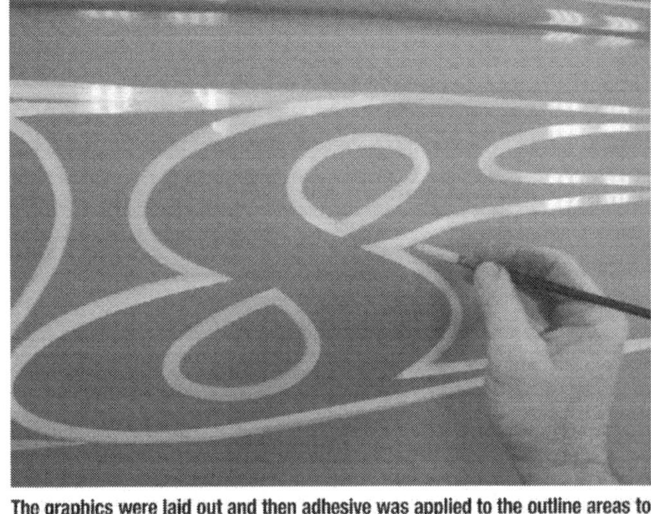

The graphics were laid out and then adhesive was applied to the outline areas to be covered in silver leaf.

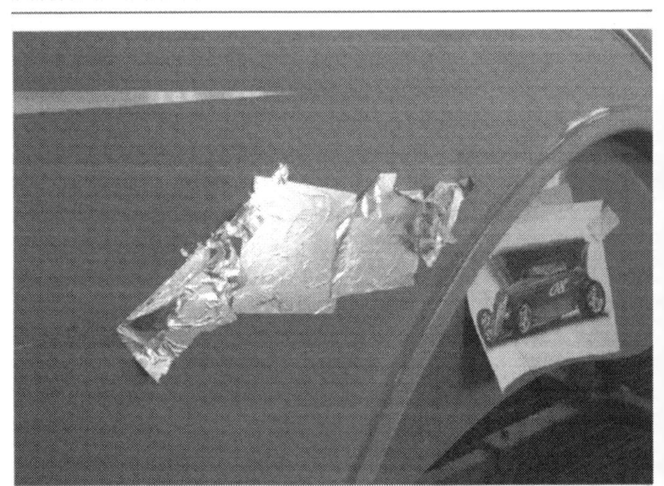

Silver leaf was applied to the adhesive and allowed to cure.

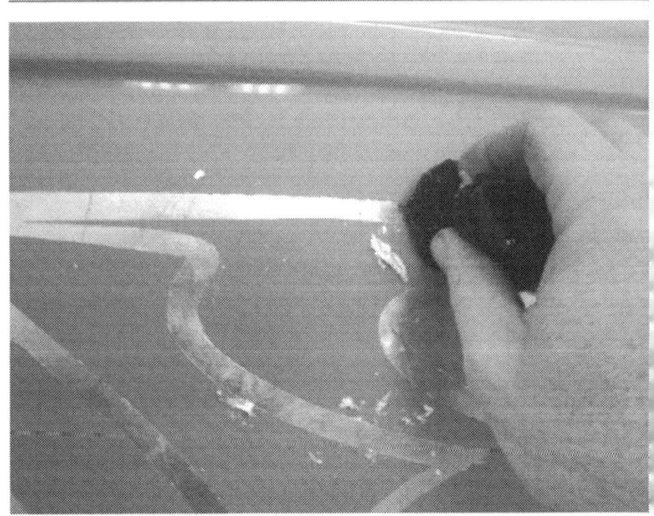

After curing, the excess leaf was carefully brushed away.

The finished outlines provide a unique texture and pattern that only leaf can provide.

With the leaf work finished, the numbers were filled in with contrasting paint.

The finishing touch was a pinstripe around all the edges.

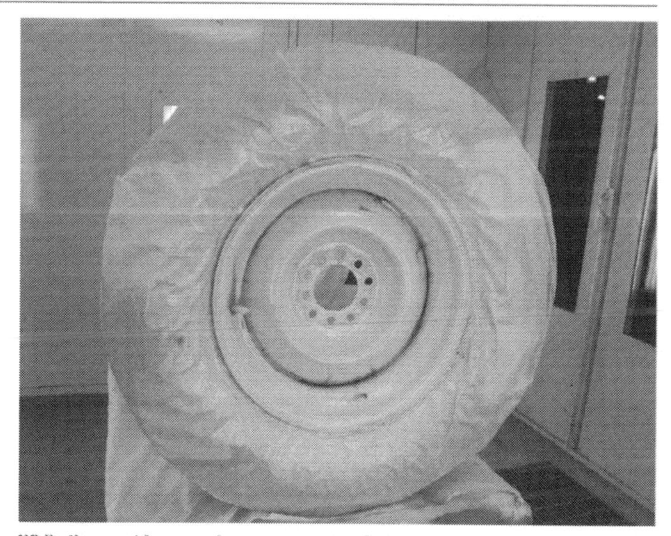

While the graphics were in progress a set of Wheel Vintiques solids were given a unique patina finish.

cases painters will use a guide coat, such as PPG's SXA1030 Guide Coat Black, to allow the painter to apply a layer of color to a primed surface that will guide them in identifying high and low spots during sanding. Once the block sanding is done, sealer is applied, followed by the topcoat materials.

FINALS

After the Speed33 had been treated to primer, primer surfacer, sealer, a stunning coat of Niles Blue Green base coat, and super-smooth layer of Vibrance clear, anyone would have been happy with the results, but the Roadster Shop wasn't quite done. Still to come were the silver leaf graphics. That process consisted of sanding the clear in the areas to be done with 600 grit paper. The patterns for the graphics were laid out, adhesive was applied, and then the leaf was pressed in place. Once cured, the leaf was carefully dusted off the areas without adhesive, the numbers and letters were painted and pinstriped, then the areas were cleared, color sanded and buffed. The final result certainly speaks for itself. ■

With the graphics finished more clear was applied, followed by color sanding and buffing.

Chapter 10
THE ELECTRICAL SYSTEM

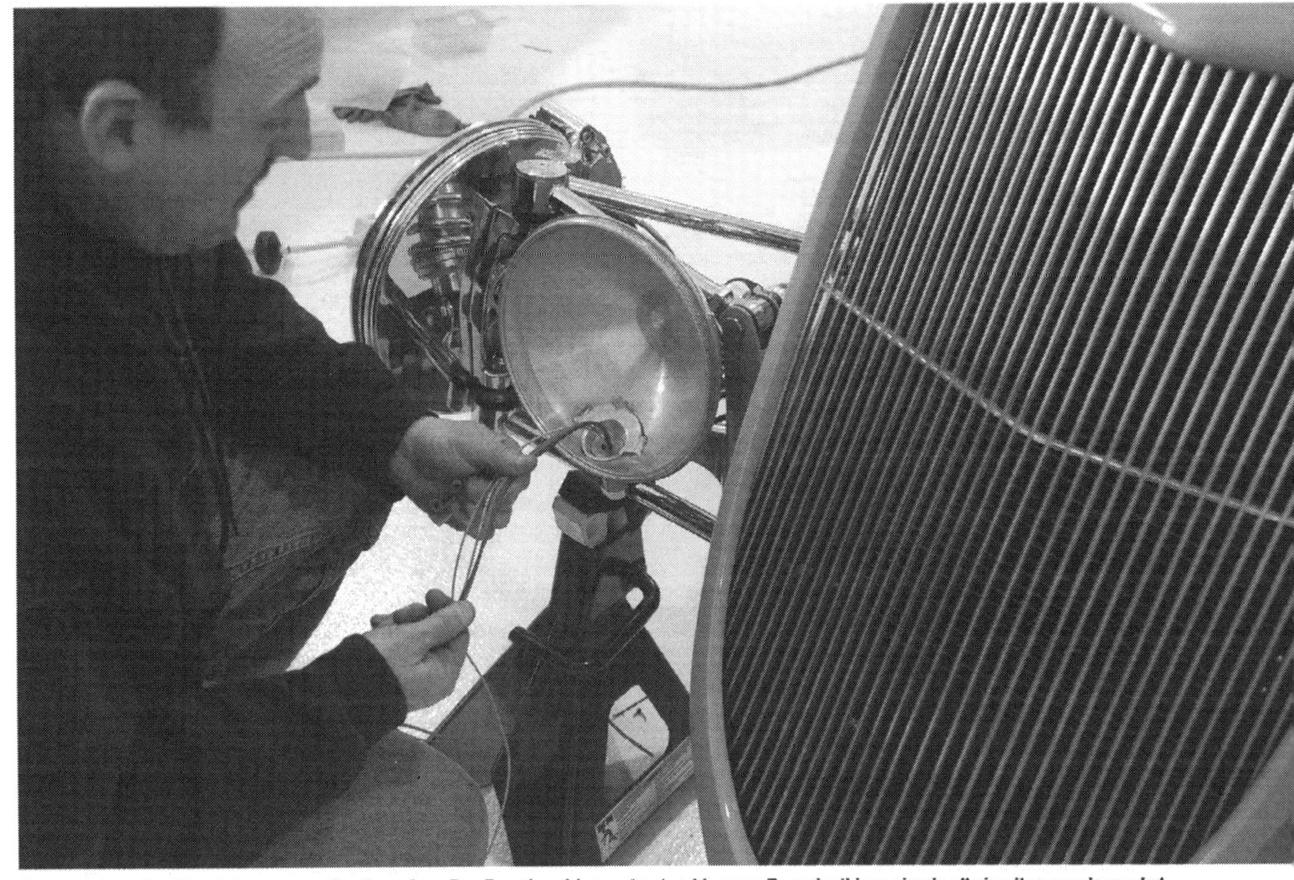

Thanks to installer-friendly harnesses, like those from Ron Francis, wiring a street rod is easy. To make things simple all circuits are color-coded.

When Model 40 Fords were new, the electrical system was quite simple and consisted of little more than starting, charging, and lighting systems. And while there is something to be said for keeping electrical systems simple, the creature comforts we've come to know and love, like air conditioning and heat, halogen headlights, sound systems, electric wipers, power windows, and so on all require electricity. So much for simplicity.

CHOOSING A WIRING KIT

Wiring a street rod from scratch, particularly when multiple electrical accessories are involved is a daunting task for most street rodders. Prior to the introduction of street rod wiring kits it wasn't unusual for street rods to be wired with cut-down harnesses from a donor car, or if they were wired from scratch to have the same color wire from one end to the other for every circuit. But contemporary wiring kits make it easy to have a neat, effective, and most importantly, sa electrical system in your street rod.

Ron Francis was one of the first to offer wiring kits for street rods in the '70s, and today the company that bears his name offers harnesses for virtually a specialty car application.

When it comes to the design of street rod wiring harnesses, there are basically two schools of thought. Some manufactures connect all the wires to t fuse panel, then, during installation, al the wires are run to wherever they go a are connected. Ron Francis uses what

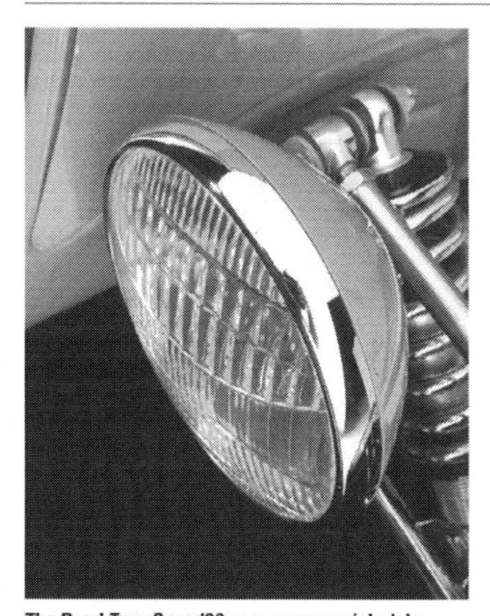
The Road Tour Speed33 uses commercial-style headlights with screw-on retainers from Jesse Greening. Halogen bulbs and turn signals have been incorporated into the reflectors.

The newest system from Ron Francis is the Express. This one is specifically for Ford-powered vehicles. It includes a fan relay and multi-connection battery junction block to reduce the number of wires going to the starter.

Ron Francis offers wiring kits for every conceivable need. This is the Bare Bonz kit for cars with basic needs.

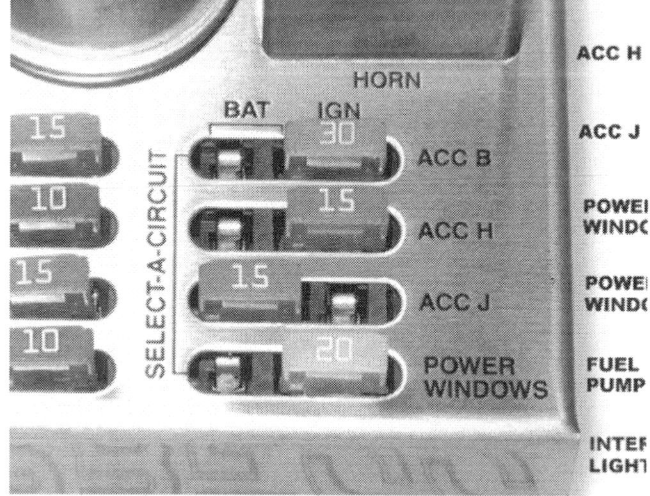

The Select-A-Circuit feature allows the supply source of the circuit to be changed from battery to switched by simply moving the fuse.

he calls front loading technology. Wires are run from the loads so the wires can be cut to the proper length for a neat installation and all connections are made at the panel. All terminals are clearly marked and the high-temperature wire is color coded to the terminals on the panel. To really make things simple, even the instructions are color-coded. Another unique feature is that all kits have an individual serial number.

We've found Ron Francis kits easy to install and they are trouble-free; that's why we chose one for the Road Tour Speed33.

ALTERNATOR/BATTERY/STARTER

For the alternator, battery, and starter we turned to Powermaster. They have an extremely diverse line of all three products making it easy to select the proper component for your application.

ALTERNATOR ADVICE FROM POWERMASTER

While modern electrical systems are generally referred to as 12-volts, in operation with the engine running voltage will be in the area of 13.5 and 14.4-volts. What makes the current flow is voltage; think of it as the push that makes the electrons move. If you have a one-wire alternator on your rod, try this: Start the engine and let it idle

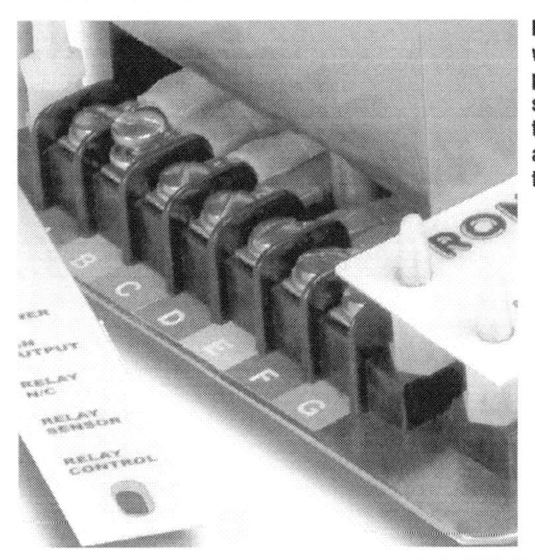

Hooking up wires to the panel is made simple by terminals that are color-coded to the wires.

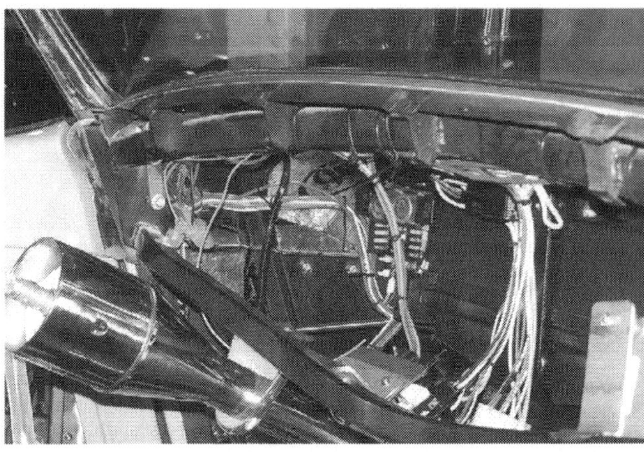

Part of the challenge when wiring a street rod is keeping the harness neat. The Roadster Shop used plenty of wire ties and grouped wires that were going to common areas.

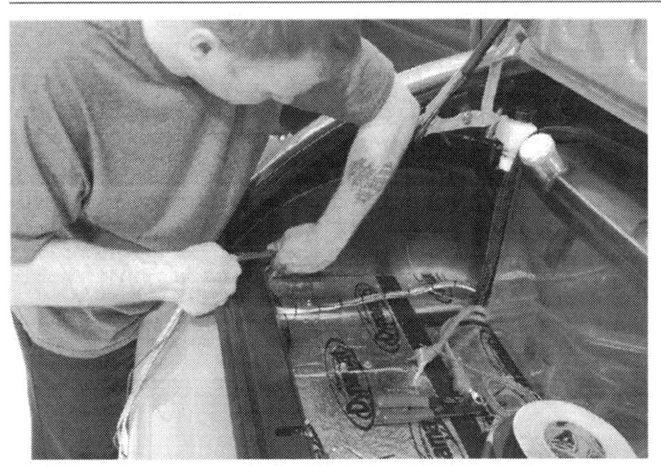

Wiring to the rear of the car was run inside the body to protect it from damage. Wires for stoplights, turn signals, license plate lights, and so on are color-coded and labeled.

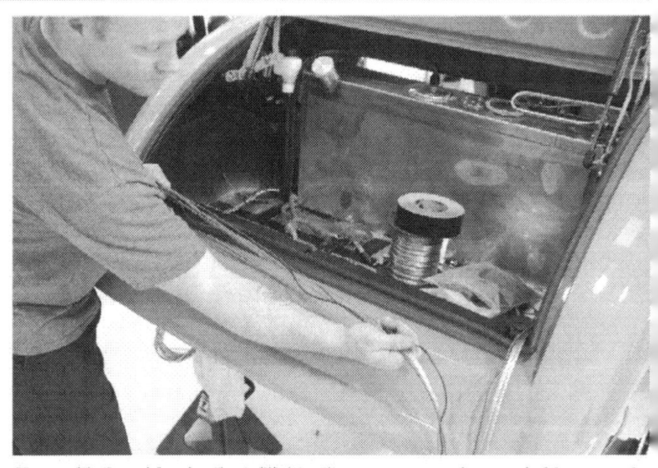

Along with the wiring for the taillights, there were a number needed to connect the stereo system.

and note the voltmeter reading (assuming your car has one), then turn the lights on. Rev the engine to the point the alternator begins to charge and two things should happen—the voltage will increase and the lights will get brighter. What's happening is the increased voltage is pushing more current through the electrical system; consequently, the lights become brighter.

Normally all the power for the electrical system is delivered by the alternator when the engine is running. The only time that this isn't the case is when current capacity of the alternator is exceeded, which may happen at very low idle speeds with all the electrical accessories turned on, or if the alternator isn't "excited." Last things first. Many one-wire alternators have to turn a certain rpm (generally around 1,400 rpm) before the internal voltage regulator will turn on (or excite) the charging system. We've seen cases where rodders have driven some distance only to find the battery voltage has dropped to the point where the engine almost quits because the alternator hasn't been spun fast enough to begin charging. A "blip" of the throttle may be necessary to rev the engine high enough to "turn on" the alternator.

Believe it or not, a similar problem can occur with too much gear. Combine tall rear gears, large diameter rear tires and an overdrive transmission, and engine speeds when cruising on the highway may be low enough that the alternator can't keep up with the electrical systems demands. There are a few simple strategies to prevent the preceding problems. First, don't use under drive pulleys that slow down the alternator; make sure the alternator exceeds the maximum current requirements; and finally, use an alternator that is capable of delivering its maximum output at an appropriate rpm.

Alternators are spoken of as a 65-amp or 100-amp alternator. When replacing the alternator on the family car, this is probably the only information that is necessary. After all, all one needs is an alternator that matches the original. But when building a custom car from the ground up, a deeper understanding of the

BASIC ELECTRICITY

Buying electrical components can often be confusing. There are terms thrown about to describe what these components are, what they do, and how to install them properly that are easily misunderstood. So, before you start wiring your street rod, here are some terms you should know.

Electricity: In simple terms, electricity is the flow of electrons, which are parts of an atom, through a conductor.

Voltage: Electrical pressure, or the push that sends electrons through a wire; Measured in volts, 12-volts has greater electrical pressure than 6.

Current: The volume of electrons flowing in a circuit; it's measured in amperes, or amps. If voltage is increased, more electrons flow. If you turn your car's headlights on with the engine off, as soon as you start the car and the charging system increases the system's voltage the lights get brighter; more voltage increases the current.

Resistance: The opposition to current flow. Resistance is like electrical friction, and as a result it can create heat. In the case of a light bulb, the element gets so hot it glows white-hot, which creates light. Increasing resistance reduces current flow; if your car's headlight switch has a dimmer for the dash lights, rotating the knob increases resistance, which reduces current flow and the lights dim. Resistance is measured in ohms and is represented by the symbol omega.

Conductor: Something that current can flow through. However, some conductors are better than others. Copper has less resistance than aluminum, so copper is a better conductor of electricity.

Insulator: Something current can't flow through. The porcelain on a spark plug is an example of an insulator. However, keep in mind some things can be a conductor or an insulator. As an example, air can be an insulator; the 12-volts of an automotive battery won't make a spark jump the gap of an ordinary spark plug, but after the coil boosts the voltage to 20,000-plus volts it will.

TYPES OF CIRCUITS

The term electrical circuit is heard regularly and what it means is the path the electricity takes. In an automobile that means electricity travels from the source (the battery) usually through a switch to the load (the device that uses electricity, like a light bulb) to ground (the metal body or frame) that's used as a return path to the battery.

Some other terms that are heard in reference to circuits are the following:

Series: This is where electricity flows through one load, then another. As an example, if light bulbs were wired in series and one bulb burned out, both would go out.

Parallel: Headlights, as an example, are wired in parallel. Wires from the switch split and go to each headlight separately; if one goes out, the other is not affected.

Open: An open circuit is one that is not complete; a switch opens and closes a circuit. A broken wire or a burned-out bulb also opens a circuit.

Short: A short is a complete circuit that goes to ground before the load. The danger in a short is this—because it goes to ground before the load, or the resistive device that consumes electricity, the resistance in the circuit is drastically reduced; as a result, current flow increases, which can create enough heat to melt the wire, or in the worst case scenario, start a fire.

When splicing wires, invest in a quality crimping tool. Note these connectors lack the usual plastic barrel.

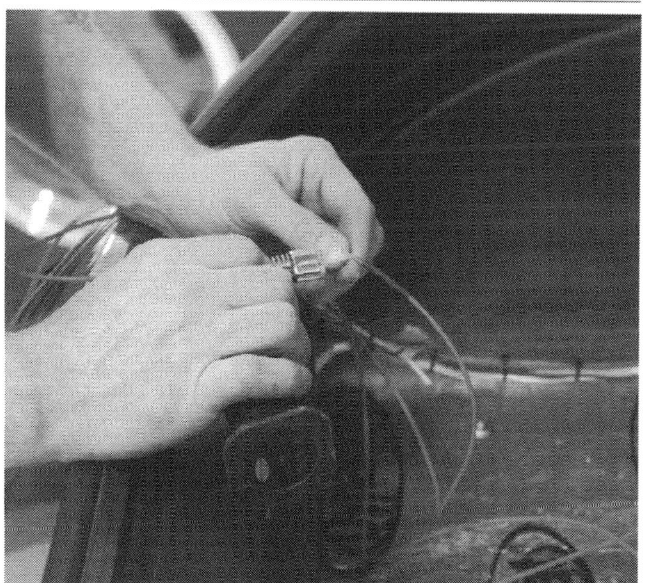

For a neat, weathertight connection, all the splices were covered with shrink tubing.

A hydraulic brake light switch was installed in one of the outlets in the Wilwood Master cylinder.

Electric instruments require senders; the canister with the wire leading to it is the oil pressure sender.

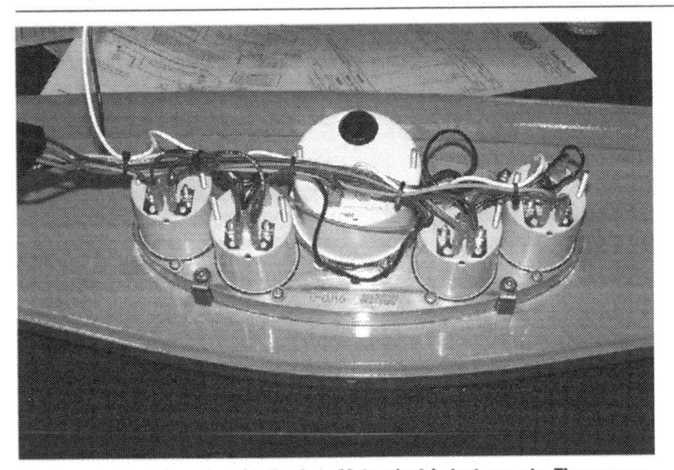

The harness includes wires for the Auto Meter electric instruments. The gauges require switched power, input from the sender, and a ground. Instrument lighting requires a feed from the light switch and a ground. (See detail chapter for instrument wiring diagrams.)

On the left are the controls for the Vintage Air system. The Flaming River column plugs in to the harness, and the instrument panel insert for the Auto Meter gauges is from Lokar. Note all the polished components have been covered with masking tape to protect them during assembly.

power curve of an alternator is required. When selecting an alternator, you must know how many amps the electrical system consumes.

This, of course, varies from car to car and can be figured two different ways. One way is to add the total amp requirements of all components together. Generally all electrical items will have their supply demands included with the instructions. Typically headlights will draw 3 to 10-amps each, ignition systems 6 to 10-amps, electric fuel pumps 7 to 10-amps, electric fans 15 to 30-amps. Another way is to use an inductive ammeter with a "peak hold" function clamped around the battery cable while the car is running. While the latter method would be more accurate since it would be testing the electrical system as a whole in real world conditions, it's not always the most practical. The point is that when everything is turned on at the same time, the amperage demands on the electrical system can be surprisingly high, so select an alternator accordingly.

An alternator's output is dependent on speed, but this can be deceiving because this output is not linear. Instead, it follows a curve. Each alternator has a unique curve, and at idle small changes in the alternator's speed can make a big difference in its output capacity. Because of the preceding, pulley ratios are very important, so steer clear of under drive pulleys on the street.

Another consideration is that an alternator rated at 80A is capable of producing 80A maximum. It does not produce power all the time, but rather only when it is needed and only in the amount needed. Therefore, if a car used 52-amps continuously a 60-amp alternator could be used. However, an 80A alternator would work better. Why? Because the 80-amp alternator is working at 65% of its capacity whereas the 60-amp is working at 87% of its capacity.

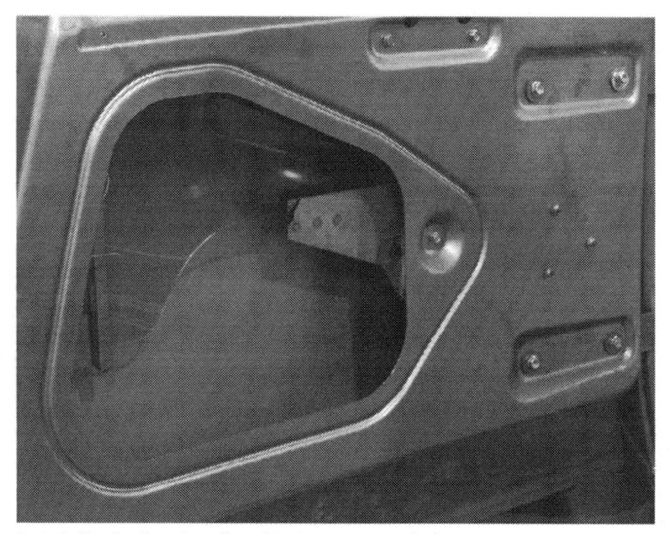

Included in the American Speed body are power windows.

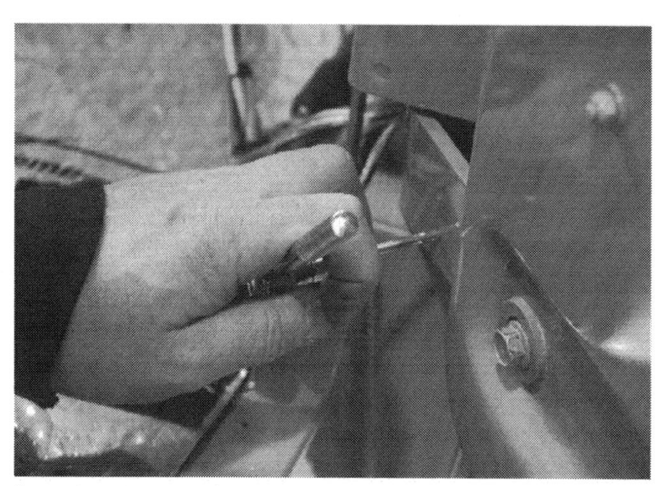

To supply power to the window motors, wires were run along the lower door hinges, which were drilled and tapped to mount wire looms.

This percentage, or duty cycle, affects the voltage that the alternator is able to maintain. The 60-amp unit will typically produce the 52-amp at a lower voltage than the 80-amp unit in the same situation. Therefore, it is good to get the alternator with the highest amp rating available for that particular mounting situation.

BATTERY

The battery we used is a new XS Power Cell from Powermaster. Using AGM (absorbed glass mat) technology, the electrolyte is suspended in an absorbent fiberglass material, eliminating the need to flood the battery with water. This unique design of an AGM enables it to be spill-proof and vibration-resistant while having ultra-low internal resistance. These batteries can be mounted in any position; however, upside-down is not recommended.

PROPER CARE TIPS FOR POWERMASTER'S AGM BATTERY

Proper charging is crucial to the life of the battery. Ensure that charge voltage never exceeds 2.5 volts per cell, or 15v for a 12-volt battery.

When using a battery charger, it is best to use a microprocessor-controlled charger like the XS Power Intellicharger. This will insure the fastest and fullest re-charge by allowing the appropriate amperage for the given battery size.

In deep cycling applications, it is important to note that a battery should not be discharged below 10.5v. Doing so may cause damage to the battery.

Before storing a battery away for the off-season, it is important that it is fully charged. Leaving them for long periods of time in a low state of charge may cause damage to the battery.

Take special care when handling batteries. Because they are tightly packed with lead, they are unusually heavy for

ELECTRICAL DEVICES

There are all sorts of electrical devices found in automobiles. The common ones are:

Fuses: These are protective devices that open the circuit when current flow exceeds a specified amount. Fuses are rated by the circuit's current-carrying capacity, and one of the most dangerous things that can be done is to increase the amp rating of a fuse to keep it from "blowing." The result can be more current flowing through the wire than it is capable of carrying, which can cause the wire to burn before the fuse opens.

Relays: A relay is an electrically controlled switch that lets a light duty circuit control a heavier circuit. Used on loads that draw lots of current, such as an engine-cooling fan, a light duty switch with relatively light wire can turn the relay on and off. The relay uses heavier wire from the battery to the load, and it turns the fan on and off.

Solid State Devices: The term solid state means that an electrical device has no moving parts other than electrons. Some of the common solid-state devices found in cars are:

Diodes: These are one-way electrical valves; current can flow one way but not the other. Diodes are found in a number of places, most notably in alternators; they help transform alternating current to direct current.

Light Emitting Diode: Becoming more common all the time, LEDs have a small lens built in. The flow of electrons generates energy released in the form of light. Unlike a conventional bulb, no heat is created.

Transistors: These are solid-state switch used in applications like electronic ignitions to turn a circuit on and off, or in a stereo to strengthen a radio signal.

Resistors: Used to limit current flow, resistors can have a fixed value or they can be adjustable (also called a potentiometer).

Capacitors: A capacitor can store an electric charge. The condenser in a point style ignition is actually a capacitor. Some electronic ignition systems use a capacitor to store an electrical charge that is released all at once.

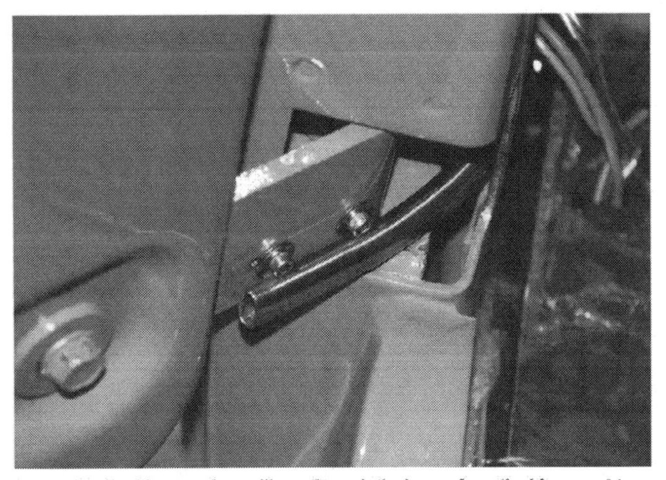

Secured to the hinges, wires will run through the looms from the hinge post to the switches in the doors.

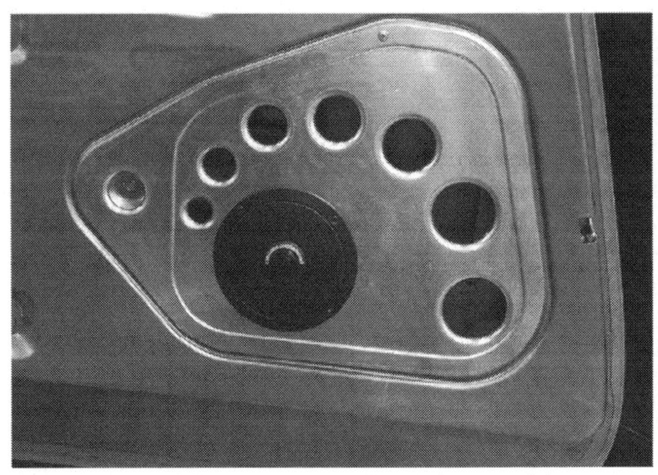

Custom filler panels in the doors mount speakers for the Custom Autosound system.

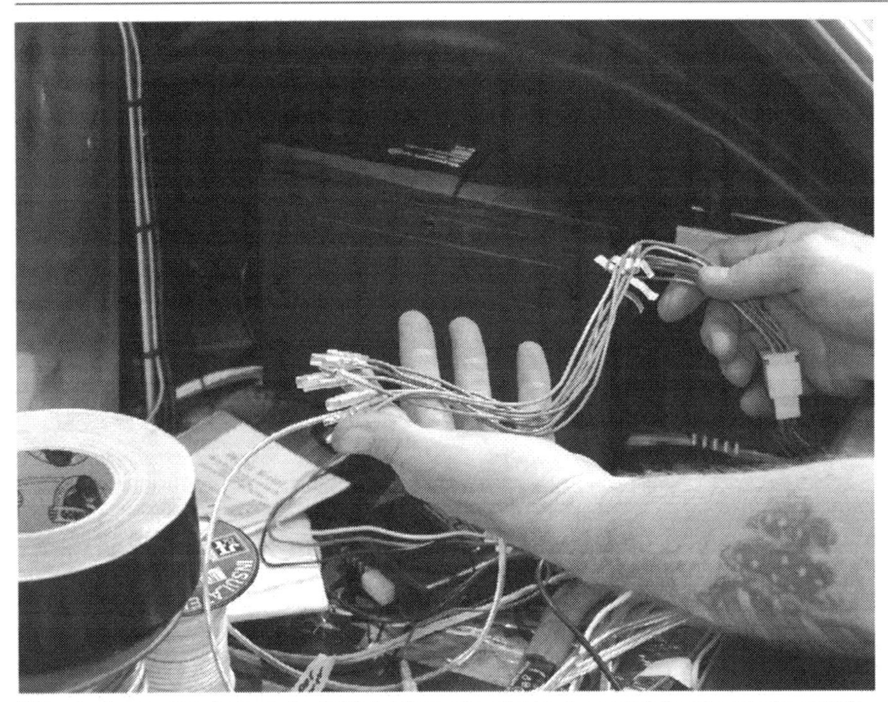

Wiring for the sound system was clearly labeled. It runs from the trunk-mounted disc player to the controls in the passenger compartment.

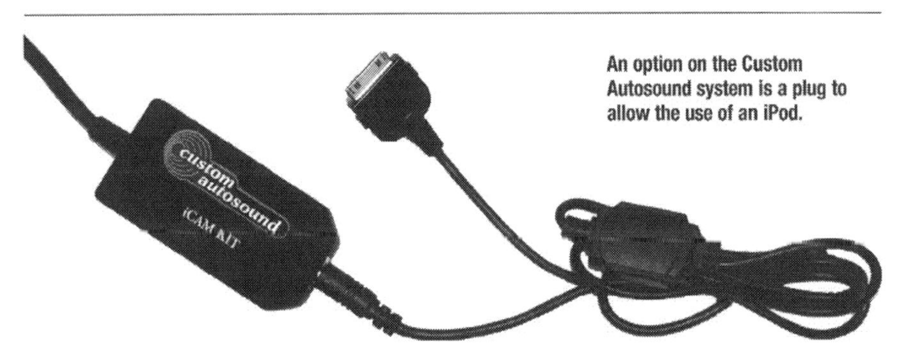

An option on the Custom Autosound system is a plug to allow the use of an iPod.

their size and sometimes difficult to handle. Do not use batteries that have been dropped.

It is important to pay close attention to the torque specs when tightening the battery terminals to prevent slippage and allow maximum connectivity.

Shielding your battery from high heat sources like headers will extend the life of the battery greatly.

STARTERS

Powermaster offers a variety of starters with varying torque ratings. All have adjustable mounting blocks (except Mopar #9130) and will work with most headers and oil pans.

POWER-MAX

With 160 lb-ft of torque, these starters are perfect for stock engines with up to 10:1 compression.

MASTERTORQUE

These starters produce 180 lb-ft of torque and are capable of spinning engines with up to 12:1 compression.

XS TORQUE

Producing 200-lb/ft of torque, these starters will handle up to 18:1 compression. These starters are recommended where space is a concern and heat soak is a problem.

ULTRA TORQUE

Able to crank engines with over 18:1 compression, these starters produce 3.4 horsepower. They are available for a variety of applications, including Diesels.

IGNITION SYSTEM

To fire the fuel in our Boss Ford we used MSD ignition components, including the distributor, control unit, and coil.

MSD offers a variety of distributors including:

Ready-to-Run, E-Curve and HEI Distributors: These are distributors have a built-in module. No ignition control is required and they will provide more than adequate spark output for street/strip applications.

Pro-Billet Distributors: Most MSD Distributors must be used with an MSD Blaster Ignition, 6, 7, 8, or 10 Series Ignition Control.

All MSD distributors use polished steel shafts that receive a QPQ, or Tuftride coating that reduces friction and resists corrosion. For accuracy MSD uses a sealed ball bearing located at the top of the housing. At the bottom of the housing, an extra-long sintered bushing controls the shaft. This combination keeps the shaft spinning smoothly and accurately throughout 10,000+ rpm.

Magnetic Pickup: All of the MSD Distributors (except crank trigger models) use a high output magnetic pickup to trigger the ignition system. This pickup is

A FEW WIRING TIPS FROM RON FRANCIS

- Don't use glass fuses, they were replaced 25 years ago for good reason.
- When installing a factory type connector, take the time to run the wire directly into the connector housing; don't splice to the wire if it can be avoided.
- Never use extension harnesses to make something fit. Extensions require either splices or extra connections, and you don't want either.
- Never fuse one item with more than one fuse (not counting a maxi-fuse).
- Never hook to the battery cable with a ring terminal to power an accessory.
- Splices are only for when there is no other choice. Little or no solder should be used to prevent the connection from becoming brittle.
- Grounds are critical; ground the battery to the block, block to the frame, and block to the body.

The Custom Autosound CD changer and power unit fit inside the right rear quarter panel—an upholstered panel will hide them.

What is a good connection? Pull-test your crimps before you install them. OEM terminals must meet these pull-test specifications

OEM Terminals must meet these Pull Test Requirements:

Wire Gauge	Minimum	Maximum
18 Ga.	30 lbs.	50 lbs.
16 Ga.	40 lbs.	60 lbs.
14 Ga.	60 lbs.	80 lbs.
12 Ga.	75 lbs.	95 lbs.
10 Ga.	85 lbs.	105 lbs.
8 Ga.	100 lbs.	120 lbs.

And for the rest of us: Give it a good healthy tug, and if it doesn't come off...

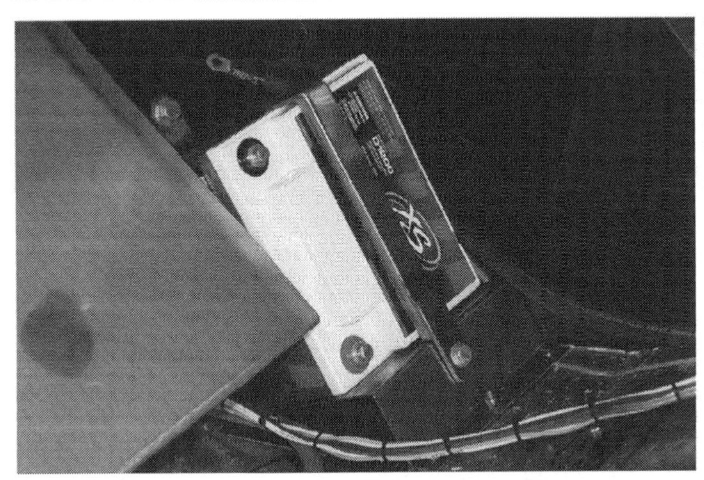

A Powermaster D1200 AGM (absorbed glass mat) battery is mounted behind the seat. It's held in place by a custom mount and retainer.

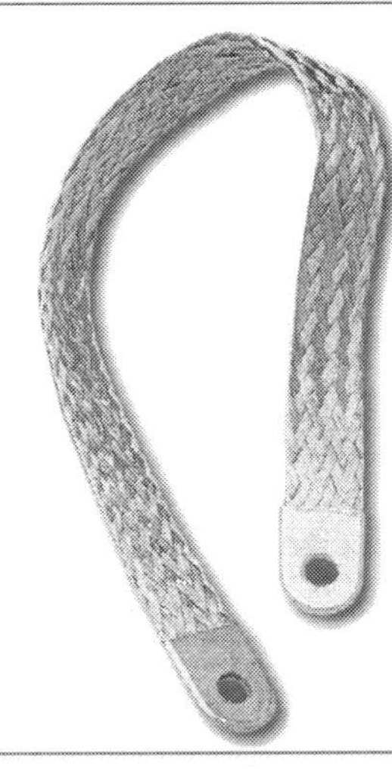

Grounding is an important part of every electrical system. Straps should be used between the engine and chassis and the body and chassis.

Providing the spark to fire our Boss Ford is an MSD Pro-Billet distributor. The magnetic pickup design requires an MSD control unit.

An MSD Blaster coil is attached to the pan rail on the right side of the engine.

completely maintenance-free, requiring no adjustment. The pickup is mounted to the base of the distributor housing and plugs directly into your MSD Ignition Control. A trigger signal is created as a precision-made reluctor (attached to the shaft) passes by. The reluctor has a "paddle" for each cylinder and when the paddle passes the pickup, a signal is created.

Adjustable Mechanical Advance: One of the most important features of the MSD Distributors is the adjustable mechanical advance assembly. The advance assembly allows you to accurately modify the advance curve to match your specific application. To start with, the advance plate is stamped and machined from chromemoly. Weight pins are then staked in and TIG-welded in place. This assembly—along with the weights—then receives a corrosion-resistant QPQ coating. Nylon weight pads are installed under the weights to ensure smooth movement as the weights are pushed out from centrifugal force to advance the timing. A variety of advance springs and stop bushings are supplied, with each distributor giving you the ability to set up to 24 different curves.

CARB Approved Distributors: MSD offers distributors that have been approved by CARB for use in all the states. Each distributor features a vacuum advance for street economy.

CONTROL UNITS

For our application we chose a Pro Billet distributor and an MSD 6 Series capacitive discharge ignition system. The majority of stock ignition systems are inductive, which means the coil must store and step up the voltage to maximum strength in between each firing. At higher rpm, since there is less time to charge the coil to full capacity, the voltage falls short of reaching maximum energy, which results in a loss of power or top end miss. The MSD Ignition features a capacitor that is quickly charged (within one millisecond) with 460-480 volts and stores it until the ignition is triggered. With the CD design, the voltage sent to the coil is always at full power even at high rpm.

The MSD 6 Series produces full power multiple sparks for each firing of a plug. The number of multiple sparks that occur decreases as rpm increases; however, the spark series always lasts for 20° of crankshaft rotation. Above 3,000 rpm there is simply not enough "time" to fire

Bigger alternators need bigger charge wires. Here are Powermaster's recommendations.

Recommended Charging Cable Gauge From Powermaster Size:

AMPS	Up to 4'	4' - 7'	7' - 10'	10' - 13'	13' - 16'	16' - 19'	19' - 22'	22' - 28'
35 - 50	12	12	10	10	10	8	8	8
50 - 65	10	8	8	6	6	6	6	4
65 - 85	10	8	8	6	6	4	4	4
85 - 105	8	8	6	4	4	4	4	2
105 - 125	6	6	4	4	2	2	2	0
125 - 150	6	6	4	2	2	2	2	0
150 - 175	4	4	4	2	2	0	0	0
175 - 200	4	4	2	2	0	0	0	0

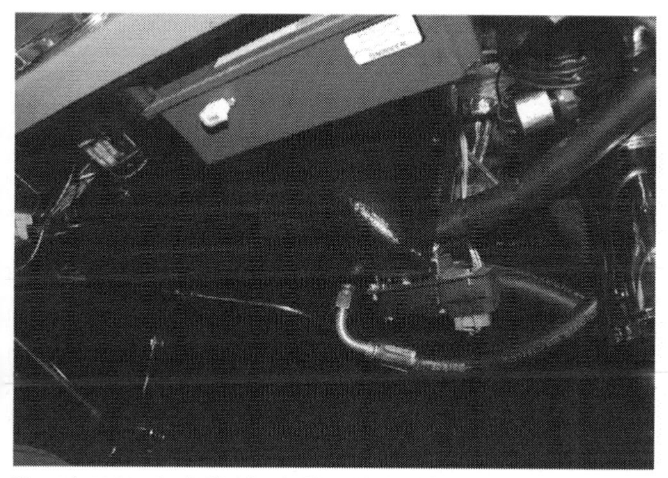

The rectangular plug behind the dashboard is the MSD 6AL ignition control.

The custom taillights. Like the headlights, screw-on rings retain the lenses.

the spark plug more than once, so there is only one powerful spark.

GAUGES

For instruments we selected Auto Meter's Street Rod Old Tyme White II series for their classic lettering and needle design. While these gauges look classic, inside they are state-of-the-art. These all-electric instruments use sending units signal to quick-reacting air core movements in the gauges while keeping all the hazardous fluids out of the passenger compartment. Electrical connections consist of three wires. ■

As a theft deterrent and a safety device, Ron Francis offers this master battery disconnect switch, part number MS-I.

There are a variety of senders for electronic speedometers. Some have additional cable drives for cruise controls.

Chapter 11
INTERIOR

This is an interior that not only looks great but also is a pleasure to spend time in. The seat is a Wise Guys; Twin City Upholstery in Bloomington, IL, handled the remainder of the coverings.

hile the outside of a street rod is what first gets your attention, for the passengers the interior is just as important, if not more so. There are a number of elements that make up a comfortable passenger compartment, and they have a huge impact on the drivability of a street rod—uncomfortable cars spend their time in the garage or on trailers; comfortable cars are driven.

A/C-HEAT

One of the obvious advantages of the Speed33's design is the top that drops for open air cruising, but let's not forget the advantages of running with the top up. In some cases it's just too hot to drive with the lid lowered, in others it's too cold, but a good heating and air conditioning system makes the Speed33 a pleasure to drive in all kinds of weather. To that end we chose a Gen II Compac heat and cool unit from Vintage Air.

To make the driver comfortable, a Flaming River leather-wrapped steering wheel and tilt steering column were used. Instruments are Auto Meter i Lokar Insert. Rear view mirror is from Yogi's.

Gen II Technology adds a long list of features to aftermarket air conditioning that was previously found only on modern OEM systems:

* Fully electronic servo operation provides increased butterfly door travel and more positive sealing, delivering dramatic gains in airflow and system flexibility.

* Gen II design provides superior defrost performance and true bi-level operation in both heat and A/C modes

* Improved coil technology and CAD-designed case provides greater cooling/heating capacity and a more efficient air mixing chamber in the smallest possible overall case size.

* Electronic operation of Gen II system means no reliance on vehicle vacuum, increasing reliability and simplifying installation.

* New Servomotor-operated heater control valve provides true temperature blending in all modes of operation, delivering OEM quality, year-round comfort.

In simple terms, the heater portion of any heat and cool system passes hot water through a mini-radiator, and a fan blows air through it to provide warmth to the passengers. While that's simple enough to understand, cooling the air is a little more complicated—the layman's explanation is air conditioners make the air cold by removing heat. Here's how the experts at Vintage Air explain the procedure:

There are seven basic components needed to air-condition any car with a conventional system: Compressor, compressor bracket, evaporator (inside car unit), condenser (outside heat exchanger), hoses and fittings, the dryer, and a safety switch.

Beginning with the compressor, it pumps refrigerant, in gas form, into the high-pressure gas discharge line. This gas is loaded with heat it has absorbed from the air flowing over the evaporator coil inside the vehicle. As the heated high-pressure gas reaches the condenser, the air flowing through the condenser carries off the heat. The refrigerant condenses into a liquid, which becomes heavier and requires less space. The more efficiently the refrigerant is condensed, the less room it uses in the system. This affects the refrigerant to lower pressures in the high-pressure side of the air conditioner. The liquid refrigerant then pours into the receiver/dryer, where it falls to the bottom of the receiver. A pick-up tube fits into the receiver/dryer, almost reaching the bottom of the tank. The open end of the tube is always below the liquid level in the receiver/dryer, if the system is fully charged. This provides pure liquid to the liquid line (between the dryer pick-up tube and the expansion valve). The expansion valve is an orifice that varies in size according to the temperature of the evaporator coil. By changing size, it meters the

Arguably one of the best street rod accessories to come along are aftermarket heat and air conditioning units. Vintage Air supplied the complete system for the Road Tour Speed33.

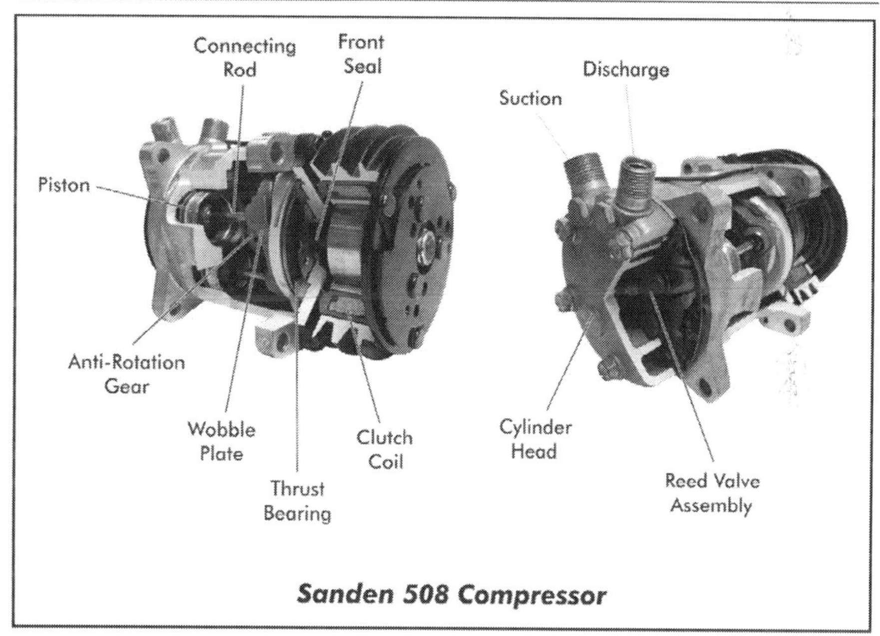

Modern A/C compressors are quiet and efficient and considerably smoother that the old upright style. Note the pistons and connecting rods.

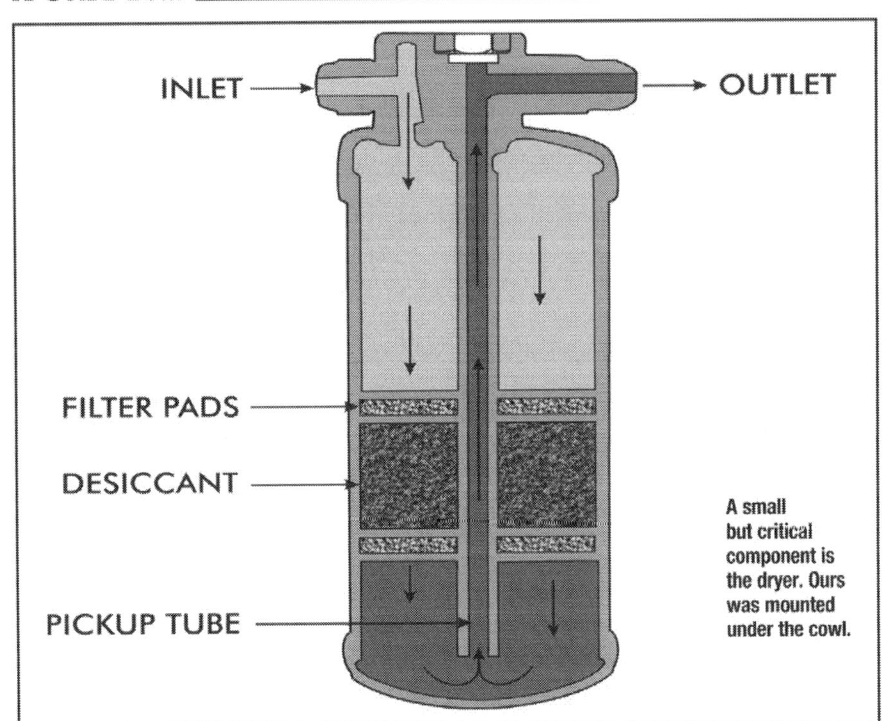

A small but critical component is the dryer. Ours was mounted under the cowl.

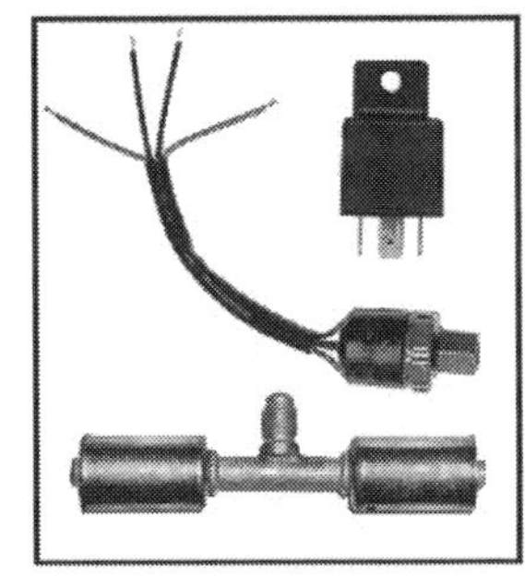

All systems should include one of two types of safety switch. A binary switch shuts off the compressor to prevent damage to the system if the pressure exceeds 406 psi on the high side or 30 psi on the low side. A trinary switch does that, plus it provides an electric engine cooling fan engagement signal at 254 psi on the high side. The trinary switch shown includes a fan relay and an installation port to be placed in the hose.

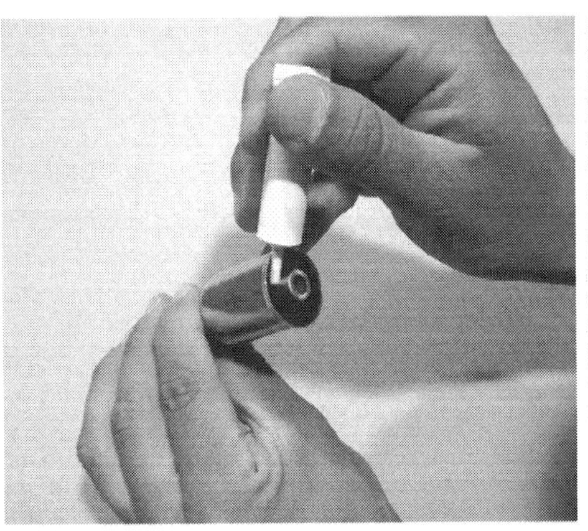

Because of the pressures involved the installation of hose ends must be done correctly. The prescribed lubricant should be applied to the fittings before they are installed on the hose.

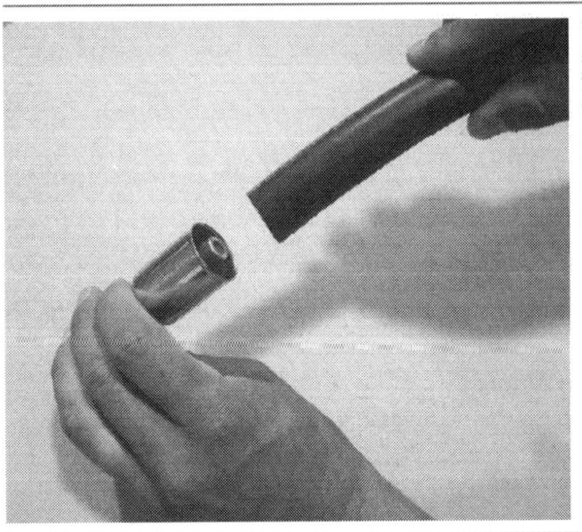

For R134a systems, the proper barrier hose must be used to prevent the loss of refrigerant.

refrigerant according to the demands of the evaporator. When warm, the orifice is largest and gets smaller as the evaporator gets colder. This orifice provides a pressure drop with the resulting drop in refrigerant temperature. The high-pressure liquid pours into the larger opening of the evaporator and the low-pressure liquid droplets begin to pick up heat, which expands the refrigerant to a low pressure (super-heated) gas which then returns to the compressor to start the cycle all over again.

SELECTING A CONDENSER

The most difficult problem is getting a condenser large enough in a place where the air is cool enough, and can be flowed across it well enough to condense the refrigerant adequately. The condenser has to provide a low resistance path for the condensed liquid to flow so pressure build-up can be avoided on the existing refrigerant. (Pressure here tends to reduce heat loss, which tries to reduce condensation.)

The old vertical vs. horizontal tubes in the condenser comes into play here. Horizontal is best, and a condenser that will fit with the tubes running horizontal is recommended. Why? Because oil flows with the refrigerant in the system and will settle in the lower loops of the condenser, thereby obstructing the flow of liquid. We have seen this single factor increase the internal pressure of the high-pressure part of the air conditioner by fifty percent, reducing its ability to work. A general rule for surface area for an R-12 system is a minimum of 210 square inches on a two row, 5/16-inch copper tube and aluminum fin condenser. This is a general rule; it is not absolute. But it is a place to start. HFC-134a requires about

DOZEN WAYS 'O SCREW UP A 'ERFECTLY GOOD IR CONDITIONER

HINK OF THIS AS A OW *NOT* TO DO IT

It goes without saying that no one utting together a street rod intentionally crews something up, but as veterans of long list of building blunders, we know uff happens. Case in point: Not long go we were on the Road Tour with our uddy Rick Love of Vintage Air.

As we wandered around one of the ops looking at cars, Rick glanced

wards a very nice coupe that had lled up and parked and said, "I'll bet e heater valve in that car is installed ckwards." Sure enough, a subsequent nversation with the car's owner vealed that the air conditioning system s not performing as it should and a ick inspection revealed that the heater lve was indeed installed incorrectly.

At about the time we decided to k Rick to use his new physic powers to give us a winning lottery number he made a confession. "Did you see the big puddle of water under that car?" he asked. "When that much water comes out of the A/C drain on a day that's not at all humid, it's a sure sign something's wrong. Usually it's the way the heater valve is installed, we see that all the time."

At this point we were struck by two things: First, here was a really nice car that appeared to be well built, yet a simple mistake was made during its construction; secondly, Rick's ability to spot and diagnose a common problem so rapidly got us to wondering how many other mistakes are easily made when installing A/C.

So, with help from Rick and Vintage Air, we've put together the following list of simple ways an air conditioning installation can be screwed up (as well as ways to avoid it). Just think of this as a how not to do it.

DON'T CHARGE THE SYSTEM PROPERLY

The easiest way to make an air conditioning system not work properly is to incorrectly charge the system; the simplest way to do that is to treat a contemporary system as if it were the old R12 type. When charging is necessary, just dump in a couple cans of refrigerant and watch the sight glass in the drier for bubbles.

Unlike the "old days" with R-12 refrigerant, the "bubbles" in the sight glass that you see with 134A are actually small oil droplets, not air bubbles. Today's systems must be charged by weight with a good scale or preferably a charging station. Vintage Air's standard charge recommendation is 1.8 lbs. (28 ounces) of 134A refrigerant. This charge will be correct for most standard installations (dash-mounted systems). For a trunk-mounted system with a liquid line of more than 12 feet, some additional refrigerant will be required.

DON'T USE A/C GAUGES

A truly gifted method of screwing up an A/C system is the "by guess and by golly system." The guess part is the system needs more refrigerant; the golly part is finding out later it really didn't. To accurately determine if an A/C system is charged properly, dedicated, high-

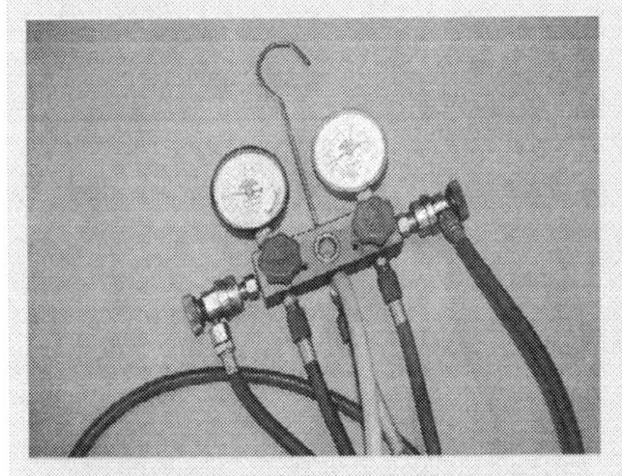

quality gauges are required. Most street rod systems use an expansion valve and a fixed displacement compressor (CCEV system). The low side pressure should be 7 to 12 lbs. when correctly charged under the following test conditions: engine rpm 1,200-1,500 RPM; doors and windows closed; blower on medium with fan in front of the radiator for air flow across the condenser and radiator. An overcharged system (too much refrigerant or oil) results in higher system operating pressures and poor performance. An undercharged system will show lower operating pressures and poor performance as well.

JUST ADD OIL

New compressors sometimes come with extra oil. So, despite the fact that all new Sanden compressors come filled with the correct type and the proper amount of lubricant for proper system operation, if you want to screw things up, add some more. That will result in increased system pressures and poor performance.

The smart move here is to save any extra oil for use if and when the system needs to be recharged (unless you're like us and can't find it when you need it, but that's another story).

DON'T EVACUATE THE SYSTEM

Leaving air and water in the system is a guaranteed method to reduce the efficiency of an A/C system.

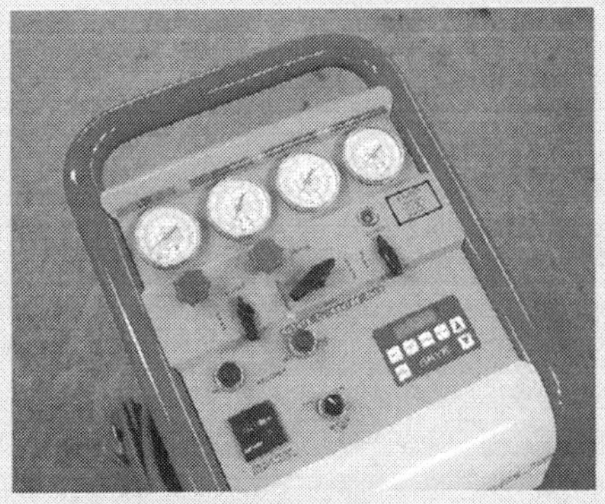

Evacuating the system for a minimum of 30 minutes at 75° F with a vacuum pump accomplishes two things—it removes air from the system while the vacuum lowers the boiling point of water, so any moisture in the system boils away. However, if it is cold there is still an opportunity to mess up the process; all components must be at 75° F for proper evacuation. If the components are colder than that, run the engine or heat them with a hair drier to get them up to temperature.

DON'T INSULATE OR SEAL THE VEHICLE

This sounds silly, but think of cold as the absence of heat. Now think of an air conditioner as something that doesn't make the air cold, but removes heat from it. If you can come to terms with those statements, it stands to reason that providing more heat for an A/C system

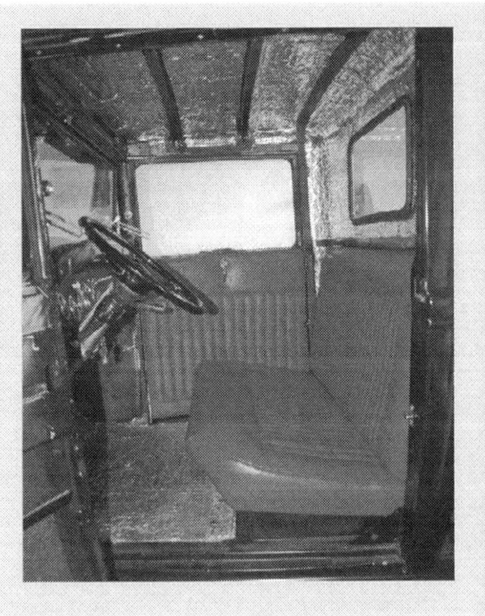

to remove will make its job that much more difficult. This can be done by not insulating or sealing the firewall, floor, doors, and all the other sources of heat that enter the passenger compartment.

An A/C system works by taking in air from a confined area and pushing it across a coil in the under-dash evaporator, where the heat is absorbed and the humidity converted to droplets that drain to the outside. Cooled air is then pushed out through the vents onto the occupants while the heat is carried to the condenser in front of the radiator.

Simply put, if you don't keep the hot air out of the vehicle, no A/C system will

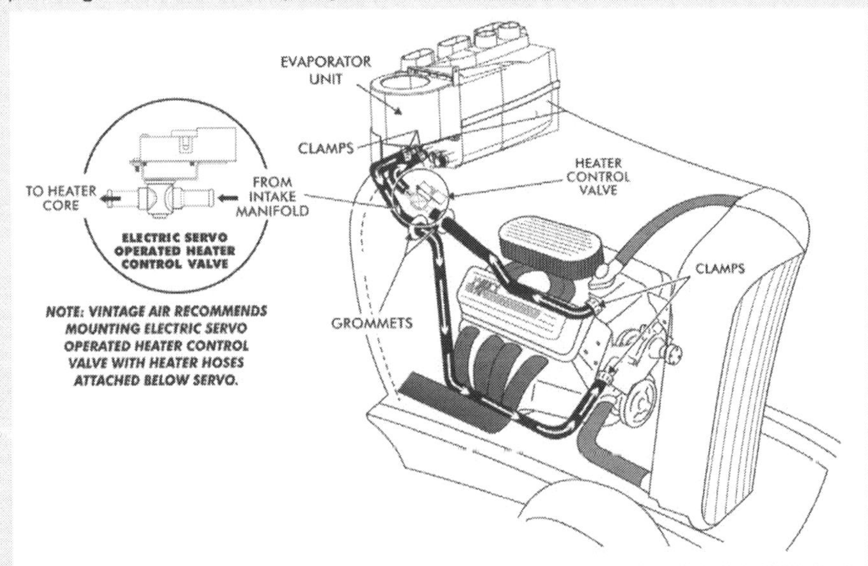

ever be able to cool off your vehicle. It's like running the A/C system in your home with the windows open.

NSTALL THE HEATER CONTROL VALVE INCORRECTLY

A very effective way to make the A/C less efficient is to install the heater control valve backwards or in the wrong hose. This allows hot water to circulate through the heater core, warming the air that the A/C is trying to cool.

Most heater control valves are directional and must be correctly oriented in the high-pressure heater hose.

Most water pump heater hose outlets are on the low-pressure (suction) side of the pump. The intake manifold outlet is the high-pressure side of the system. As water pressure in the hose helps the valve seal, if they are installed backwards, or in the wrong hose, they will not shut off completely and some hot water will continue to flow.

MOUNT THE LOUVERS/VENTS SO THE COOLED AIR DOESN'T BLOW ON THE OCCUPANTS

Outlets are simple enough to screw up. Find some that are real restrictive (even if they look good) and point them at the floor. A couple more tricks that will reduce A/C efficiency are capping off unused vents in the evaporator housing (it results in "cold spots" in the coil and rapid coil freeze-up) and bunching up the duct hose.

When deciding on louvers, make sure they are open and adjustable, then place them so cool air can be directed at the occupants' faces. Stretch duct hoses for smoothest airflow path, with no droops.

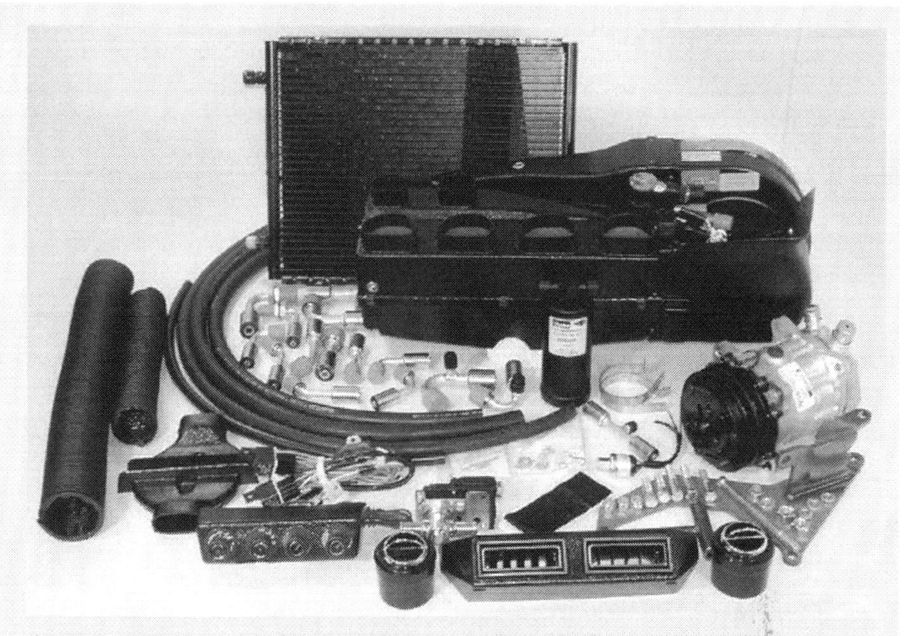

DON'T BUY A MATCHED SYSTEM

This isn't easy to do if you buy a complete system, but if you buy components individually it can be done. As we said earlier, an air conditioning system works by removing the heat and humidity from an enclosed space. If the evaporator is too small for the amount of interior area to be cooled, the results will be less than satisfactory.

In fairness, using the wrong condenser is a mistake often made accidentally. Radiators may come with an A/C condenser as part of a package, but that doesn't mean the condenser will be appropriate for the rest of the A/C system.

As we said earlier, the condenser dissipates the heat that was absorbed inside the vehicle to the outside air. As the gaseous refrigerant condenses to a liquid, it transfers the heat to the condenser tubes and the tubes then transfer the heat to the fins, where the air flowing through the fins can carry it away.

For years condensers used copper tube/aluminum fin construction and it is this style that may be found with aftermarket radiators. Unfortunately, these old style condensers are not efficient when using 134A refrigerant. The best choice is aluminum parallel flow condenser as they provide increased surface area in the same size package size and, therefore, are much more efficient. Vintage Air always suggests using the largest condenser that will fit the radiator core.

DON'T INCLUDE A COMPRESSOR SAFETY SWITCH

Excessive high side pressure can cause damage to the compressor or rupture a hose (the latter is always a crowd pleaser).

A binary compressor safety switch will disengage the clutch if the system pressure gets too high (above 406 psi). Also, a binary switch will not allow the

compressor to engage if the high side system pressure is below 30 psi, which indicates refrigerant loss. Since an air conditioning system relies on the refrigerant to help carry lubricant through the system, if the refrigerant is lost, so is the compressor's lubricant supply. As can be guessed, allowing the compressor to run without lubrication can cause it to be damaged or to lock up.

CONNECT THE ELECTRIC ENGINE FAN TO THE A/C CLUTCH

With this arrangement, when the A/C is on, so is the engine cooling fan. But the engine fan doesn't normally have to be on at highway speeds and the A/C compressor working doesn't change that.

If your vehicle relies on an electric fan for cooling there should be two things that activate it, engine temperature and/or A/C system pressure. Along with an engine temperature switch of some sort, a trinary compressor safety switch should be part of the A/C system.

A trinary switch provides the same high and low pressure protection as a binary switch, but also includes a fan engagement signal at 254 psi. It should be wired in parallel to the same relay as the engine temperature switch. This way, either engine temperature or A/C system pressure will turn on the fan.

MOUNT COMPONENTS INCORRECTLY

Part of the A/C process is condensing a gas to a liquid. That's a process that can be made less efficient by mounting the condenser upside down or on its side. Mounting the receiver/dryer near a heat source is also a good way to make a good system struggle to keep you cool.

When installing a parallel flow condenser, the tanks should be vertical, and the tubes horizontal. It is also critical that the gaseous refrigerant pumped from the compressor (the larger #8 fitting) be on top, and the liquid line (smaller #6 fitting) on the bottom. As a gas is being condensed into a liquid, the system will work more efficiently if it's not trying to push a liquid up through the condenser.

Another factor is refrigerant flow through the receiver/dryer. The path is from the compressor, through the condenser, the dryer and finally to the evaporator. Make sure the arrow on the receiver/dryer matches the direction of flow.

Remember the idea is to get rid of heat, so you don't want the refrigerant to absorb heat under the hood. Mounting the dryer where it will be

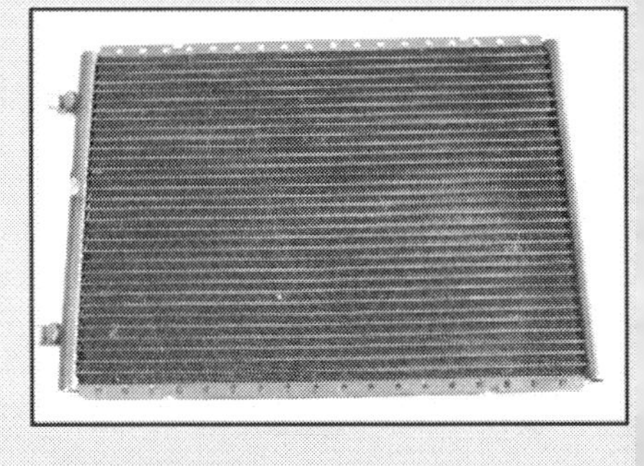

exposed to cool air or inside the car is the best option.

AND OF COURSE, DON'T READ THE INSTRUCTIONS

This last tip practically guarantees your A/C won't work as it should, plus it will make you really popular with the guys on the tech line when you call for help. Most manufacturers go to great lengths to provide instructions for their products. So, since they think they are important, a great way to screw up almost anything is to totally disregard them. About the only way to improve upon this screw-up is to not mail in the warranty card.

Before you begin installation of an A/C system, read all the instructions, warnings, labels and any other printed material included; it really is there for a reason. Then, familiarize yourself with all the components before your start. And if you still have questions, get them answered before proceeding. The tech guys would rather prevent a problem than cure one.

20% more capacity, which means with a conventional tube and fin condenser you need about 20% more size. Our Super Flow condensers give that increase in capacity without additional size. By using flat tubes manifolded together so that the refrigerant flows through multiple tubes each pass, we get virtually 100% contact of the refrigerant with the condenser tube walls. This design also offers very low restriction in the pathway through the condenser and is up to 40% more efficient than a comparable size copper tube and fin type condenser.

ERGONOMICS

The foundation of the Road Tour program is the concept that street rods are made to be driven and it's the ergonomics that can make a it a pleasure or a pain to drive. When automotive designers use the term ergonomics they are talking about everything from the location of the steering wheel, door handles, switches, pedals and the buttons on the radio to shape of the seats and the door openings. Of course, some things are fixed when working with a street rod, but there are a number of items that still require thought.

Of course, one of the key ingredients in comfort is the seating. The seat bottoms should provide to support to the backs of your legs as there's nothing more uncomfortable that sitting on your tailbone for a long period of time. In addition the backrest should be at a comfortable angle. We chose a seat

There are two types of fittings commonly used on A/C hoses, barb, or beadlock. Each type of fitting requires a specific crimping tool.

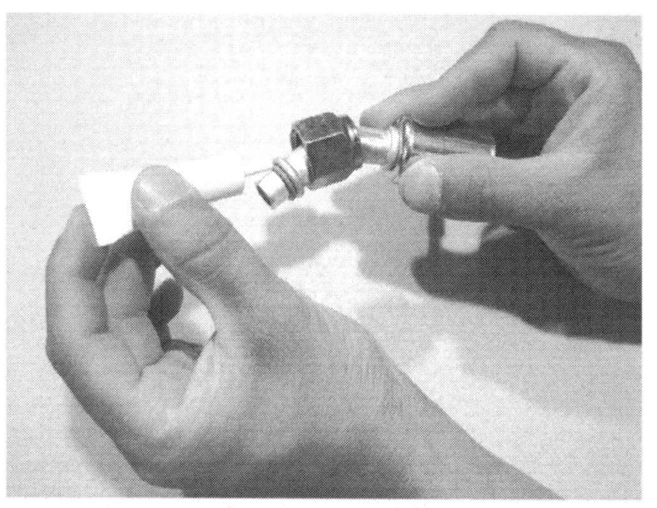

When installing completed hoses, it is important that the proper O-rings are used and that they are coated with appropriate lubricant.

from Wise Guys because they have long, comfortable bottom cushions and the seatbacks are fully adjustable, so setting them to the ideal angle is simply a matter of flipping a lever.

Another important ergonomic item is the steering column. In terms of placement, one of the design elements found on many high performance cars is that the steering column is at a very slight angle that follows the driver's line of sight to the center of the lane in front of the car. While it's something that is normally not noticeable, driving a car in which the steering column points noticeably to the left or right side of the road can be disconcerting, even if you don't know why. Thanks to the adjustability of the Flaming River steering column, the wheel can be positioned as needed.

Another important ergonomic consideration is the placement of the pedals. The area around the bottom of the column can get crowded, particularly in a car with a manual transmission. The Roadster Shop pedals and Lokar throttle are ideally placed so the movement from gas to brake and the reverse is easy.

With all the controls positioned, the next issue for most street rodders is the positioning of the switches. In some cases, a clean dash is worth hiding things like the light and ignition switches. In the Road Tour Speed33, the ignition

When routing heater and A/C hoses keep them out of harms way, particularly headers. Note the service ports in the A/C hoses for charging the system.

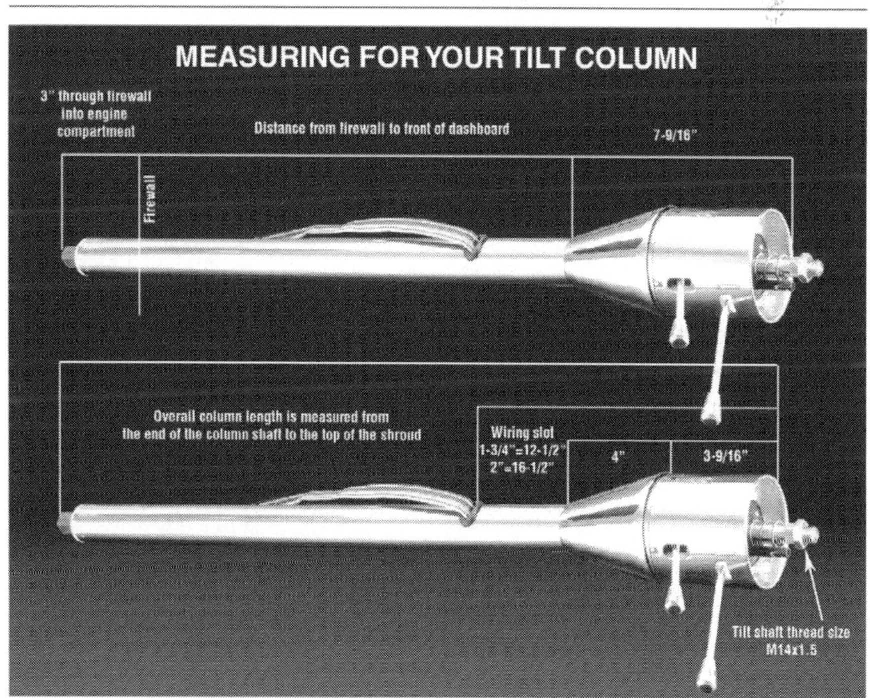

Adequate airflow is necessary for proper operation, so a good fan is necessary to help at low speeds.

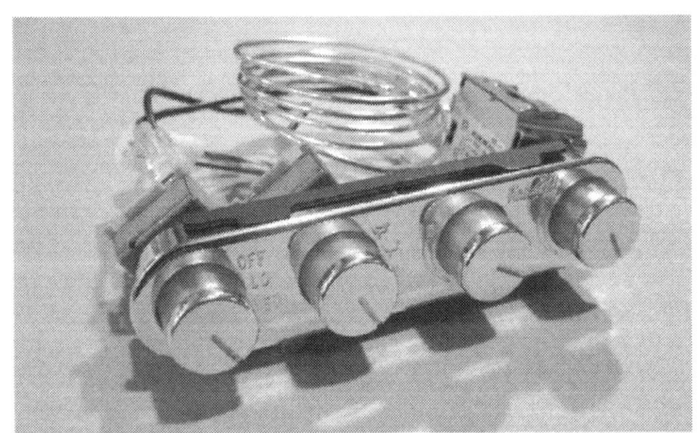
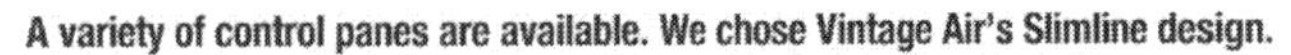

A variety of control panes are available. We chose Vintage Air's Slimline design.

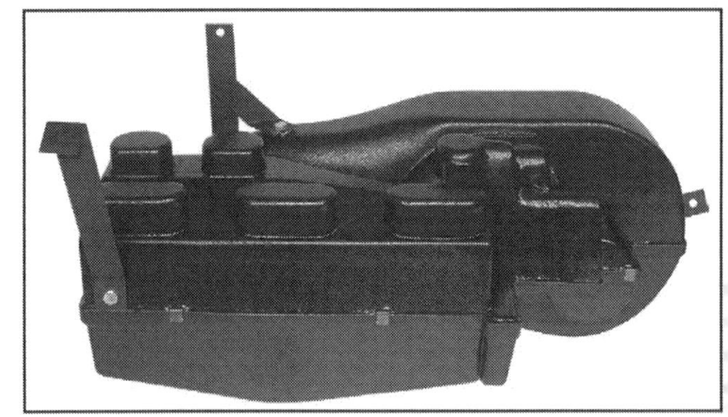

As an installation aide, Vintage Air offers lightweight mock-up cases that lack internals.

and headlight switches mount below the dash to the right of the steering column.

Another consideration when building a street rod is the positioning of the instruments so one or more isn't blocked from view by the steering wheel. We certainly won't have that problem with our centrally located Lokar panel and Auto Meter instruments.

INSULATION

One of the most important factors in interior comfort is the reduction of vibration and road noise. According to Scott Whitaker of Dynamat, a thin viscoelastic damper best controls vibration while thermal control takes some thickness of material that entraps air.

For the best results a quality sound damper should be applied to all interior

INSULATION FAQS

From Scott Whitaker of Dynamat

Q: What kind of tools do I need to install Dynamat?

A: Installing Dynamat requires only a few tools: razor knife or scissors, heat gun (for Dynamat Original only), roller tool, rags, and a solvent-based cleaner (rubbing alcohol also works). When installing Dynaliner, TacMat, or Extremeliner on vertical or upside-down surfaces, you will need a spray adhesive. An upholstery adhesive is best; 3M makes an excellent aerosol adhesive available from your local hardware store.

Q: My floorboard gets hot during long drives. Is there anything I can do?

A: Heat coming from a hot exhaust or headers is a common problem. Fortunately, Dynamic Control has a solution. First, apply Dynamat Xtreme to the floor and firewall, and then install Extremeliner, both underneath the floor's carpet.

Q: What part of the vehicle should I do first?

A: We recommend applying Dynamat to any surface you can easily reach. In general, we recommend treating your vehicle in the following order: doors, trunk, rear deck, floors, roof, hood.

Q: Should I use Dynamat Original or Xtreme?

A: Dynamat Xtreme is our best-performing material for controlling vibration. Dynamat Xtreme damps four times better than Dynamat Original and weighs at least 50 percent less. Dynamat Xtreme's aluminum-constraining top layer also makes it well suited for situations where heat is a problem, such as on the floor and firewall near an exhaust or header. Dynamat Xtreme is recommended anywhere Dynamat can be applied.

Dynamat Original is our entry-level damping material and offers the best compromise between damping efficiency and cost. It is recommended for floors, doors, side panels, and the floor of the trunk. For best installation and performance, use a heat gun during installation. Dynamat Original is not recommended for locations requiring upside-down installation (such as car roofs). For those locations, use Dynamat Xtreme.

Q: How does Dynamat stop road noise?

A: As a car operates, it generates noise. This noise is caused by the transference of energy (vibration) from the internal components and from the road to the vehicle's chassis. The chassis (doors, floors, roof etc.) transforms this vibration into audible noise. Dynamat transforms the energy (vibration) into silent energy.

Q: How much will Dynamat quiet my car?

A: Even a small amount of Dynamat can cause a profound noise reduction. For example, applying Dynamat to the doors of your vehicle can reduce road noise from 3–6 dB. Complete coverage of an average vehicle can reduce road noise 9, 12, even as much as 18dB.

Q: How much Dynamat do I need to use to be effective?

A: You can apply Dynamat in patches (25–50 percent area coverage) to keep a specific panel from resonating, or you can apply it over an entire area (such as the floor, doors, or trunk) to create a sound barrier and thermal insulator.

Q: What is Dynamat?

A: Dynamat is a thin, flexible, easy to cut and mold sheet that actually stops noise causing resonance and vibration by using visco-elastic qualities that promote vibro-acoustic energy conversion. In short, that means noise becomes silent energy.

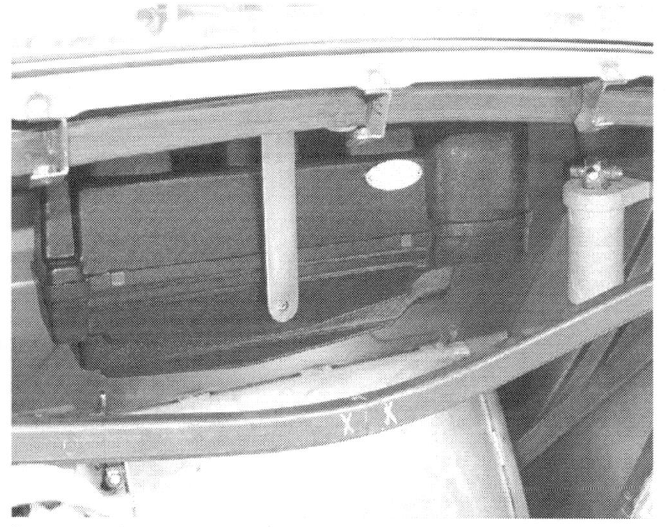

Proper mounting of the evaporator case is important; note the support strap the Roadster Shop attached to the case. That's the dryer mounted to the right side of the cowl.

The compressor is securely mounted by the Vintage Air Front Runner system. Formed refrigerant lines lead to the right side of the engine.

This is the hot water valve; note it has a directional arrow on it. It must be installed in the correct hose in the proper orientation.

Wise Guys offers a complete line of seats, buckets and bench as well as bench style bottoms with bucket backs.

These are examples of the various round outlets available.

Also available from Wise Guys are fixed and adjustable mounting brackets.

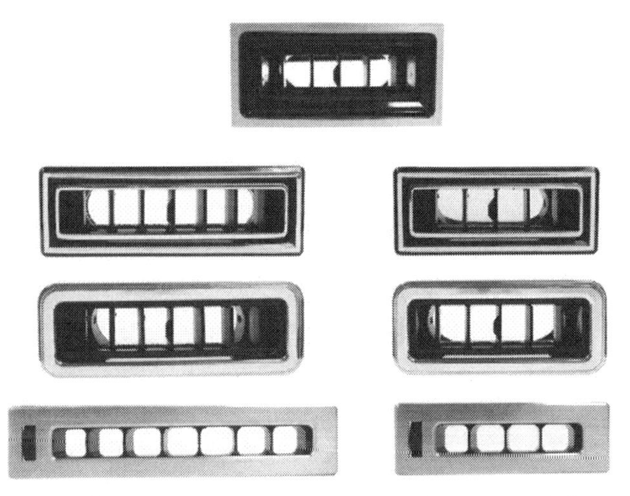

In some applications the rectangular style fits better; in any case, outlets in the evaporator case should never be blocked off or just allowed to blow out under the dash.

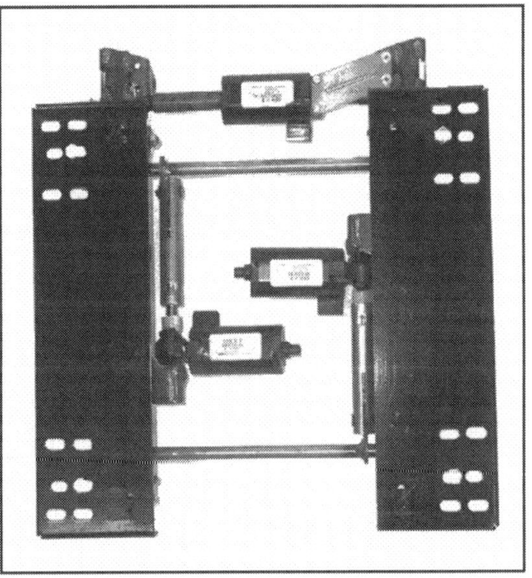

For the ultimate in convenience, power-operated bases are also available.

As well as upholstered seats, Wise Guys sells bare frames and frames with foam installed. This example comes with mounts for a shoulder harness.

Wise Guys has a number of accessories, such as this armrest, to make building an interior easer.

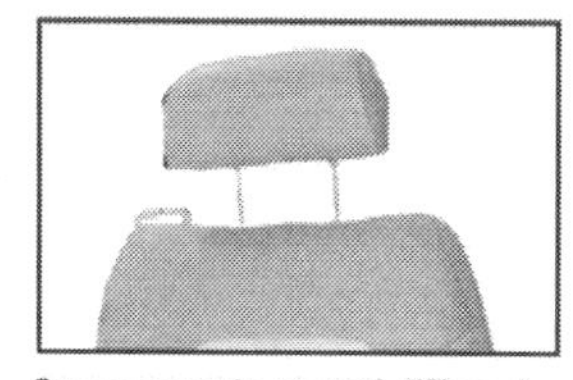

On some seats several different headrest styles are offered.

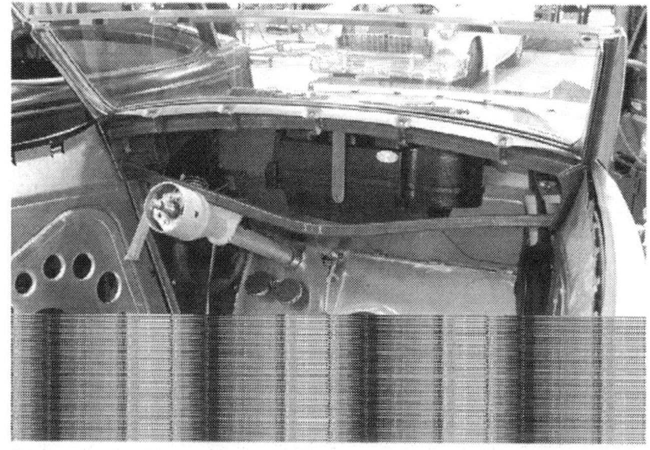

It takes planning to lay out comfortable driver controls. Here, the Flaming River column has been mounted. Note the location of the pedals; often cramped in a rod with a clutch pedal, the Roadster Shop pedals provide plenty of foot room.

sheetmetal or fiberglass for a solid, quiet, comfortable ride. Thermal insulation is needed most where engine-generated heat is greatest, like the firewall and floor.

Dynamic Control has a variety of sound and heat control products for various applications. Dynamat and Dynaliner should be used on all interior surfaces for general-purpose insulation. With some insulating materials moisture can be a problem; however, Dynamat and Dynaliner are actually moisture proof. In addition, they meet FMVSS 302 (Federal Motor Vehicle Safety Standard 302) and are tested by UL.

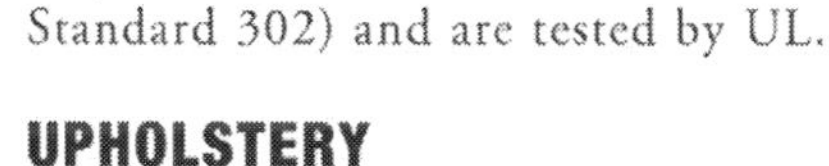

UPHOLSTERY

One of the few jobs not done in-house at the Roadster Shop was the interior. Wise Guys supplied the seat, and staff at Twin City Upholstery handled the rest of the interior. It looks great, is extremely comfortable, and has the unmistakable aroma of leather.

After covering the inside of the body and floor with Dynamat and installing the speakers for the Custom Autosound stereo, the Twin City crew covered the floor in the passenger compartment and trunk with cut pile carpeting and the upholstery panels in leather furnished by Wise Guys, so it would be the same as that found on the seat. ■

Before the interior was installed, Dynamat was applied to every accessible surface.

Dynamat was installed in the truck as well, even on the gas tank.

The steering column was secured to the floor by a custom tube mount. Lokar supplied the spoon throttle.

A Flaming River swing mount attaches the column to the square tube structure that runs from one side of the body to the other.

A Lokar cable, mounting bracket, and return spring are at the other end of the throttle pedal.

The Flaming River tilt column lacks a shifter, although they are available. Turn signal wiring is standard GM.

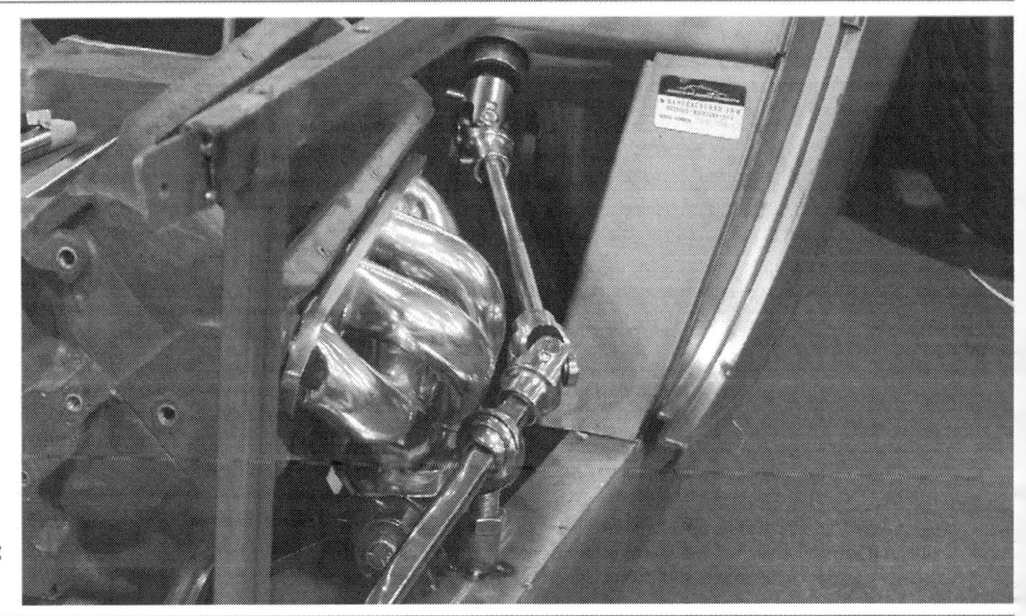

As it often happens, positioning the column for driver comfort complicates the hook-up to the steering gear. In this case, multiple Flaming River U-joints and a support bearing solve the problem.

With the exception of the seat, the crew at Twin City Upholstery was responsible for the interior.

All the necessary interior panels were fabricated from thin mahogany or plastic, then covered in leather supplied by Wise Guys and cut plie carpet.

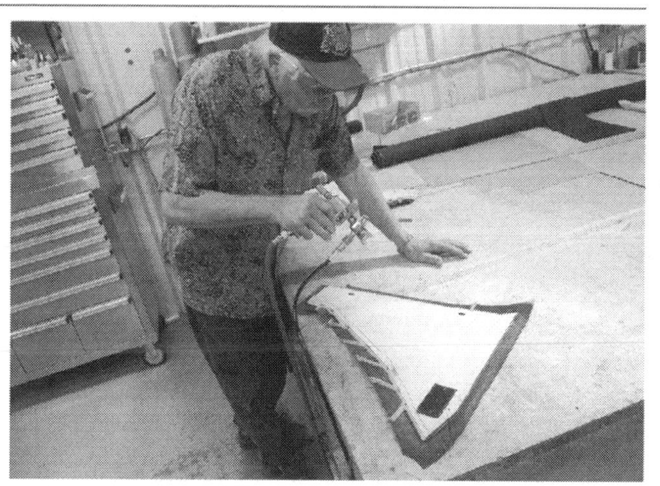

After the material was applied to foam cut to shape and pleated. Upholstery adhesive was sprayed on the front and along the edges on back, the upholstery was then put in place and wrapped around the edges.

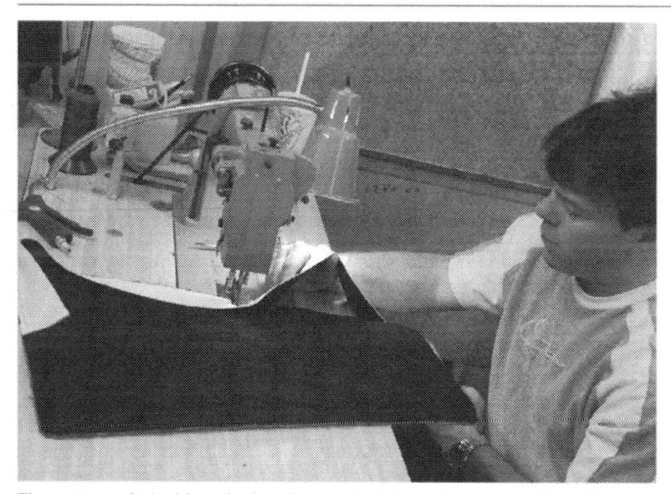

The pattern stitched into the interior panels follows the theme of the Wise Guys seats.

The aluminum panels in the door had cutouts for the speakers and dimpled holes for styling. Black material was attached to the backside of the panels to close off the holes.

With the carpeting down, the panels in the quarters are next. Note how the top folds in the area behind the seat.

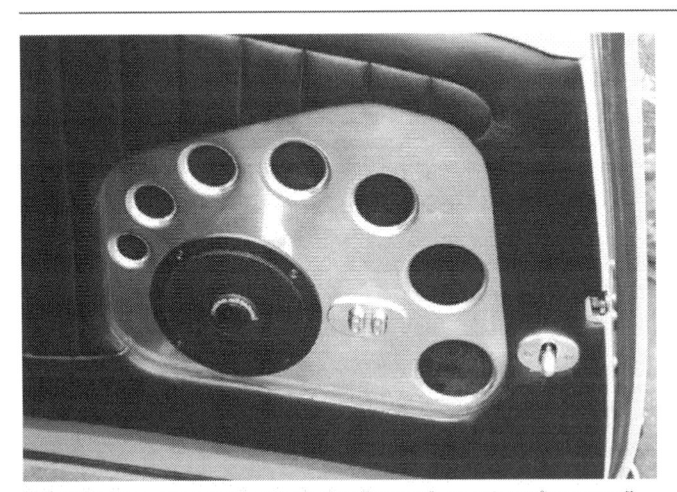

Giving the door panels a unique look, the alloy panels mount speakers as well as the power window switches.

A nice feature on those long road trips is a fold-down armrest. Other options available from Wise Guys include inflatable lumbar supports, heaters, power outlets, and power operated adjustment.

Lonnie King and Kent Biedehyharn prepare to put the seat in place. Wise Guys offers a variety of upholstery colors and patterns.

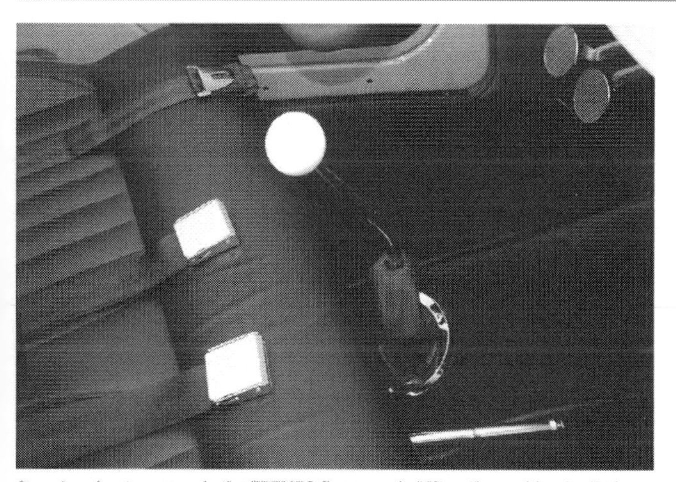

A custom boot surrounds the TREMEC five-speed shifter; the parking brake lever is from Lokar.

Behind the left side trunk panel is the reservoir for the hydraulic clutch.

Chapter 12
FINAL DETAILS/SOURCES

here are many companies involved in making the Road Tour Program a success and helping us to present the construction of a quality street rod like the '08 Speed33. However, the real beauty of this program is that you can duplicate the car you see in this book.

This year's Road Tour Sponsors are:

SPONSOR	OFFICIAL PRODUCT
AEROMOTIVE	FUEL SYSTEM
AMERICAN SPEED COMPANY	BODY
AMSOIL	LUBRICANTS AND FILTRATION/PRESENTING SPONSOR
AUTO METER PRODUCTS	GAUGES
CLASSIC MOTORSPORTS GROUP (CLASSIC CHEVY 5 SPEED)	5-SPEED TRANSMISSION CONVERSION KIT
COKER TIRE	TIRES
CUSTOM AUTOSOUND	AUDIO ELECTRONICS
DYNAMAT	INSULATION AND NOISE CONTROL
FLAMING RIVER	STEERING COMPONENTS
FORD RACING	PRESENTING SPONSOR
FORD RACING	ENGINE
HEIDT'S HOT ROD SHOP	FRONT SUSPENSION
HUSHPOWER (FLOWMASTER)	EXHAUST SYSTEM WITH MUFFLERS
LOKAR	SHIFTER AND CABLES
NSRA	EVENT
PPG INDUSTRIES	TITLE
PPG INDUSTRIES	PAINT
RIGHT COAST ASSOCIATION	EVENT
ROADSTER SHOP	CHASSIS
ROADSTER SHOP	OFFICIAL BUILDER
RON FRANCIS WIRING	WIRING
SANDERSON HEADERS	HEADERS
STRANGE ENGINEERING	SHOCKS
STRANGE ENGINEERING	COMPLETE REAR END
U.S. RADIATOR	RADIATOR AND FAN
VINTAGE AIR, INC.	AIR CONDITIONING AND ACCESSORY DRIVE SYSTEM
WHEEL VINTIQUES	PRESENTING SPONSOR
WHEEL VINTIQUES	WHEEL
WILWOOD BRAKES	OFFICIAL BRAKES
WISE GUYS SEATING & INTERIOR	SEATING AND INTERIOR
YOGI'S	RETAIL STORE
CLASSIC AUTOMOBILIA	TOUR SPONSOR
VINTAGE AIR, INC.	TOUR SPONSOR
SACRAMENTO VINTAGE FORD	TOUR SPONSOR
NHRA MOTORSPORTS MUSEUM	TOUR SPONSOR

LOKAR	TOUR SPONSOR
GOLDEN RODTRONICS	TOUR SPONSOR
EDELBROCK	TOUR SPONSOR
COKER TIRE	TOUR SPONSOR

There is a big list of small parts required to build the Speed33; most of what we used came from Yogi's. Here is that list:

YOGI'S PARTS LIST

COMPANY	PART	DESCRIPTION
AFCO	AD37750	In Line Transmission Cooler
Billet Specialties	BLT55220	License Plate Frame w/light
Billet Specialties	BLT72120	Rear View Mirror Mount
Billet Specialties	BLT73520	Oval Mirror Head, Rear View Mirror
Billet Specialties	BLT75120	Radiator Cap
Dakota Digital	ANT-1	No Show Antenna and Remote Entry
Juliano's	LL01	Seat Belt, Chrome lift latch, black (2)
Lokar	DLR-2100	Universal Door Latch Cable Release
Lokar	EC80FHT	Emergency Brake Cables, Stainless Steel
Lokar	EHB7000F	Emergency Hand Brake
Lokar	EHB7001	Emergency Brake Warning Switch kit
Lokar	IDH2001	Interior Door Handles
Lokar	SPO6070	Gas Pedal, spoon type
Lokar	SPO6071	Brake Pad, Chromed Steel
Lokar	SRK4000	Throttle Bracket & Springs, Stainless Steel
Lokar	TC1000U36	Throttle Cable kit, 36"
Russell	PLY4780	Braided Brake Hoses
Specialty Power Windows	FWC-BA	Flex Wire Conduits w/aluminum ends
Specialty Power Windows	SPW-C12	Wiper Blades (2)
Specialty Power Windows	SPW-ST	Wiper Arms (2)
Specialty Power Windows	WWK2I	Windshield Wiper kit w/intermittent motor
Taylor	TAY70051	Spark Plug Wires, Black, 90 degree
Total Cost Involved	204-2016-02	King Pint Kit, Stainless Steel
Vintique	RO10	Radiator Overflow Tank, 13" Polished Stainless
Watson's Streetworks	SW-L39BOS	Power Window Switch, single
Watson's Streetworks	SW-L39BOD	Power Window Switch, double
Wilwood	260-3278	2# Residual Valve
Wilwood	260-8419	Proportioning Valve

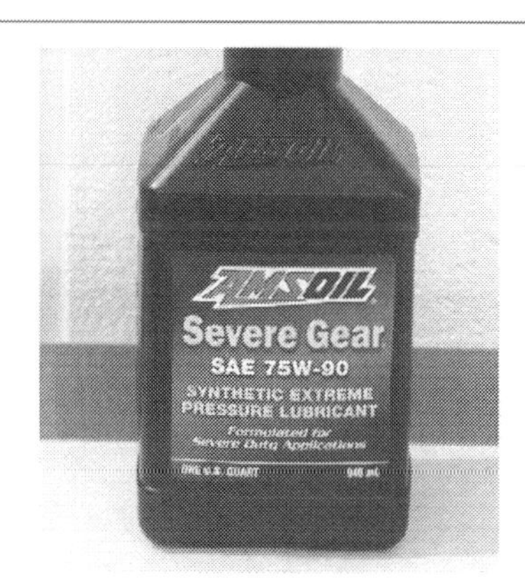

For all the necessary lubricants and fluids to make the Road Tour car function, we turned to the leaders in synthetics, AMSOIL. One of their newest products is the Dominator line of Racing Oil

AMSOIL also has a complete line of oil and air filters. These are some of their cleanable and reusable air filters.

FUEL GAUGE TIPS FROM AUTO METER

- Be sure that the sending unit has a second wire coming off of it and going to a common chassis ground. Make sure that wire is in good shape and is making a good, clean connection.

- Verify the model number of the gauge to make sure its resistance range matches the resistance range of the sending unit in your vehicle.

- Measure the empty and full resistance range of your sender if you are unsure of its range.

- Verify 12 volts, measuring across the "I" and "GND" terminals on the back of the gauge with the key on.

COMMON PROBLEMS:

If Auto Meter does not offer a fuel level gauge to work with the sender, use a universal sender under model number 3262. It operates from 240 ohms at empty and 33 ohms at full. It is adjustable from 5 to 24-inches tank depth and uses a 5-bolt mounting flange. In most cases, it may be necessary to cut a new hole in the top of the tank to use this sender. It does not replace spin lock or ring type factory sending units.

Another option is if you are using the Cobalt, C2, Ultra Lite, Phantom, or Sport Comp series full sweep programmable fuel level gauges (not the standard short sweep version). The full sweep programmable unit may be custom calibrated to operate with nearly any variable resistance to ground sender that has a range between 0 and 270 ohms.

If the fuel level gauge always reads past full

First we need to determine the model number of the gauge to know what the calibrated resistance range is of the gauge in question. You may either check our catalog or use the Ask A Question feature to find out what the range of operation of the gauge is.

Next, we need to determine whether that gauge is a match for the sending unit that you are using. For example, a 0 to 90 ohm fuel level gauge will not operate correctly on a universal sender with

AUTO METER WIRING DIAGRAMS

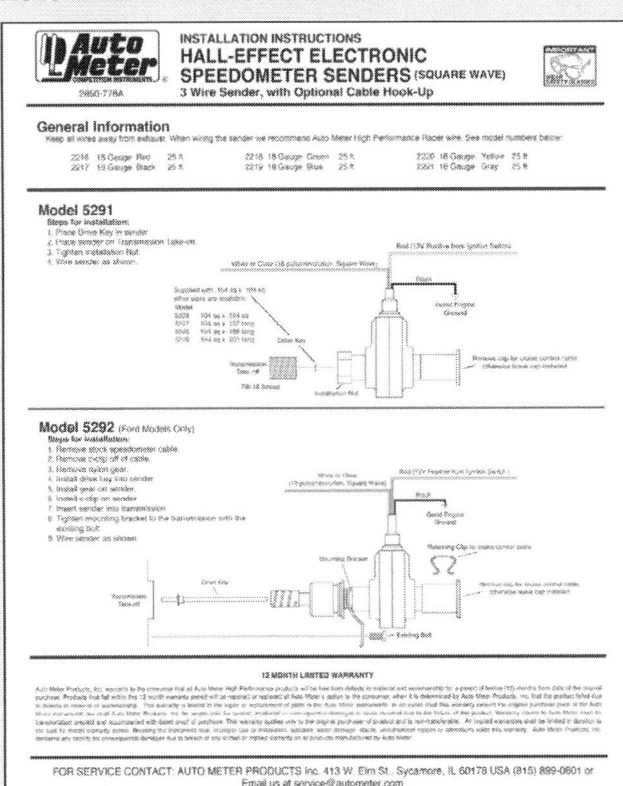

Auto Meter

INSTALLATION INSTRUCTIONS

HALL-EFFECT ELECTRONIC SPEEDOMETER SENDERS (SQUARE WAVE)

3 Wire Sender, with Optional Cable Hook-Up

2650-776A

General Information

Model 5291

Model 5292 (Ford Models Only)

12 MONTH LIMITED WARRANTY

FOR SERVICE CONTACT: AUTO METER PRODUCTS Inc. 413 W. Elm St., Sycamore, IL 60178 USA (815) 899-0601 or Email us at service@autometer.com

INSTALLATION INSTRUCTIONS

SHORT SWEEP ELECTRIC GAUGES

CAUTION FOR ALL GAUGE INSTALLATION

Mounting

Wiring

Temperature Gauges

Pressure Gauges

Ammeter

Read before installing. Must be installed by experienced mechanic.

WARNING

Have your maximum alternator output tested. Choice of improper ammeter rating and/or wire size, and any loose connections can cause dangerous overheating, which could lead to a fire in the vehicle. Ammeter and wire should have a capacity of at least 10 amps more than your vehicle's maximum alternator output.

1. 10-gage wire or larger must be used.
2. **IMPORTANT:** Verify that base nuts on both meter terminals are tight. Tighten these nuts prior to installing terminal lugs and wires. Connect ammeter as shown.

CAUTION: *DO NOT CONNECT THE AMMETER ACROSS THE BATTERY.*

Wiring

Example wiring of a typical Ammeter installation. Consult vehicle Mfr. for specific wiring details and safety considerations.

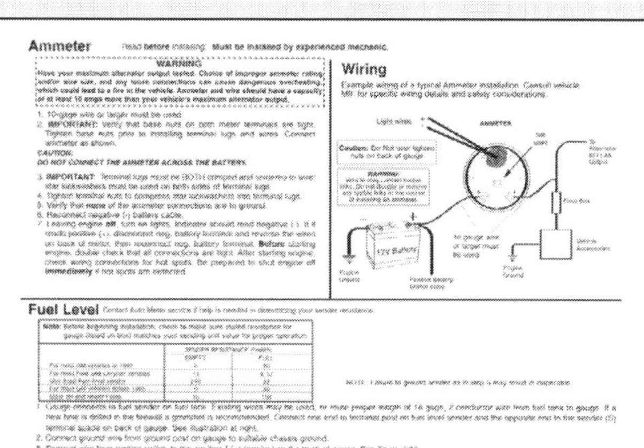

Fuel Level

Voltmeter

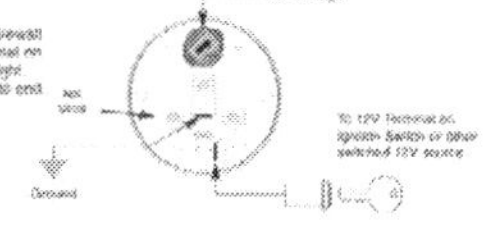

Questions?

If you have questions regarding the operation or installation of your instrument(s), please contact Auto Meter Technical Service at 815-899-0801.
You may also email us at service@autometer.com.
Additional information can also be found at http://www.autometer.com

SERVICE

12 MONTH LIMITED WARRANTY

FOR SERVICE CONTACT: AUTO METER PRODUCTS Inc. 413 W. Elm St., Sycamore, IL 60178 USA (815)899-0801 or
Email us at service@autometer.com

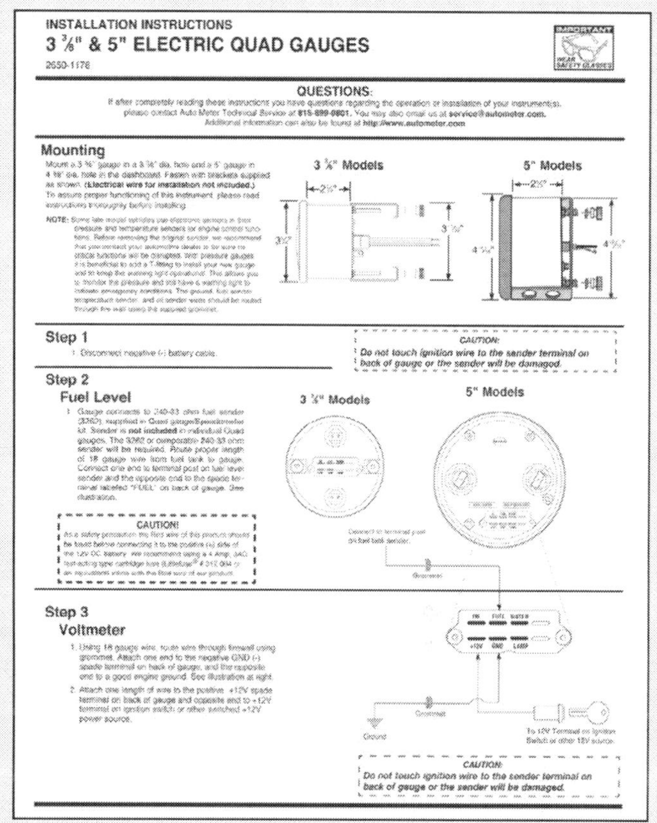

INSTALLATION INSTRUCTIONS

3 3/8" & 5" ELECTRIC QUAD GAUGES

2650-1178

QUESTIONS:

If after completely reading these instructions you have questions regarding the operation or installation of your instrument(s), please contact Auto Meter Technical Service at 815-899-0801. You may also email us at service@autometer.com. Additional information can also be found at http://www.autometer.com

Mounting

3 3/8" Models | 5" Models

Step 1

1. Disconnect negative (-) battery cable.

CAUTION: ***Do not touch ignition wire to the sender terminal on back of gauge or the sender will be damaged.***

Step 2
Fuel Level

3 3/8" Models | 5" Models

CAUTION!

Step 3
Voltmeter

1. Using 18 gauge wire, route wire through firewall using grommet. Attach one end to the negative GND (-) spade terminal on back of gauge, and the opposite end to a good engine ground. See illustration at right.
2. Attach one length of wire to the positive +12V spade terminal on back of gauge and opposite end to +12V terminal on ignition switch or other switched +12V power source.

CAUTION: ***Do not touch ignition wire to the sender terminal on back of gauge or the sender will be damaged.***

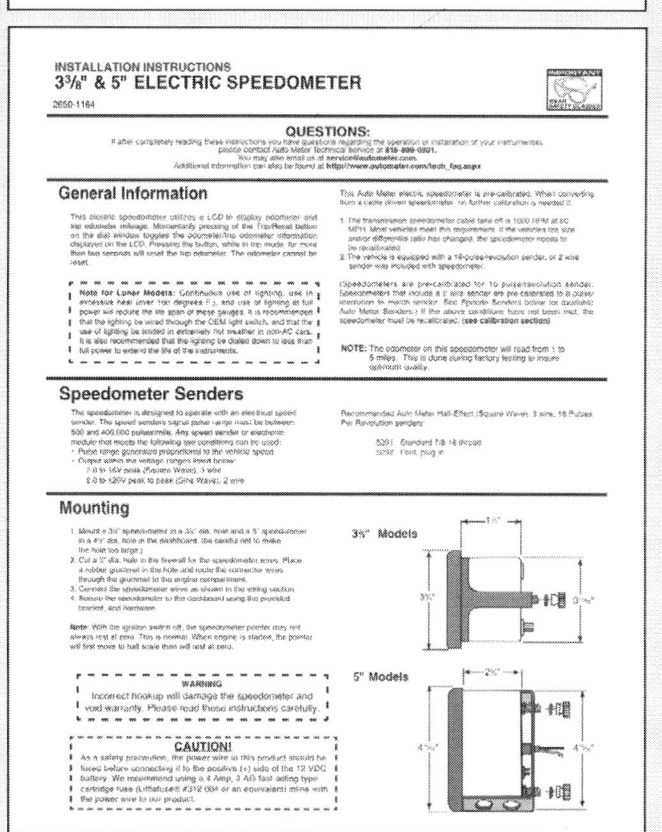

INSTALLATION INSTRUCTIONS

3 3/8" & 5" ELECTRIC SPEEDOMETER

2650-1164

QUESTIONS:

General Information

Speedometer Senders

Mounting

3 3/8" Models

5" Models

WARNING

Incorrect hookup will damage the speedometer and void warranty. Please read these instructions carefully.

CAUTION!

As a safety precaution, the power wire to this product should be fused before connecting it to the positive (+) side of the 12 VDC battery. We recommend using a 4 Amp, 3 AG fast acting type cartridge fuse (Littelfuse® #312 004 or an equivalent) inline with the power wire to our product.

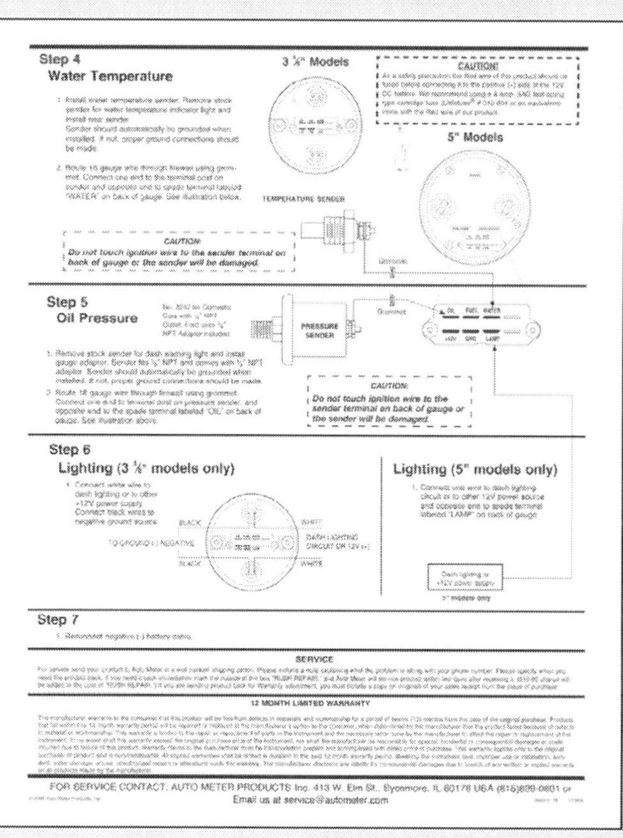

Step 4
Water Temperature

3 3/8" Models

CAUTION!

5" Models

TEMPERATURE SENDER

CAUTION: ***Do not touch ignition wire to the sender terminal on back of gauge or the sender will be damaged.***

Step 5
Oil Pressure

PRESSURE SENDER

CAUTION: ***Do not touch ignition wire to the sender terminal on back of gauge or the sender will be damaged.***

Step 6
Lighting (3 3/8" models only)

Lighting (5" models only)

Step 7

1. Reconnect negative (-) battery cable.

SERVICE

12 MONTH LIMITED WARRANTY

FOR SERVICE CONTACT: AUTO METER PRODUCTS Inc. 413 W. Elm St., Sycamore, IL 60178 USA (815)899-0801 or
Email us at service@autometer.com

DYNALINER SPECIFICATIONS

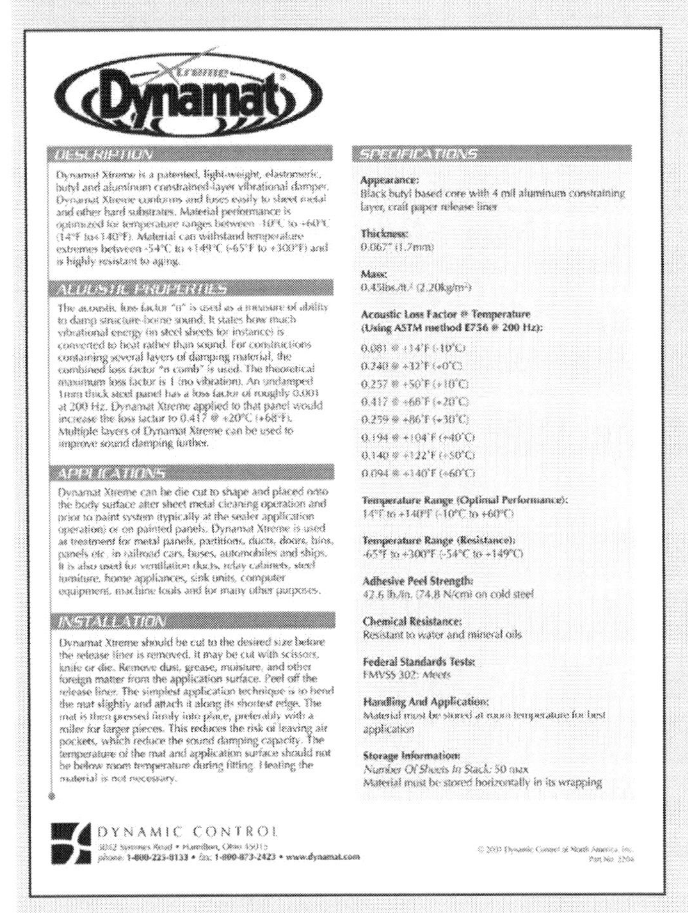

Dynamat Xtreme

DESCRIPTION

Dynamat Xtreme is a patented, light-weight, elastomeric, butyl and aluminum constrained-layer vibrational damper. Dynamat Xtreme conforms and fuses easily to sheet metal and other hard substrates. Material performance is optimized for temperature ranges between -10°C to +60°C (14°F to +140°F). Material can withstand temperature extremes between -54°C to +149°C (-65°F to +300°F) and is highly resistant to aging.

ACOUSTIC PROPERTIES

The acoustic loss factor "n" is used as a measure of ability to damp structure-borne sound. It states how much vibrational energy (in steel sheets for instance) is converted to heat rather than sound. For constructions containing several layers of damping material, the combined loss factor "n comb" is used. The theoretical maximum loss factor is 1 (no vibration). An undamped 1mm thick steel panel has a loss factor of roughly 0.001 at 200 Hz. Dynamat Xtreme applied to that panel would increase the loss factor to 0.417 @ +20°C (+68°F). Multiple layers of Dynamat Xtreme can be used to improve sound damping further.

APPLICATIONS

Dynamat Xtreme can be die cut to shape and placed onto the body surface after sheet metal cleaning operation and prior to paint system (typically at the sealer application operation) or on painted panels. Dynamat Xtreme is used as treatment for metal panels, partitions, ducts, doors, bins, panels etc., in railroad cars, buses, automobiles and ships. It is also used for ventilation ducts, relay cabinets, steel furniture, home appliances, sink units, computer equipment, machine tools and for many other purposes.

INSTALLATION

Dynamat Xtreme should be cut to the desired size before the release liner is removed. It may be cut with scissors, knife or die. Remove dust, grease, moisture, and other foreign matter from the application surface. Peel off the release liner. The simplest application technique is to bend the mat slightly and attach it along its shortest edge. The mat is then pressed firmly into place, preferably with a roller for larger pieces. This reduces the risk of leaving air pockets, which reduce the sound damping capacity. The temperature of the mat and application surface should not be below room temperature during fitting. Heating the material is not necessary.

SPECIFICATIONS

Appearance:
Black butyl based core with 4 mil aluminum constraining layer, craft paper release liner

Thickness:
0.067" (1.7mm)

Mass:
0.45lbs./ft.² (2.20kg/m²)

Acoustic Loss Factor @ Temperature (Using ASTM method E756 @ 200 Hz):

0.081 @ +14°F (-10°C)
0.240 @ +32°F (+0°C)
0.257 @ +50°F (+10°C)
0.417 @ +68°F (+20°C)
0.259 @ +86°F (+30°C)
0.194 @ +104°F (+40°C)
0.140 @ +122°F (+50°C)
0.094 @ +140°F (+60°C)

Temperature Range (Optimal Performance):
14°F to +140°F (-10°C to +60°C)

Temperature Range (Resistance):
-65°F to +300°F (-54°C to +149°C)

Adhesive Peel Strength:
42.6 lb./in. (74.8 N/cm) on cold steel

Chemical Resistance:
Resistant to water and mineral oils

Federal Standards Tests:
FMVSS 302: *Meets*

Handling And Application:
Material must be stored at room temperature for best application

Storage Information:
Number Of Sheets In Stack: 50 max
Material must be stored horizontally in its wrapping

DYNAMIC CONTROL
3042 Symmes Road • Hamilton, Ohio 45015
phone: 1-800-225-8133 • fax: 1-800-873-2423 • www.dynamat.com

© 2003 Dynamic Control of North America, Inc.
Part No. 2204

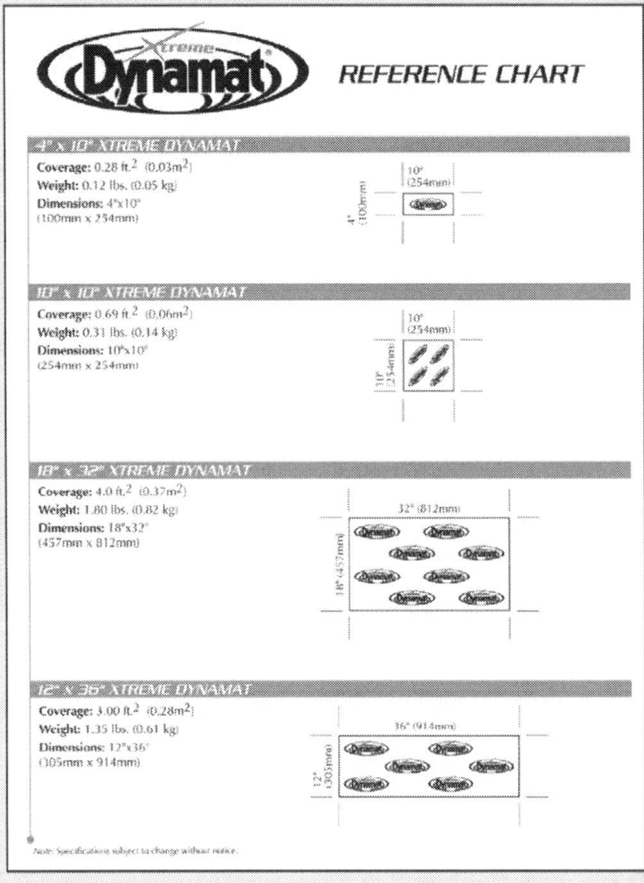

Dynamat Xtreme REFERENCE CHART

4" x 10" XTREME DYNAMAT

Coverage: 0.28 ft.² (0.03m²)
Weight: 0.12 lbs. (0.05 kg)
Dimensions: 4"x10"
(100mm x 254mm)

10" x 10" XTREME DYNAMAT

Coverage: 0.69 ft.² (0.06m²)
Weight: 0.31 lbs. (0.14 kg)
Dimensions: 10"x10"
(254mm x 254mm)

18" x 32" XTREME DYNAMAT

Coverage: 4.0 ft.² (0.37m²)
Weight: 1.80 lbs. (0.82 kg)
Dimensions: 18"x32"
(457mm x 812mm)

12" x 36" XTREME DYNAMAT

Coverage: 3.00 ft.² (0.28m²)
Weight: 1.35 lbs. (0.61 kg)
Dimensions: 12"x36"
(305mm x 914mm)

Note: Specifications subject to change without notice.

a range of 240 to 33 ohms.

If the gauge increases in resistance from empty to full, such as 0 to 90, 0 to 30, or 16 to 158, and assuming that the gauge is properly matched to the sender, then read on. The most common cause of this type of gauge to read over full is typically due to no ground at the sender, an open circuit, or break in the wire going from the gauge to the sender. A quick and easy way to check the gauge is to remove the sender wire off of the back of the gauge, leave the power and ground hooked up and use a jumper wire to connect the "S" terminal of the gauge to ground. Turn the power on. If the gauge responds by going to E, then you have proven that the gauge responds well. Jumping the "S" terminal to ground is the same as 0 ohms of resistance to ground.

Having no wire or jumper on the "S" terminal is infinite resistance to ground, which is much greater than the gauge's F reading, which then will cause the gauge to read past full. If, when you jumpered the "S" terminal to ground and the gauge did not respond by going to E, you will then check power, check ground, check the ground you jumpered to, then lastly check the model number on the gauge to see if you have the correct one (it should go up in resistance reading as the fuel level increases).

If the gauge you have decreases in resistance from Empty to Full, such as a 73 to 10, or 240 to 33, and assuming that the gauge is matched to the sender, then read on. The most common cause of a fuel level gauge of this type to read only past full is if the "S" of the gauge is somewhere shorted to chassis ground or of the sender is internally shorted to ground. A quick and easy way to check the gauge is to remove the sender wire from the back of the gauge, leave the power and ground hooked up and turn the power on.

With nothing attached to the "S" terminal, the gauge should read Empty. If the gauge responds by going to empty, then the gauge is likely fine. You will then want to make sure the gauge you have matches the sender in your vehicle. While the sender wire is off the gauge, you may use an ohmmeter to measure the resistance of the sender. Hook the red wire of the ohmmeter to the sender wire while it is off of the gauge and the negative lead of the ohmmeter to ground. This will tell you what the gauge is seeing from the sender for resistance and will help determine whether you have a gauge problem or a sender problem/wiring problem. ■

AUTOMOTIVE

DESCRIPTION

Dynaliner is an ultra-lightweight closed cell high-performance insulation. Dark gray in color, Dynaliner is available in 1/8", 1/4" and 1/2" thicknesses. Dynaliner is self-adhesive with a high-temperature acrylic adhesive. Dynaliner is optimized for temperatures from -30°F to 200°F (-34°C to 94°C) and meets both UL and FMVSS flame resistance.

ACOUSTIC AND THERMAL PROPERTIES

Dynaliner is the perfect ultra-lightweight insulator to use on top Dynamat. This durable, crush and tear resistant material has the highest heat blocking properties available in a single layer synthetic foam-type material. Dynaliner is not affected by oil and does not absorb water.

APPLICATION

Easy to install, Dynaliner provides acoustic isolation and excellent thermal insulation for roof, interior firewall, floor, quarter panels, doors and even under hood. Dynaliner can be used in place of carpet pad.

INSTALLATION

Cutting: Dynaliner can be cut to a desired size and shape with a pair of scissors or razor knife. Dynaliner is self-adhesive. Make sure area is free from dirt oil and debris. For best results, work evenly from one side to the other applying even pressure.

AVAILABLE SIZES

Dimensions: 32" x 54" (81cm x 137cm)
Coverage: 12.0 ft² (1.1m²)
Available 1/8", 1/4" and 1/2" (3mm, 6mm and 6mm) thickness

TYPICAL MATERIAL PROPERTIES*

Part#	11101	11102	11103
Material Thickness:	0.125 in.(3.18mm)	0.250 in.(6.35mm)	0.500 in.(12.70mm)
Weight:	0.042lb./ft² (0.21kg/m²)	0.084lb./ft² (0.41kg/m²)	0.168lb./ft² (0.82kg/m²)
Density:	4.0lb./ft³ (64.6kg/m³)	4.0lb./ft³ (64.6kg/m³)	4.0lb./ft³ (64.6kg/m³)
Adhesive Strength:	tba	tba	tba
Tensile Strength:	tba	tba	tba
Tear Strength:	tba	tba	tba
Temperature Range: (Maximum)	-30°F to 200°F (-34°C to 93°C)	-30°F to 200°F (-34°C to 93°C)	-30°F to 200°F (-34°C to 93°C)
Temperature Range: (Optimal)	-30°F to 200°F (-34°C to 93°C)	-30°F to 200°F (-34°C to 93°C)	-30°F to 200°F (-34°C to 93°C)
STC:	N/A	N/A	N/A
FMVSS302:	Meets	Meets	Meets
UL Rating:	UL 94 HF-1	UL 94 HF-1	UL 94 HBF
R Value:	0.42°Fft²hr/Btu (0.07Km²hr/W)	0.83°Fft²hr/Btu (0.15Km²hr/W)	1.7°Fft²hr/Btu (0.3Km²hr/W)

* Material properties have tolerances of ±10% unless otherwise noted
Parentheses denote metric measurements.

The data provided in the material summary are typical of average values based on testing conducted by Dynamic Control or independent laboratories. They are indicative only of the results obtained in such tests and should be used for reference only. Materials used in situations not recommended must be tested under actual service to determine their suitability for that purpose.

DYNAMIC CONTROL
3042 Symmes Road • Hamilton, Ohio 45015
phone: 1-800-225-8133 • fax: 1-800-873-2423 • www.dynamat.com

Part No. 2211

INSTALLATION INSTRUCTIONS FOR VINTAGE AIR SAFETY SWITCHES

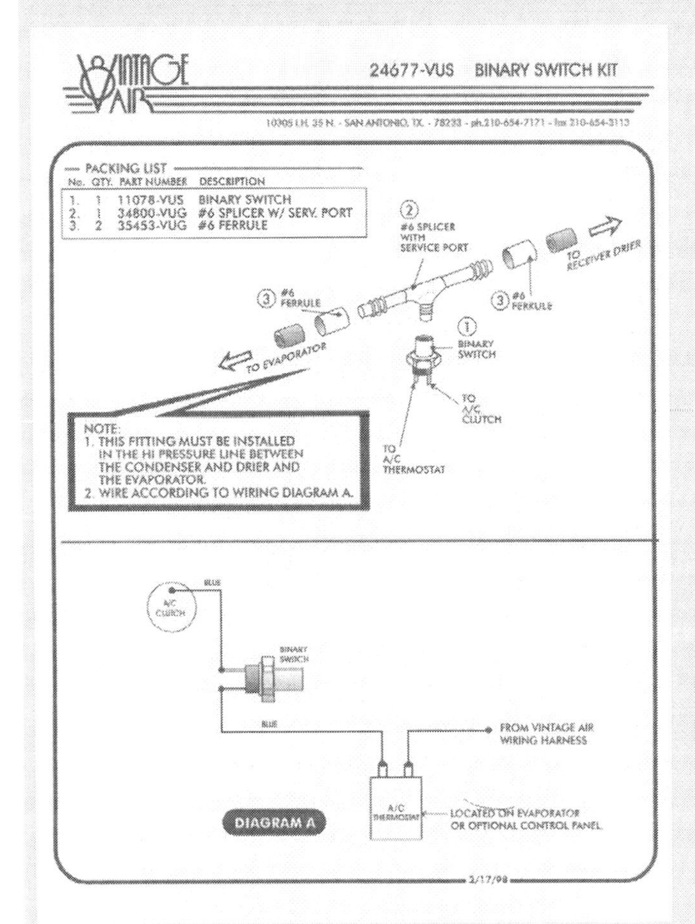

VINTAGE AIR — 24677-VUS BINARY SWITCH KIT

10305 I.H. 35 N. - SAN ANTONIO, TX. - 78233 - ph.210-654-7171 - fax 210-654-3113

— PACKING LIST —

No.	QTY.	PART NUMBER	DESCRIPTION
1.	1	11078-VUS	BINARY SWITCH
2.	1	34800-VUG	#6 SPLICER W/ SERV. PORT
3.	2	35453-VUG	#6 FERRULE

NOTE:
1. THIS FITTING MUST BE INSTALLED IN THE HI PRESSURE LINE BETWEEN THE CONDENSER AND DRIER AND THE EVAPORATOR.
2. WIRE ACCORDING TO WIRING DIAGRAM A.

2/17/98

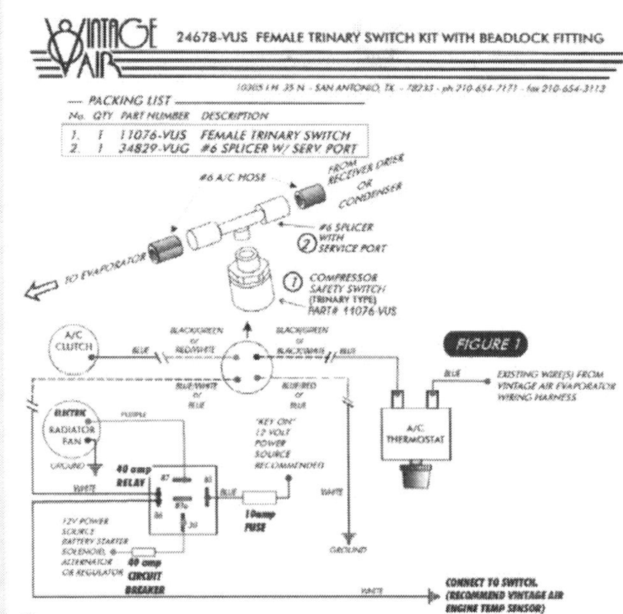

① INSTALL #6 SPLICER WITH SERVICE PORT IN THE HIGH PRESSURE LINE BETWEEN THE CONDENSER AND DRIER OR BETWEEN THE DRIER AND EVAPORATOR. THE TRINARY MAY ALSO BE INSTALLED DIRECTLY INTO THE DRIER, IF THE DRIER HAS THE PROVISION. **NOTE: IF THE SYSTEM IS CHARGED WITH REFRIGERANT, YOU MUST EVACUATE THE SYSTEM BEFORE REMOVING THE TRINARY SWITCH PORT PLUG LOCATED IN THE DRIER. INSTALL THE TRINARY ADAPTER WITH O-RING INTO THE DRIER AND TIGHTEN. INSTALL THE TRINARY SWITCH ONTO THE ADAPTER. HOLD THE ADAPTER WITH ONE WRENCH AND TIGHTEN THE TRINARY WITH A SECOND WRENCH.**

② TRINARY FUNCTION SWITCH WILL SPLICE INTO THE BLUE WIRE WHICH RUNS FROM THE A/C THERMOSTAT TO THE A/C CLUTCH. THE THERMOSTAT IS LOCATED ON THE EVAPORATOR .... IF YOU HAVE STANDARD DASH PANEL. IF YOU ARE USING A PROLINE PANEL, THE THERMOSTAT IS LOCATED ON THE BACK OF THE PANEL.

- CONNECT TRINARY FUNCTION SWITCH BLACK/WHITE OR BLACK/GREEN WIRE TO BLUE WIRE CONNECTED TO A/C THERMOSTAT ON THE EVAPORATOR OR THE CONTROL PANEL.
- CONNECT TRINARY FUNCTION SWITCH RED/WHITE OR BLACK/GREEN WIRE TO BLUE WIRE WITH BULLET PLUG RUNNING TO COMPRESSOR CLUTCH.
- CONNECT TRINARY FUNCTION SWITCH BLUE/RED OR BLUE WIRE TO GROUND.
- CONNECT TRINARY FUNCTION SWITCH BLUE/WHITE OR BLUE WIRE TO PIN #86 ON RELAY.

WIRING DIAGRAM

FIGURE 1.

WIRING SCHEMATIC FOR THE CUSTOM AUTOSOUND SECRET AUDIO

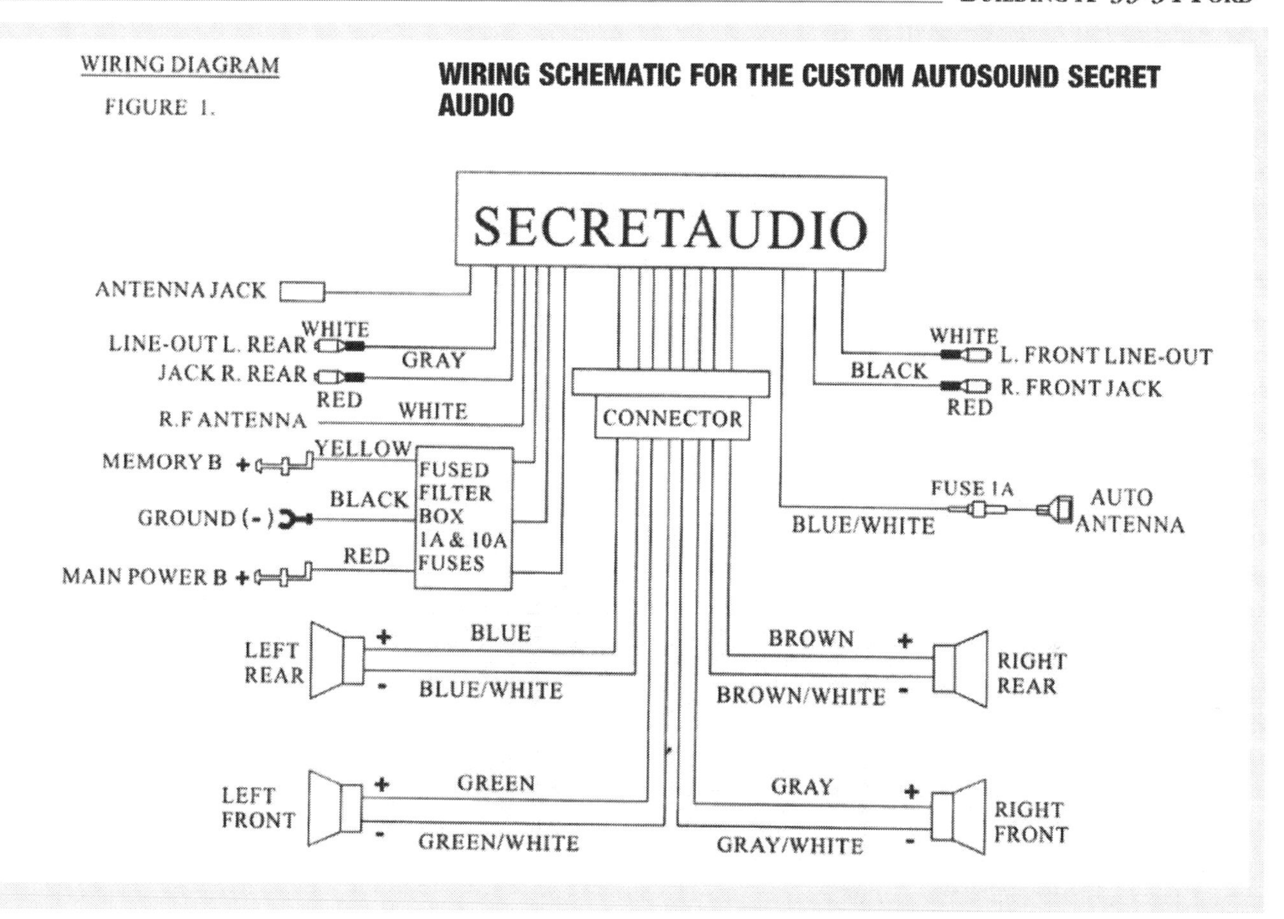

CONTROLS FOR THE CUSTOM AUTOSOUND SYSTEM

LCD DISPLAY CONTROLS

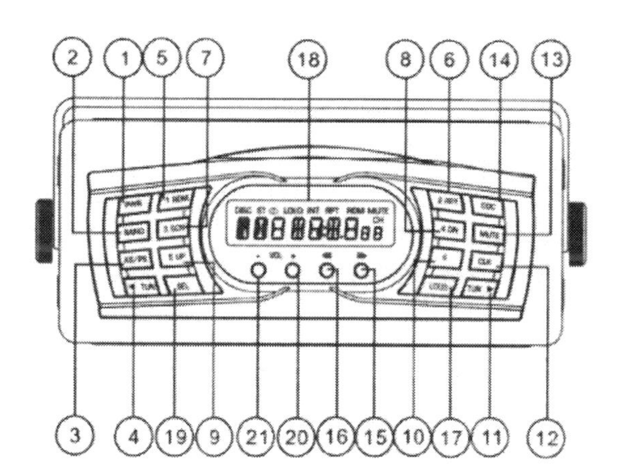

1. Power On/Off.
2. FM 1/FM 2/FM 3/AM1/AM2 band selector.
3. Tuner PRE - SET scan/auto store.
4. Tuner seek down//CD track down/Fast reverse.
5. CDC RDM / Radio preset 1.
6. CD track repeat/Radio preset 2.
7. CDC Scan/Radio preset 3.
8. CD disc down/Radio preset 4.
9. CD disc up/Radio preset 5.
10. Radio preset 6.
11. Tuner seek up/CD track up/Fast forward.
12. Clock setting button.
13. Mute selector.
14. CD changer On/Off.
15. Manual tune down.
16. Manual tune up.
17. Loudness selector.
18. LCD display.
19. Change mode for volume, treble, bass, balance, fader.
20. Volume up, raise bass & treble ,balance right, fader front.
21. Volume down, decrease bass & treble, balance left, fader rear.

Chapter 13
SPEED33 IS READY FOR THE ROAD

By Ron Ceridono • Photos by SRM Staff

Based on an American Speed Company Speed33 body and a Roadster Shop chassis, the 2008 Street Rodder/PPG Road Tour car is ready to roll. That subtle color is 1941 Ford Niles blue/green.

This book has dealt with the building of an American Speed Company's Speed33 convertible, a takeoff on the very popular '33-34 Ford roadster. Taking the great points of the'33-34 roadster and adding modern touches have turned the car into a convertible ideally suited for today's street rodding. Best of all, the very same car we built can be replicated down to the last detail, and used as a source for ideas and inspiration for you, our readers to build your own interpretation.

This year's car uses one of American Speed Company's amazing Speed33 convertible bodies. Skillfully designed and beautifully built, it combines the best of Ford's vintage style with today's construction techniques. The result is a final product that offers a win/win situation—the timeless appeal of the Model 40 and a body that requires very little prep work to finish. Thanks to the production tolerances, rigid inner structure, and dead-on chassis from the Roadster Shop, no shims were required to make the doors fit and panels align. And of course, to top it all off (no pun intended), the hidden folding top and roll-up windows make this a truly civilized hot rod.

Our car was obviously built in highboy fashion—something that the Roadster Shop went to great pains to perfect. The pinched rails have been contoured to complement the bottom of the body and the shape o the hood. But they haven't overlooked other building styles; they can supply a chassis for a Speed33 built in virtually a manner, including full fendered.

Oddly enough, looking at this car, it's easy to get lost in the details and the fit a finish. But for all its flash, there's an equa amount of substance. Like a prizefighter that's gone to finishing school, don't let t refined appearance fool you. The Heidt's independent front suspension, Flaming River steering, Strange coilovers, and Wlwood brakes all allow the '08 car to ta roadwork in stride. The Boss Ford engin and five-speed transmission provide plent of punch. ■

This car looks good coming or going. It rolls on Coker/Firestone 8.20x18 grooved rear tires and Coker/Firestone Deluxe Champion 5.00x16 ribbed fronts wrapped around polished wheels from Wheel Vintiques.

American Speed has done a masterful job of incorporating a hidden, folding top and roll-up windows into the Speed33 body without diluting the character of the original design.

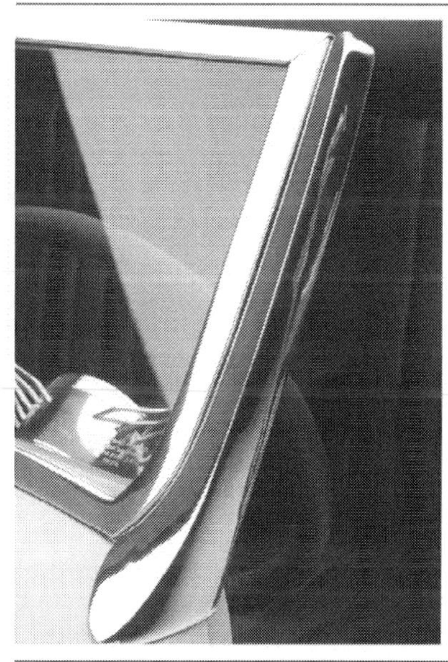

The polished stainless steel windshield posts and frame are works of art. The design challenge here was to put a sealing surface into the posts for the roll-up windows without making them bulky.

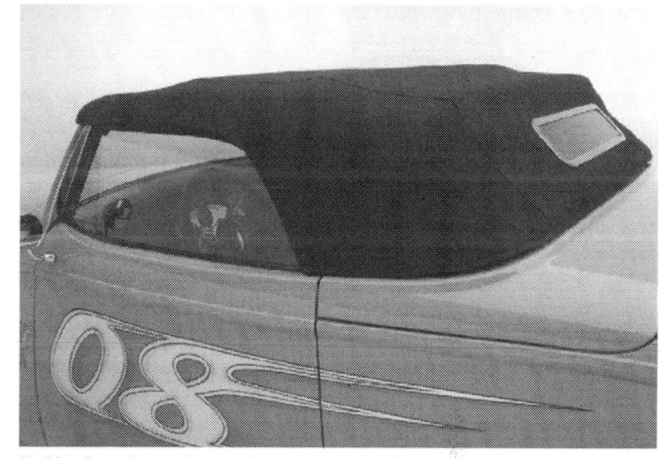

Nothing is makes or breaks the shape of a top like the rear bow. The traditional hot rod shape is achieved by leaning the rear bow forward to make it slightly lower than the center bow, while adding to the forward slope of the back panel. In our opinion, this is how a top is supposed to look.

A variety of frontend options are available on the Roadster Shop frames for Speed33 bodies. We opted for a pinched front and Heidt's IFS. This construction shot shows the extra long A-arms to provide the proper tread width with the narrower framerails.

Stopping power up front is provided by Wilwood 11-inch, cross-drilled and slotted rotors squeezed by four-piston polished calipers. Coilovers are from Strange, and the rack-and-pinion steering is from Flaming River.

At the rear of the chassis is a Strange rearend and center section holding a U.S. Gears ring-and-pinion. A Roadster Shop triangulated four-bar and Strange coilovers complete the package.

Wilwood discs are used on the rear as well. Note the shoes and parking brake assembly mounted to the backing plate. The drum for the parking brake is the inside of the rotor's hat.

Strange coilovers feature adjustable damping as well as preload adjustment collars at the base of the springs. The damping adjustment knob can be seen at the top of the shock.

The BOSS is back. Providing more than adequate power is a 347-inch Boss Ford small-block. A new offering from Ford Racing, they can be built in a variety of displacements including the legendary 302 configuration.

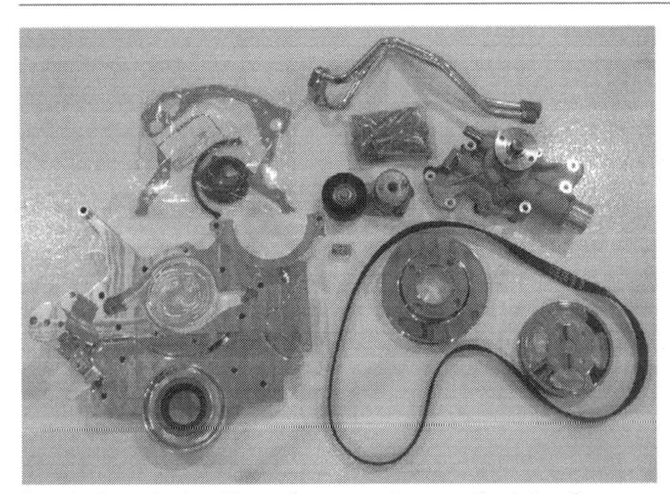

To make the packaging of the engine accessories compact and attractive, we chose to install a Front Runner system from Vintage Air. All the brackets, mounts, and pulleys are included.

A special compressor designed for use with the Front Runner shortens the overall length of the engine considerably.

Ignition is provided by MSD. This distributor requires a separate control box. It was mounted behind the dashboard.

Topping off the engine is a Holley 650-cfm double-pumper with vacuum secondaries. Aeromotive supplied the fuel log, pump, and filter.

Backing up the small-block is a Tremec five-speed. The gearbox, pressure plate, disc, shifter, and the hydraulic throwout bearing came from Classic Motorsports.

Because of the pinched frame and the location of the Flaming River steering shaft, a block-off plate, and a remote oil filter were necessary.

Another feature of the pinched frame is a cove built into the left side 'rail to accommodate the rack-and-pinion steering shaft and U-joint.

Flaming River supplied the U-joints, shafts, and support bearing necessary to hook the steering column to the rack-and-pinion. Headers are Sanderson.

Only those lucky enough to own a turn-key Roadster Shop creation will have one of these on the firewall of their car.

Surprisingly little bodywork was required to get the Speed33 body ready for paint. Here, the gap between the tonneau cover and body is being massaged.

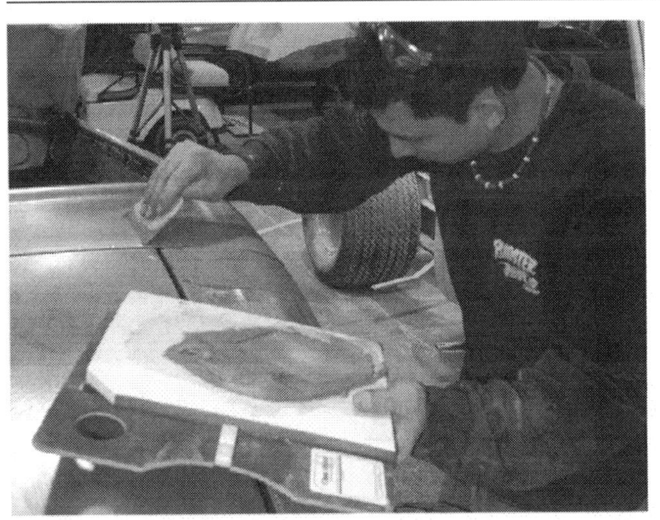

In a few areas, a skim coat of filler was applied, much of which was removed in the block-sanding process.

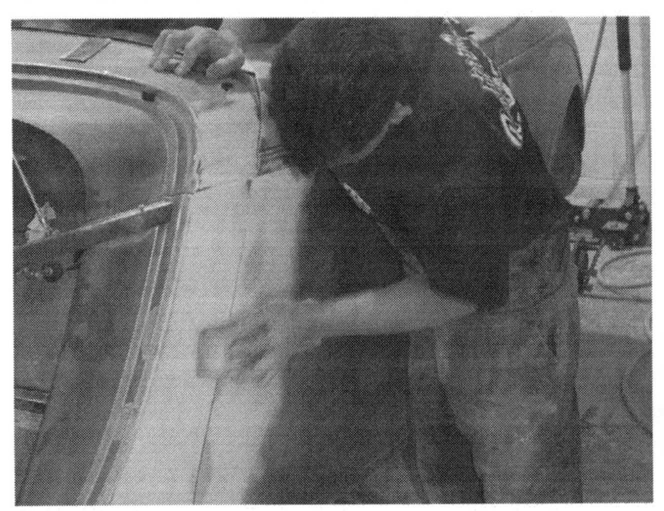

Long sanding blocks are used to get the flanks super straight. Sanding across the gaps, as shown, results in doors that fit perfectly.

A rotisserie makes it much easier to finish off the bottom of the body, which in fact is just as nice as the top. The perfect door alignment without being bolted to the frame is testament the body's strength.

After the bodywork was done, PPG DP90 sealer was applied, followed by MK217 sealer, then NCP270 final primer. The body was then block-sanded several times to make it super straight.

As in years past, PPG products were used exclusively on the Road Tour Car

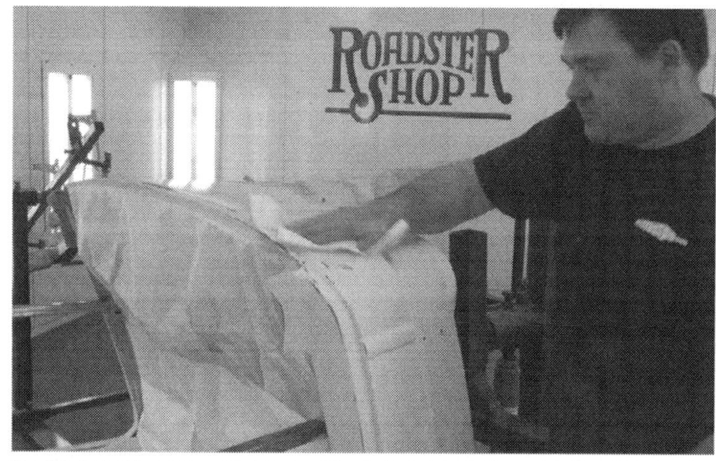

The Roadster Shop does virtually everything in-house, including paint. Here the primed body is being wiped down in preparation for color application.

Following an application of NCS2002 Pre-Paint Sealer, the DBC base color was applied followed by Vibrance clear.

Fresh from the paint booth, the body was bright as a new penny, but there was more to come—the addition of gold leaf graphics.

The first step in applying the gold leaf was to wet sand the clear with 600-grit paper.

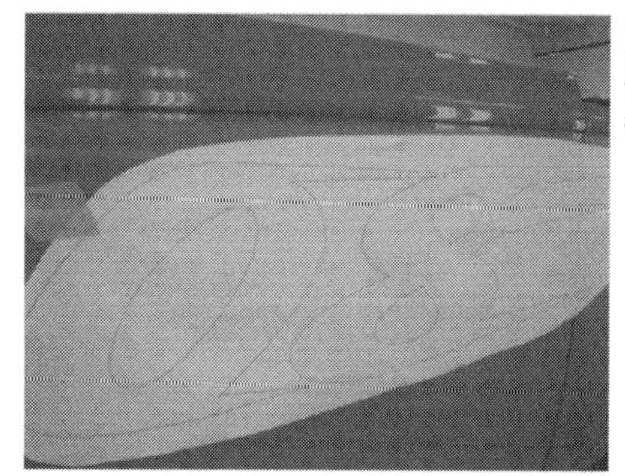

Next, the pattern is positioned, trimmed to shape, and the adhesive applied.

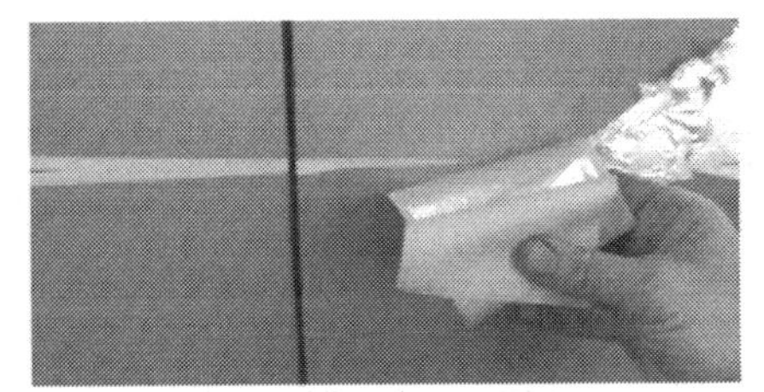

The gold leafing is carefully applied and pressed down.

It doesn't look like much at this stage, but carefully dusting off the areas without adhesive will yield surprising results.

Here the area between the gold leaf outline has been painted and the edges pinstriped. All that remains is to clearcoat the area, color sand, and buff.

Keeping the engine cool is a custom radiator supplied by the Roadster Shop; it's equipped with an overflow tank from Vintique. The A/C condenser is part of the Vintage Air heat-and-cool package. Powermaster supplied the alternator and starter.

Although the A/C compressor is on the driver side of the engine compartment, the preformed lines of the Vintage Air Front Runner system run to the passenger side to make connections easier. The short hose connecting the compressor and condenser includes a service port.

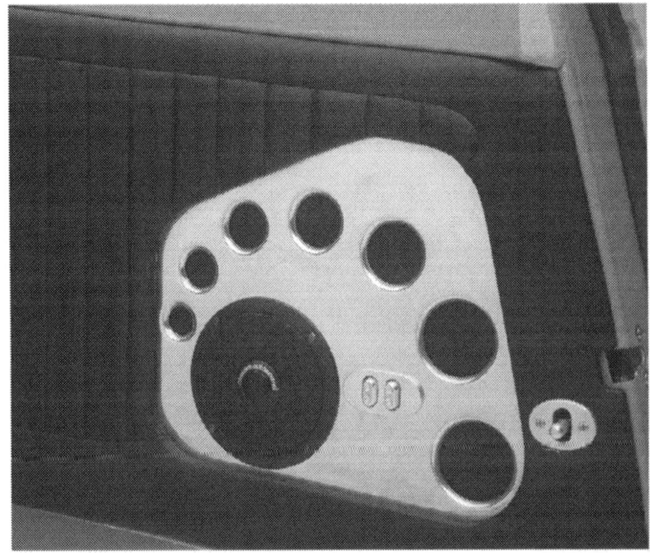

The Custom Autosound Secret Audio speakers and electric window controls are captured within a metal panel located on the door.

Tucked under the dash is a Vintage Air heat-and-cool unit. The firewall as well as the rest of the interior was insulated with Dynamat.

With the advent of AGM (absorbed glass mat) technology that allows batteries to be mounted next to the gas tank on their side, finding a spot for them has become much easier. Our Powermaster D1200 battery is secured behind the seat with a custom retainer.

Ron Francis supplied the wiring harness, the panel was mounted so it was easily accessible. The steering column and drop are from Flaming River.

Wise Guys supplied the upholstered bench seat. The remainder of the interior is the handy work of Twin City Upholstery.

With the Dynamat insulation and carpet installed, Lonnie King and Kent Biedenharn slide the seat in place.

Wise Guys seats are available with a host of options including a fold-down armrest, reclining lumbar supports, heaters, and 12-volt accessory outlets.

To ensure the interior panels all matched the seat, Wise Guys supplied the additional leather necessary to complete the interior.

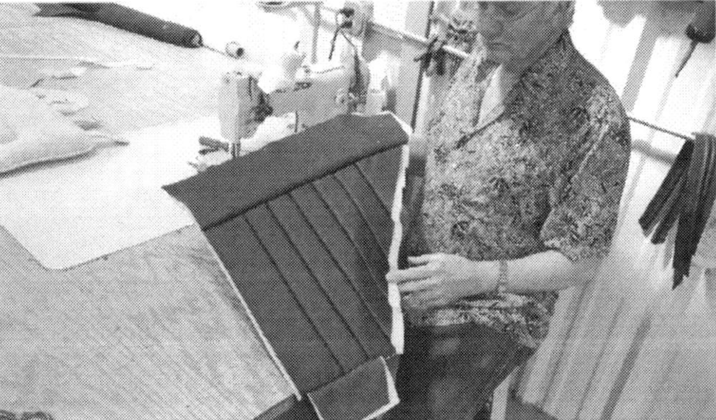

Dwain Haskins holds one of the trunk panels. Mahogany or ABS is used to provide the basic shape, 1/4-inch thick foam is used to make the 2-inch wide pleats.

Perfect is the only way to describe the stance of the Roadster Shop chassis. They will be offering everything from frames to turnkey versions of the Speed33.

)f the several dashboard options, we chose Auto Meter instruments in a .okar panel.

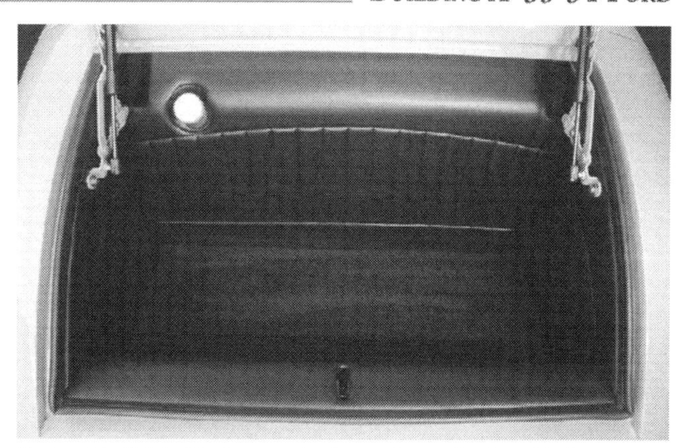

The trunk is finished in the same leather and carpeting found in the passenger compartment. Behind the pleated panel is the gas tank; the filler is at the upper left.

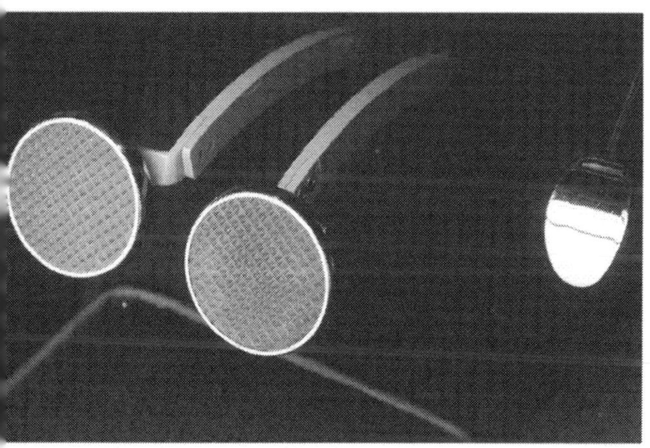

here's a laundry list of Lokar products on the Road Tour car—throttle and arking brake cables, hand brake, interior door handles, pedal pads, and the poon throttle.

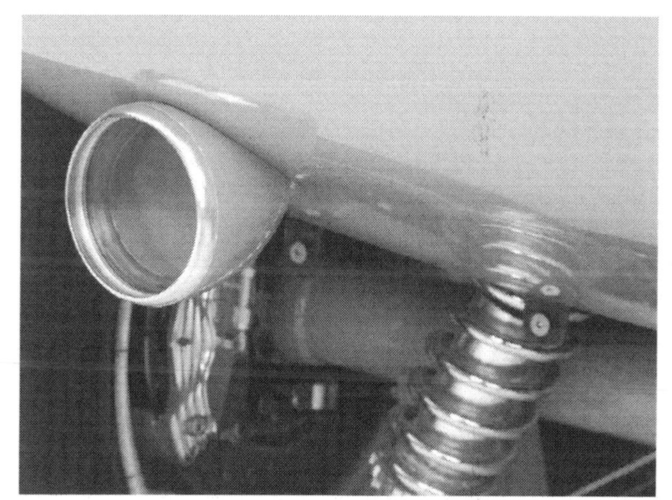

Those cool '37-esque taillights fit the style of the car perfectly.

he exhaust system is a combination of Sanderson headers, Hushpower ıufflers and pipes. Thanks to the mufflers' Cool-Case design, heat transfer to ıe passenger compartment is virtually eliminated.

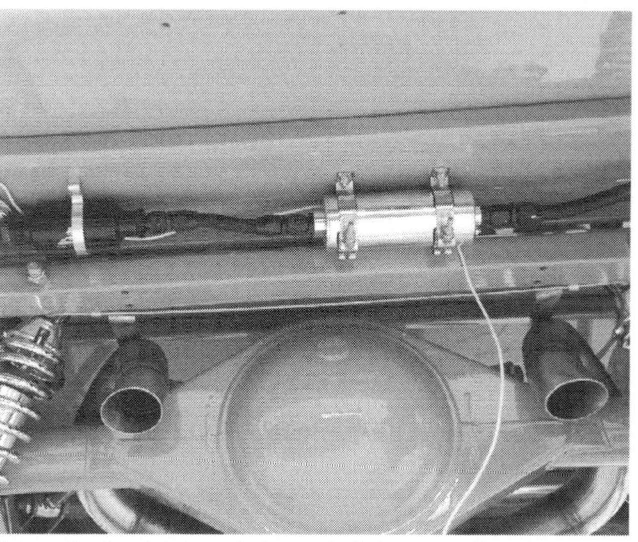

This construction shot shows the Aeromotive fuel pump and filter. Note the bracket that holds the pump (left) and the clamps (right) that allow the fuel pump to be changed quickly and easily.

The sculpted grille of the '33 Ford has long been thought to be more stylish than the '34, but that is personal taste. American Speed Company has taken the design even further, and with a painted grille shell, has made the convertible's appearance even more appealing.

Yogi's supplied a number of accessories such as the eternal rearview mirror.

AMSOIL synthetic products protect everything on the Road Tour car that relies on lubrication, such as the engine, transmission, and rearend. We also used their brake fluid and oil filter.

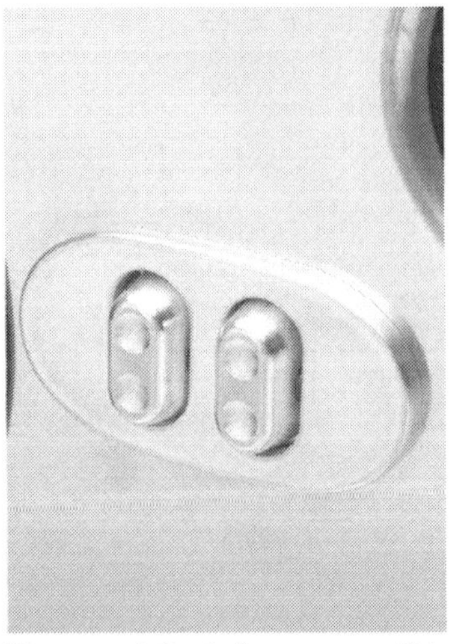

The power window buttons were supplied by Yogi's.

The key is part of the Ron Francis wire kit, while the Dakota Digital remote control handles the power chores such as doors and decklid. All came from Yogi's.

Just for fun, we swapped out the Wheel Vintiques billet models and replaced them with a set of its own steel wheels. A completely different look that works equally as well.

SOURCES

AMSOIL INC.
715-392-7101
www.amsoil.com

AEROMOTIVE INC.
913-647-7300
www.aeromotiveinc.com

AUTO METER PRODUCTS
815-899-0800
www.autometer.com

AMERICAN SPEED COMPANY
734-451-1141
www.americanspeedcompany.com

CLASSIC MOTORSPORTS GROUP
760-438-2244
www.classicchevy5speed.com

COKER TIRE
866-251-6336
www.coker.com

CUSTOM AUTOSOUND MFG.
(800) 888-8637
www.casmfg.com

POWERMASTER MOTORSPORTS
865-688-5953
www.powermastersports.com

DYNAMAT
513-860-5094
www.dynamat.com

FLAMING RIVER INDUSTRIES, INC.
800-648-8022
www.flamingriver.com

FORD RACING
800-FORD-788
www.fordracingparts.com

HEIDTS HOT ROD SHOP
800-841-8188
www.heidts.com

HUSHPOWER
877-EXHAUST
www.hushpower.com

LOKAR PERFORMANCE PRODUCTS
877-469-7440
www.lokar.com

PPG INDUSTRIES
www.ppgrefinish.com

THE ROADSTER SHOP
847-949-RODS
www.roadstershop.com

RON FRANCIS WIRING
800-292-1940
www.ronfrancis.com

SANDERSON HEADERS
800-669-2430
www.sandersonheaders.com

STRANGE ENGINEERING
847-663-1701
www.strangeengineering.net

VINTAGE AIR INC.
800-862-6658
www.vintageair.com

WHEEL VINTIQUES
559-251-6957
www.wheelvintiques.com

WILWOOD ENGINEERING
805-388-1188
www.wilwood.com

WISE GUYS SEATING & ACCESSORIES
866-494-7348
www.wiseguys-seats.com

YOGI'S INC.
800-373-1937
www.yogisinc.com

Made in the USA
Lexington, KY
12 May 2010